Excel

Get the Results You Want!

Year 5 NAPLAN*-style Literacy Tests

Alan Horsfield &
Elaine Horsfield

* This is not an officially endorsed publication of the NAPLAN program and is produced by Pascal Press independently of Australian governments.

Reprinted 2011
New NAPLAN Test question formats added 2012
Reprinted 2015
Conventions of Language questions updated 2017
Reprinted 2017, 2018

Revised in 2020 for the NAPLAN Online tests

Reprinted 2020, 2021, 2022, 2023, 2024

ISBN 978 1 74125 364 1

Pascal Press Pty Ltd
PO Box 250
Glebe NSW 2037
(02) 9198 1748
www.pascalpress.com.au

Publisher: Vivienne Joannou
Project editor: Mark Dixon
Edited by Rosemary Peers
Answers checked by Dale Little and Peter Little
Cover and page design by DiZign Pty Ltd
Typesetting by Precision Typesetting (Barbara Nilsson) and lj Design (Julianne Billington)
Printed by Vivar Printing/Green Giant Press

Contents

NAPLAN AND NAPLAN ONLINE

WHAT IS NAPLAN?

- NAPLAN stands for National Assessment Program—Literacy and Numeracy.
- It is conducted every year in March and the tests are taken by students in Years 3, 5, 7 and 9.
- The tests cover Literacy—Reading, Writing, Conventions of Language (spelling, grammar and punctuation)—and Numeracy.

WHAT IS NAPLAN ONLINE?

Introduction

- In the past all NAPLAN tests were paper tests.
- From 2022 all students have taken the NAPLAN tests online.
- This means students complete the NAPLAN tests on a computer or tablet.

Tailored test design

- With NAPLAN paper tests, all students in each year level took exactly the same tests.
- In the NAPLAN Online tests this isn't the case; instead, every student takes a tailor-made test based on their ability.
- Please visit the official ACARA site for a detailed explanation of the tailored test process used in NAPLAN Online and also for general information about the tests: https://nap.edu.au/online-assessment.
- These tailor-made tests mean broadly, therefore, that a student who is at a standard level of achievement takes a test mostly comprised of questions of a standard level; a student who is at an intermediate level of achievement takes a test mostly comprised of questions of an intermediate level; and a student who is at an advanced level of achievement takes a test mostly comprised of questions of an advanced level.

Different question types

- Because of the digital format, NAPLAN Online contains more question types than in the paper tests. In the paper tests there are only multiple-choice and short-answer question types. In NAPLAN Online, however, there are also other question types. For example, students might be asked to drag text across a screen or listen to an audio recording of a sentence and then spell a word they hear.
- Please refer to the next page to see some examples of these additional question types that are found in NAPLAN Online and how they compare to questions in this book. As you will see, the content tested is exactly the same but the questions are presented differently.

NAPLAN ONLINE QUESTION TYPES

<table>
<tr><th>Additional NAPLAN Online question types</th><th>Equivalent questions in this book</th></tr>
<tr><td>Sequencing
Drag these events to show the order in which they happened in the text.
Use the tab to read the text.
1 Jenny heard a noise against the outside wall.
2
3
4
Ms Mann didn't believe Jenny's story.
The class started laughing.
Jenny signed the Signing Out sheet.
Jenny heard a noise against the outside wall.</td><td>Write the numbers 1 to 4 in the boxes to show the correct order in which events happened in the text.
The first one (1) has been done for you.
☐ Ms Mann didn't believe Jenny's story.
☐ The class started laughing.
☐ Jenny signed the Signing Out sheet.
1 Jenny heard a noise against the outside wall.</td></tr>
<tr><td>Click
Choose two options.
Another word for flutes would be
grooves. ☐
cracks. ☐
cuts. ☐
lines. ☐
holes. ☐
ridges. ☐</td><td>Choose two options. Another word for flutes would be
A grooves.
B cracks.
C cuts.
D lines.
E holes.
F ridges.</td></tr>
<tr><td>Drag and drop
Which word correctly completes the sentence?
There wasn't ______ water in the birdbath after the rain.
many   some   much   no   plenty</td><td>Which word correctly completes the sentence?
There wasn't ______ water in the birdbath after the rain.
A many   B some
C much   D no
E plenty</td></tr>
<tr><td>Text entry
Craig said, "We were ______ the grass when the storm struck."
Click on the play button to listen to the missing word.
0.08 / 0.09
Type the correct spelling of the word in the box.</td><td>Ask your teacher or parent to read the spelling words for you. The words are listed on page 147. Write the spelling word on the line below.
<table><tr><th>Word</th><th>Example</th></tr><tr><td>levelling</td><td>Craig said, "We were levelling the grass when the storm struck."</td></tr></table>
______</td></tr>
</table>

MAXIMISE YOUR RESULTS IN NAPLAN ONLINE

STEP 1: USE THIS BOOK

How *Excel* can help you prepare for NAPLAN Online

Tailored test design

- We can't replicate the digital experience in book form and offer you tailored tests, but with this series we do provide Standard, Intermediate and Advanced NAPLAN Online–style Literacy tests—both mini tests and the longer sample tests.
- This means that a student using these tests will be able to prepare with confidence for tests at different ability levels.
- This makes it excellent preparation for the tailored NAPLAN Online Literacy tests.

Remember the advantages of revising in book form

There are many benefits to a child using books to prepare for the online test:

- One of the most important benefits is that writing on paper will help your child retain information. It can be a very effective way to memorise. High-quality educational research has shown that writing by hand is more effective than using a keyboard for remembering what you write and assisting in learning.
- Students will be able to prepare thoroughly for topic revision using books and then practise computer skills easily. They will only succeed with sound knowledge of topics; this requires study and focus. Students will not succeed in tests simply because they know how to answer questions digitally.
- Some students find it easier to concentrate when reading a page in a book than when reading on a screen.
- It can be more convenient to use a book, especially when a child doesn't have ready access to a digital device.
- You can be confident that ***Excel*** books will help students acquire the topic knowledge they need, as we have over 30 years experience in helping students prepare for tests. All our writers are experienced educators.

STEP 2: PRACTISE ON *Excel Test Zone*

How *Excel Test Zone* can help you practise online

We recommend you go to www.exceltestzone.com.au and register for practice in NAPLAN Online–style tests once you have completed this book. The reasons include:

- for optimal performance in the NAPLAN Online tests we recommend students gain practice at completing online tests as well as completing revision in book form
- students should practise answering questions on a digital device to become confident with this process
- students will be able to practise tailored tests like those in NAPLAN Online, as well as other types of tests
- students will also be able to gain valuable practice in onscreen skills such as dragging and dropping answers.

Remember that ***Excel Test Zone*** has been helping students prepare for NAPLAN since 2009; in fact we had NAPLAN online questions even before NAPLAN tests went online!

We also have updated our website along with our book range to ensure your preparation for NAPLAN Online is 100% up to date.

ABOUT THE LITERACY TESTS AND THIS BOOK

THE YEAR 5 NAPLAN ONLINE LITERACY TESTS

About the tests

In Literacy there are three NAPLAN tests:

- **Reading** (comprehension)—there are 39 questions in this test
- **Conventions of Language** (spelling, grammar and punctuation)—there are 50 questions in this test
- **Writing** (written expression)—there is one piece of writing in this test.

About the report

- When your child completes the NAPLAN tests, you and your child's school will receive a report indicating their standard of proficiency in literacy and numeracy. There are four levels of achievement:
  - **Exceeding** (advanced proficiency)
  - **Strong** (average to high-average proficiency)
  - **Developing** (not yet proficient)
  - **Needs additional support** (help is needed).

The report will also show the national average.

ABOUT THIS BOOK

The Mini Reading and Conventions of Language Tests

In the first part of the book you will find ten tests for each subject. These tests are divided into three levels of difficulty:

- Standard level
- Intermediate level
- Advanced level.

- You will be able to see what level your child is at by finding the point where they start having consistent difficulty with questions. For example, if your child answers most questions correctly up to the intermediate level and then gets most questions wrong from then onwards, it is likely your child's ability is at an intermediate level.
- You will be able to see your child's strengths and weaknesses in different topics by completing the **Strengths and weaknesses chart** (see page viii).
- You will also be able to give your child intensive practice in short tests which have time limits based on the actual Reading and Conventions of Language test times.
- There are quick answers for every question so you can easily mark your child's work.
- For the **Reading tests**, line references and explanations are provided. The line references will help you find exactly where the answer to the question is found in the text. Questions in the reading answer section have been divided into five types: fact-finding, inferring, judgement, language and synthesis. Explanations are provided within these answer scaffolds to help you teach your child how to answer the different types of reading questions. If you turn to the inside back cover you will see all these types of explanations explained fully.
- For the **Conventions of Language tests**, tips and explanations are provided. Your child can then learn to apply these general tips to similar questions and the explanations will help you explain the answers to your child.

The Mini Writing Tests

- There are three **Writing tests**.
- There are tips specific to the type of text of each question. These tips will provide guidelines for your child's writing.
- Each Writing test has writing samples at standard, intermediate and advanced levels. From this you will be able to see which level your child is writing at. For example, if your child's writing closely resembles the intermediate writing sample then their writing is at the intermediate level.
- Marking checklists are also provided so you can go through your child's writing and check that they have covered all of the necessary points.

The Sample Online-style Literacy Tests

- In the second part of the book we provide you with three sample tests which are modelled on actual NAPLAN Online Literacy tests.
- For the Conventions of Language and Reading tests there are answers, tips and explanations, and also a list of each question's level of difficulty.
- For the Writing tests there are marking checklists and writing samples, one each at standard, intermediate and advanced levels. From this you will be able to see what level your child is writing at by comparing their writing to the writing samples.

STRENGTHS AND WEAKNESSES CHART

- As your child completes each test, mark it using the answer section at the back and then fill in this chart to record their progress.
- You will be able to see at a glance your child's strengths and weaknesses in different topics and different strands of Literacy.
- If you find your child needs more practice on specific topics, use the checklist of ***Excel*** books on the back cover to find the book to help them.

Area of Learning	Level	Mini test	Mark
Spelling	Standard	1	/18
Spelling	Standard	2	/18
Spelling	Intermediate	3	/18
Spelling	Intermediate	4	/18
Spelling	Intermediate	5	/18
Spelling	Intermediate	6	/18
Spelling	Advanced	7	/18
Spelling	Advanced	8	/18
Spelling	Advanced	9	/18
Spelling	Advanced	10	/18
Grammar	Standard	1	/18
Grammar	Intermediate	2	/18
Grammar	Intermediate	3	/18
Grammar	Advanced	4	/18
Grammar	Advanced	5	/18
Punctuation	Standard	1	/18
Punctuation	Intermediate	2	/18
Punctuation	Intermediate	3	/18
Punctuation	Advanced	4	/18
Punctuation	Advanced	5	/18
Reading	Standard	1	/6
Reading	Standard	2	/6
Reading	Intermediate	3	/6
Reading	Intermediate	4	/6
Reading	Intermediate	5	/6
Reading	Intermediate	6	/6
Reading	Advanced	7	/6
Reading	Advanced	8	/6
Reading	Advanced	9	/6
Reading	Advanced	10	/6

SPELLING Standard level questions

Mini Test 1

Please ask your parent or teacher to read to you the spelling words on page 143.
Write the correct spelling of each word in the box.

1. The ______ dog ate all the dog food.
2. The car broke down in a ______ street.
3. "Don't ______ to take your homework," called Mel's mother.
4. I got every ______ right except the first one.
5. My grandparents went on a ______ to the South Pacific.
6. There were ______ of lightning in the western sky.
7. The new school ______ were given out on the first day of Term 1.
8. The ______ were trapped in a small pool in the creek.

The spelling mistakes in these sentences have been highlighted.
Write the correct spelling for each highlighted word in the box.

9. The **envelop** was found under the letterbox!
10. Put your name and **adress** on your exercise book.
11. Every town in Australia has a **postcoad**.
12. "That was a **truely** great film", declared Dad as he stood up.
13. The express train roars **threw** just after eight o'clock each night.

Read the text *Our planet.* Each line has a word that is incorrect.
Write the correct spelling of the word in the box.

Our planet

14. All the inner planets in our soller systems have mountains. Our
15. planet is not the only one where volcanos are found. These
16. monster mountains brethe gas, smoke, ash and fumes into the air.
17. Luckly for the creatures on Earth this does not happen all the time.
18. It usually only hapens for a short while after an eruption.

SPELLING

Standard level questions

Mini Test 2

Please ask your parent or teacher to read to you the spelling words on page 143.
Write the correct spelling of each word in the box.

1 A snail left a slimy, silver ______ right down the window.

2 My sister and I are in ______ schools in the same street.

3 Take a bucket and brush and clean up the ______ mess.

4 Mark's ______ is on the first day of the second month.

5 The hollow tree is a safe home for many bush ______.

6 The ______ was knotted through the wire and I couldn't undo it.

7 We put ______ and pickles on the sandwich.

8 "You don't need money to find ______", stated Mum.

9 The ______ on the back deck was rotting.

10 That is the ______ result for a science test I have ever seen.

The spelling mistakes in these sentences have been highlighted.
Write the correct spelling for each highlighted word in the box.

11 Heath told the class he was **sory** for being late for the concert.

12 We all smiled as the bride and **grume** left the church.

13 Dad sighed, "There are too many films about **witchs** and wizards."

14 Is it better to have wealth and **richers** rather than happiness?

Read the text *The sun*.
Each line has a word that is incorrect. Write the correct spelling of the word in the box.

The sun

15 The sun is our nearest star. It is the sauce of all our heat and

16 light. Almost everythink on Earth depends on it. The sun is made

17 up of a mixture of different tipes of gas. They are all burning. At

18 the centre of the sun the tempratures are very, very high.

Answers and explanations on pages 85–86

SPELLING

Intermediate level questions

Mini Test 3

Please ask your parent or teacher to read to you the spelling words on page 143.
Write the correct spelling of each word in the box.

1. Good ______ is more important than working late into the night.
2. Mum cannot ______ the magazine, but I can get it for her.
3. A yellow ______ whistled sadly in its cage.
4. David can't ______ which shirt to wear to the party.
5. Every ______ fruit bats head to the orchards for food.
6. Lizards were hiding in a ______ log to escape the winter frosts.
7. Don't play with ______. You could cut yourself.
8. The school has a new computer and I am ______ keyboard skills.

The spelling mistakes in these sentences have been highlighted.
Write the correct spelling for each highlighted word in the box.

9. Jan was so **mene** she wouldn't buy her mother a present.
10. Will you pass a **peace** of cake to our guest?
11. A stick **figuer** is a quick way to draw a person.
12. The children were **smileing** for the class photo.
13. I'd like to be a thin person but not a **skiny** one!

Read the text *Playing field*. Each line has a word that is incorrect.
Write the correct spelling of the word in the box.

Playing field

14. We don't train for hockey on an oval. We train on a vacent lot near
15. a desseted ten-storey building. No one has lived in the building for
16. many years but when we were hitting a ball around the ovver night
17. I saw a purson watching us from a window on the third floor. He
18. should be reported to security for trespassing on privete property.

SPELLING Intermediate level questions

Mini Test 4

Please ask your parent or teacher to read to you the spelling words on page 144.
Write the correct spelling of each word in the box.

1 The ______ of the meat was too strong for me.

2 All the players had ______ when they turned professional.

3 Our netball team was an ______ team when we won last year's final.

4 The water ______ the oval and the assembly area.

5 Have you ever seen a red ______?

6 There were cut-out ______ along the fence over Christmas.

7 I used almost a whole tin of ______ when I painted the floor.

8 Turn the ______ down! I can't think with that noise.

The spelling mistakes in these sentences have been highlighted.
Write the correct spelling for each highlighted word in the box.

9 The wheather got worse the further north the explorers travelled.

10 A wallerby is a small marsupial.

11 The dog's kennell was put in the shade of an old tree.

12 We need protection for reiny days as well as hot days.

13 The enterance to the school is through the gate in a side street.

Read the text *Magnets*. Each line has a word that is incorrect.
Write the correct spelling of the word in the box.

Magnets

14 Magnets are objects that attrack iron nails or steel pins that are

15 put nearby. The magnet holes onto them and it can take a firm,

16 gentle tug to pull them off. The magnet has an invisable force

17 that pulls the nails and pins twowards it. This force is called

18 magnetic force but it cannot be used on other mettles.

Answers and explanations on pages 87–88

SPELLING Intermediate level questions

Mini Test 5

Please ask your parent or teacher to read to you the spelling words on page 144.
Write the correct spelling of each word in the box.

1 The ______ in my trousers has lost its spring. I need a leather belt.

2 Meg is smart at science but her ______ reports are messy.

3 I was ______ for work yesterday but I'm early today.

4 Our neighbour grows roses but my parents prefer ______.

5 The ______ is a grey and pink parrot.

6 Every warehouse in this district has a ______.

7 Mum wonders if ______ will be better than joggers for our walk.

8 What do you want with your breakfast? ______ or a banana?

9 We had a choice of ______ or muesli each morning.

10 Mr Jones grows ______ and cabbages in his back garden.

The spelling mistakes in these sentences have been highlighted.
Write the correct spelling for each highlighted word in the box.

11 The orphans were raysed in a building outside the town.

12 "Here are your birthday presence," said my relatives as we sat down.

13 Bricks can be rough but steel can be smoove.

14 Many outdoor-sports people live dangrously and enjoy the thrill.

Read the text *Adam's place*.
Each line has a word that is incorrect. Write the correct spelling of the word in the box.

Adam's place

15 Adam lived with his parents across the road from a small warf. His

16 father worked in a shed over the water, reparing small boats. Often

17 a pellican or seagull would perch on the boatyard gate that Adam's

18 father had to unlock each mourning. They would watch him silently.

Answers and explanations on page 88

SPELLING

Intermediate level questions

Mini Test 6

Please ask your parent or teacher to read to you the spelling words on page 144.
Write the correct spelling of each word in the box.

1 The ______ cracked when a driver parked a council truck on it.

2 The moon ______ the Earth every twenty-four hours.

3 In our last test we had to answer questions on ______ and tables.

4 The ______ were left in the middle of the alley!

5 "Is the woman ______ or guilty?" asked the judge.

6 The chest was found in a far corner of the dusty ______.

7 It is not ______ to complete the project before Friday.

8 "To my way of thinking," said the captain, "we will ______ win."

9 The soldiers were ______ after their jungle march.

10 Tell the youth to tell the ______!

The spelling mistakes in these sentences have been highlighted.
Write the correct spelling for each highlighted word in the box.

11 James skinned his **nuckle** when he fell from his skateboard.

12 There was a **blancket** of smoke after the blaze in the mattress factory.

13 Farmers had a **plentyfull** supply of water after the spring storms.

14 Marcel had two **assinments** to do in a fortnight.

Read the text *Holly's fear*.
Each line has a word that is incorrect. Write the correct spelling of the word in the box.

Holly's fear

15 Holly has never forgoten the day she had to wait outside the playground

16 fence and she had scene the dog. To Holly, who was small, it was

17 hugue with sharp teeth, great rolling, dark eyes, and a long, dripping

18 tongue. Suddenly it raced up towards the gate to the kindergarden.

Answers and explanations on page 89

SPELLING Advanced level questions

Mini Test 7

Please ask your parent or teacher to read to you the spelling words on page 145.
Write the correct spelling of each word in the box.

1 Graham was ______ distracted during the last half of the game.

2 Grace ______ well in her half-yearly test.

3 The enemy submarine fired its ______ from ten kilometres away.

4 David went ______ at the school concert.

5 Dad complains that Mum ______ every time they go shopping.

6 An ______ of the moon is when the Earth's shadow is on the moon.

7 As the climbers ______ the mountain they became sick.

8 The school is having an ______ night for the parents.

9 Tessa's mother won a ______ prize.

10 The possum is a ______ animal.

The spelling mistakes in these sentences have been highlighted.
Write the correct spelling for each highlighted word in the box.

11 A **yatch** in the final ocean race lost a sail.

12 Kites were **saleing** through the air when the breeze dropped.

13 A **bough** wave forms at the front of a moving ship.

Read the text *Waiting room*. Each line has a word that is incorrect.
Write the correct spelling of the word in the box.

Waiting room

14 All winter I had had a sore throat. It was more than a coff. I think my

15 tonsills might have to come out. I had been to see the doctor so many

16 times she knew my name. I had read all her megazenes at least

17 once. My doctor is a specialest in ear, nose and throat complaints.

18 I hope I don't have to go to hospital to have an operashun.

Answers and explanations on pages 89–90

SPELLING

Advanced level questions

Mini Test 8

Please ask your parent or teacher to read to you the spelling words on page 145.
Write the correct spelling of each word in the box.

1 The wattle ______ made some people sneeze.

2 A dislocated ______ can be very painful.

3 After ______ the diver gasped for air.

4 An ______ is a bird that cannot fly.

5 Have you ever been ______ in class?

6 There was a ______ smell coming from the dry creek bed.

7 Animals can detect ______ people cannot smell.

8 Many ______ at the sales were at half price.

9 Teachers should not show ______ when they give out awards.

10 An ______ is a spaceman or spacewoman.

The spelling mistakes in these sentences have been highlighted.
Write the correct spelling for each highlighted word in the box.

11 A reckangeler shape has four straight sides.

12 A hexogen is a common shape for bathroom tiles.

13 At the boarder the passengers had to produce their passports.

Read the text *Wheat farmers*. Each line has a word that is incorrect.
Write the correct spelling of the word in the box.

Wheat farmers

14 Wheat farmers in Australia use large tractors and harvestors to

15 preduice crops of wheat. The wheat is then transported by large

16 trucks to stoarage silos, where it is then carried by rail to a port

17 to be shipped overcease. Within weeks it can be offloaded and

18 made into flour for the manyerfacteur of basic bread products.

Answers and explanations on pages 90–91

SPELLING

Advanced level questions

Mini Test 9

Please ask your parent or teacher to read to you the spelling words on page 146.
Write the correct spelling of each word in the box.

1. The reported ______ was caught in a police operation.
2. Did the circus magician make the rabbit ______?
3. I was ______ to be chosen as class captain in the election.
4. Our ______ is a very safe place even during the holidays.
5. The ______ star was relaxing under a palm tree during a short break.
6. Colin Brown was a ______ gymnast but now he is an announcer.
7. There are twelve hours between ______ and midnight.
8. Who was the ______ of the adventure story set in the forest?
9. Some popular herbs are ______, mint and chives.
10. "We are not ______ this any longer," declared the park ranger.

The spelling mistakes in these sentences have been highlighted.
Write the correct spelling for each highlighted word in the box.

11. The cashews, peanuts and **armonds** were in bags of mixed nuts.
12. "Don't waste your money at the **keosks**," warned my parents.
13. I have to sleep in my underwear as I have forgotten my **perjamas**.
14. Evelyn wore her new **neckelace** and sapphire earrings.

Read the text *Making plans*. Each line has a word that is incorrect.
Write the correct spelling of the word in the box.

Making plans

15 Have you ever though about getting a job or creating your own? Lots
16 of students once had deliverey rounds, especially for newspapers. There
17 are many things yunger people can do other than roaming the streets at
18 odd hours. Why not cheque out your area to see what needs doing?

Answers and explanations on page 91

SPELLING

Advanced level questions

Mini Test 10

Please ask your parent or teacher to read to you the spelling words on page 146.
Write the correct spelling of each word in the box.

1. You ______ know how to complete this survey form.
2. ______ driven aircraft are not normal but can be seen at country air shows.
3. The sights on the ______ of the rifle were aligned.
4. An ______ carnival has a variety of different events.
5. "Why is there a pile of gravel on the lawn?" ______ Dad.
6. The ______ at the western end of the swamp is polluted.
7. No ______ was available for the miners trapped underground.
8. The painters had to repaint under the ______ of the garage roof.
9. A landscape ______ can make the outside of a cottage very attractive.
10. The residents demanded lights at the busy ______.

The spelling mistakes in these sentences have been highlighted.
Write the correct spelling for each highlighted word in the box.

11. I could feel the hairs on my **scalpe** prickle as I watched the horror movie.
12. Jake ordered a seafood meal. He had prawns, **molluskes** and chips!
13. In the refrigerator were tubs of custard and cream and some **mueseli**.
14. Maria was only **fithteen** when she left on an overseas vacation.

Read the text *Newspapers*. Each line has a word that is incorrect.
Write the correct spelling of the word in the box.

Newspapers

15. Newspapers have excisted for almost five hundred years. When radio
16. and, latter, television appeared during last century, news reporting in
17. these media changed the methed it was undertaken in newspapers. There
18. was a greater urgencey to have reports written for prompt distribution.

Answers and explanations on page 92

Standard level questions

Mini Test 1

1 Which of the following correctly completes the sentence?

Karl bought a ______ present for his mother for her birthday.

A interesting **B** ugly **C** useful **D** orange

2 Which of the following correctly completes the sentence?

Where is ______ new knife I gave you for cutting meat? I cannot find it anywhere.

A a **B** an **C** what **D** the

3 Draw a line to join the beginning that correctly completes this sentence.

A Me and my mates
B Me and me mates
C My mates and I
D Me mates and I

will always be friends.

4 Which of the following correctly completes the sentence?

The old couple won a five-week cruise ______ an ocean liner.

A in **B** on **C** with **D** at **E** for

Read the text *Typists*. The text has some gaps. Choose the best option to fill each gap.

Typists

Typists in offices have many duties.

Text		A	B	C	D
Most can type very ______ , often	5	quick	quicker	quickly	quickest
______ than one hundred words	6	gooder	better	best	more better
each minute. ______ also have to	7	She	Them	But	They
file paper ______ take messages.	8	and	yet	but	which
They have to be polite ______ visitors.	9	at	to	with	among

Answers and explanations on pages 92–93

Mini Test 1 (continued)

10 Which word can be used instead of the highlighted words?

Jerry had lots of comics about his superheroes. He kept **his comics** under his bed.

A those **B** they **C** it **D** them

11 Which of the following correctly completes the sentence?

The hound dog soon discovered the ________ of the frightened rabbit.

A scent **B** sent **C** sense **D** cent

12 Which of the following correctly completes the sentence?

Trudy left the room because she ________ the movie a few weeks ago.

A had saw **B** seen **C** had seen **D** sees

13 Which of the following correctly completes the sentence?

Mum told me never to touch the switch but I know I ________ reach it if I stand on a chair.

A would **B** might **C** may **D** can

Read the text *The park*. The text has some gaps. Choose the best option to fill each gap.

The park

Churchill Park is just down our street.

Text		A	B	C	D
It's a great place for kids to ________	14	plays	play	playing	player
cricket on ________ open, grassy spaces.	15	a	an	them	the
Joggers ________ on the wide paths	16	train	trainer	trains	training
and visitors can stroll ________ the	17	over	across	among	between
many gardens or ________ the birds.	18	fed	feed	feeding	feeds

Answers and explanations on pages 92–93

Mini Test 2

1 Which of the following correctly completes the sentence?

My brother is coming ______ Monday to get his books.

A for **B** at **C** in **D** on

Read the text *Team trouble*. The text has some gaps. Choose the correct word to fill each gap.

Team trouble

Lots of hamburgers were **2** at the picnic. This was a shock for the coach **3** had warned his team about keeping fit and being prepared.

2 **A** eat **B** eated **C** eaten **D** ate

3 **A** that **B** who **C** what **D** which

4 Which sentence is correct?

A There is so much grass in the garden since it rained!
B There is so many grass in the garden since it rained!
C There are so much grass in the garden since it rained!
D There are so many grass in the garden since it rained!

5 Which of the following correctly completes the sentence?

The boys in the rock band ______ having a short break.

A is **B** are **C** am **D** was

Read the text *Kangaroos*. The text has some gaps. Choose the best option to fill each gap.

Kangaroos

The kangaroo is a large macropod.

Text		A	B	C	D
Macropods ______ big-footed marsupials.	6	are	were	is	have
Wallabies are also macropods ______	7	and	yet	because	but
they are a lot ______. Kangaroos	8	smallest	smaller	more smaller	small
roam ______ open plains of outback	9	a	an	the	that
Australia, where they can be ______ in huge herds.	10	seen	saw	seed	sawed

Answers and explanations on pages 93–94

Mini Test 2 (continued)

11 Which word can be used instead of the highlighted words?

The merry-go-round was a blaze of flashing, coloured lights.
The merry-go-round's lights could be seen across the bay.

A Them **B** There **C** It's **D** Its **E** Their

12 Which of the following should have a question mark?

A How wonderful
B How to pan for gold
C How did you escape the fires
D How you lost is not my worry

13 Which word is a collective noun? Write your answer in the box.

The children in the team put on coats for protection against the Hobart cold.

14 Which words correctly complete the sentence?

The jogger avoided the lane because there ______

A have been an oil spill.
B are an oil spill.
C were an oil spill.
D had been an oil spill.

Read the text *Sasha*. The text has some gaps. Choose the best option to fill each gap.

Sasha

Sasha was the top student in her class.

She ______ all her addition facts

	know	knew	knowed	knows
15	**A**	**B**	**C**	**D**

by the time she ______ nine. She

	were	is	was	are
16	**A**	**B**	**C**	**D**

neither watched ______ played any

	nor	but	or	and
17	**A**	**B**	**C**	**D**

sports. Her friends ______ she was

	thinks	thinked	thoughts	thought
18	**A**	**B**	**C**	**D**

a little bit odd!

Answers and explanations on pages 93–94

GRAMMAR Intermediate level questions

Mini Test 3

15 MIN

1 Which of the following correctly completes the sentence?

Sherri was looking for ______ old shoes in the garden shed.

A a **B** an **C** the **D** them

2 Which word or figures are unnecessary in this sentence?

The salesman told my father that the shirt was 100% pure silk.

A my **B** shirt **C** the **D** 100%

3 Which of the following correctly completes the sentence?

We have a choice. Either you get a video ______ we watch repeat shows on TV!

A and **B** or **C** but **D** when **E** nor

Read the text *The meal*. The text has some gaps. Choose the correct word to fill each gap.

The meal

The hiking party **4** tired and hungry after the long trip. All they wanted was a **5** rest in a warm lounge in front of television.

4 **A** was **B** is **C** were **D** are

5 **A** slow **B** large **C** long **D** big

6 Which word can be used instead of the highlighted words?

We bought a bag of cards, paper and tape at the newsagency to wrap the presents. The bag of cards, paper and tape cost more than some of the presents.

A Them **B** What **C** They **D** It

7 Which group of words can all be used as nouns?

A last, only, greener, yourself
B wisdom, Coles, breeze, gang
C fry, fanciful, careless, recall
D near, between, underneath, by

8 Which sentence is correct?

A I don't have no money so I can't buy no chips.
B I don't have any money so I can't buy any chips.
C I don't have any money so I can't buy no chips.
D I don't have any money but I can't buy any chips.

Answers and explanations on pages 94–95

Mini Test 3 (continued)

Read the text *Presents!* The text has some gaps. Choose the best option to fill each gap.

Presents!

Planning for birthdays can be difficult.

There ______ a number of questions

	A	B	C	D
9	are	is	am	was

to be decided. Last year we ______

	A	B	C	D
10	bought	buy	buyed	buying

a chair for Grandpa. It ______ a lot

	A	B	C	D
11	costed	costs	cost	costing

of money ______ he didn't like it at

	A	B	C	D
12	because	which	and	but

all! What ______ we think we should

	A	B	C	D
13	do	does	did	dose

get this year?

Read the text *School teams*. The text has some gaps. Choose the best option to fill each gap.

School teams

Meg and I are in the debating team.

Last week we had a ______, so our

	A	B	C	D
14	buy	by	bye	bi

points ______ not changed. The girls

	A	B	C	D
15	have	has	had	haven't

in the other team ______ their last

	A	B	C	D
16	win	winned	wind	won

match. It was a ______ win than

	A	B	C	D
17	best	better	good	more better

______ expected as they were late

	A	B	C	D
18	it	she	they	those

arriving at the other school.

Answers and explanations on pages 94–95

GRAMMAR Advanced level questions

Mini Test 4

1 Choose the word that describes how the crowd hissed. Write your answer in the box.

Immediately after the fumbled pass the angry crowd hissed softly at our team's poor effort.

2 Which of the following correctly completes the sentence?

Nerida said, "Your new uniform is different ______ mine."

A from **B** to **C** then **D** than

3 Which of the following best completes the sentence?

The price we paid for the new flat-screen television was ______.

A beautiful **B** remarkable **C** charming **D** majestic

4 Which of the following correctly completes the sentence?

Evan said, "Smoking is not only bad for the lungs ______ the heart."

A and **B** but also **C** but **D** and yet **E** as

5 Which sentence is correct?

A Because you went to the cinema in a bus.

B Because the men were old, and the sea was too rough.

C Because Aaron is ten, and you are his younger brother.

D Because I have the money, I will pay.

6 Which of the following correctly completes the sentence?

They don't have ______ right to give us homework on the weekend!

A no **B** any **C** what **D** not none

7 Which of the following correctly completes the sentence?

My shoes were tightly tied, however Jake's shoes were ______ tied.

A more tightly **B** tighter **C** tightest **D** tightly **E** most tightest

8 Which sentence is correct?

A Jan saw herself and me in the club news.

B Jan saw herself and I in the club news.

C Jan saw hers self and me in the club news.

D Jan saw sheself and I in the club news.

Answers and explanations on pages 95–96

Read the text *Story time*. The text has some gaps. Choose the best option to fill each gap.

Story time

On Thursday we have story time at school.

The teacher doesn't ______ us a story.

	A	B	C	D
9	told	tell	tolled	tells

We have to ______ a story. Last week we

	A	B	C	D
10	writ	wrote	write	writes

______ about a prince who killed a

	A	B	C	D
11	written	write	writes	wrote

red dragon. My prince was brave ______

	A	B	C	D
12	so	but	and	because

he fell over and ______ his sword. He

	A	B	C	D
13	lost	lose	losted	losed

had to get up and run away!

Read the text *The wharf*. The text has some gaps. Choose the best option to fill each gap.

The wharf

There is an old wharf on the river bend near our town.

I have ______ down there on Sundays

	A	B	C	D
14	going	goes	gone	goed

just to watch the yachts ______ by the

	A	B	C	D
15	sails	sail	sailed	sailing

old mill. I have to be careful ______

	A	B	C	D
16	for	cause	and	as

there is a broken ______ right near

	A	B	C	D
17	board	bored	bord	boared

the very end ______ the wharf.

	A	B	C	D
18	off	on	at	of

Answers and explanations on pages 95–96

GRAMMAR

Advanced level questions

Mini Test 5

1 Which of the following correctly completes the sentence?

When Pam went to the zoo she saw an ______.

A European owl **B** sleeping ostrich **C** awkward penguin **D** honking goose

2 Which of the following correctly completes the sentence?

"The bulldozer was operated all day," growled Dad. "______ noise interfered with my work."

A it's **B** It's **C** its **D** Its

3 This sentence contains **at least** one noun.

Unless the organisers make a decision soon our squads will not come in before sunset.

Use as many boxes as you need to write any nouns included in this sentence.

4 Which of the following correctly completes the sentence?

We must find ______ to the castle before it gets dark.

A some way **B** some-way **C** someway **D** Someway **E** yet

Read the text *The park*. The text has some gaps. Choose the correct word to fill each gap.

The park

Dad said it was safe to play **5** the park as long **6** we stayed away from the edge of the bicycle path.

5 **A** at **B** on **C** to **D** in

6 **A** for **B** as **C** that **D** while

7 Which word can be used instead of the highlighted words?

The girls in the class played chess while the boys played Monopoly.
The girls in the class and the boys all enjoyed being allowed some free time.

A They **B** While **C** Them **D** It **E** Those

8 Which sentence is correct?

A Five dollars is too much to pay for an ice cream.

B Five dollars are too much to pay for an ice cream.

C Five dollars is too many to pay for an ice cream.

D Five dollars are too many to pay for an ice cream.

Answers and explanations on pages 96–97

Mini Test 5 (continued)

Read the text *Accidents*. The text has some gaps. Choose the best option to fill each gap.

Accidents

Experts say the number of accidents has increased.

Text		A	B	C	D
Even ____ the number is increasing,	9	as	how	if	was
does it give a true picture? There ____	10	are	is	was	will be
more cars being ____ on our roads now	11	drived	drove	driving	driven
____ ever before. The population	12	then	than	even	when
____ increased greatly in recent	13	have	had	has	haved

years and is still increasing.

Read the text *Music lessons*. The text has some gaps. Choose the best option to fill each gap.

Music lessons

Most people have music lessons at some time in their childhood.

Text		A	B	C	D
Grant, Jason and ____ all want to	14	me	us	my	I
to play guitars. A new band ____	15	had	have	has	having
places ____ two more players, a	16	for	in	with	by
guitarist ____ a drummer. We have	17	but	and	or	also
____ to the leader to ask him	18	speaked	spoke	spoken	spake

to put us all in the band!

Answers and explanations on pages 96–97

Standard level questions

Mini Test 1

1 Which of the following correctly completes the sentence?

We were invited to go to the talk on skin cancer by ________ Stevens.

A doctor **B** Dr **C** Dr. **D** dr

2 Which of the following best completes the sentence?

I was stunned by the answer. It wasn't right ________

A full stop (.) **B** comma (,) **C** question mark (?) **D** exclamation mark (!)

3 Which sentence has the correct punctuation?

A Justin and Lyn joined the school choir to sing Christmas carols.
B Justin and Lyn joined the school choir to sing Christmas Carols.
C Justin and Lyn joined the School choir to sing Christmas Carols.
D Justin and Lyn joined the School choir to sing Christmas carols.

4 Which sentence has the correct punctuation?

A When I come home I will fix the door?
B When the band plays you have to stand up?
C When do you expect to get your pocket money?
D When I see a spider I scream?

5 Circle the letters to show where the missing commas (,) should go.

"These old ↑(A) boxes will be fine ↑(B) " said Mum ↑(C) as she dropped old ↑(D) books onto the floor.

6 Which of the following correctly completes the sentence?

In Tasmania, the capital ________ lights were left on all night.

A city's **B** cities' **C** citys' **D** citie's

7 Which sentence has the correct punctuation?

A Julie, my cousin will visit Fiji, in July.
B Julie, my cousin will visit Fiji in July.
C Julie, my cousin, will visit Fiji in July.
D Julie, my cousin, will visit Fiji, in July.

8 Which of the following correctly completes the sentence?

The rider just got a flat tyre. He ________ win the road race now.

A cant **B** can'not **C** ca'nt **D** can't

9 Circle the letter to show where the missing question mark (?) should go.

Where ↑(A) and when is the game this week ↑(B) When I get home ↑(C) I need to put petrol in the car ↑(D)

Answers and explanations on page 97

10 Which sentence is an example of a statement and should end with a full stop?

A Captain Smith lost his ship in the Pacific Ocean

B Quickly bring your book to me

C Would you mind passing the salt

D Exactly the same as the other girl's racquet

11 Which sentence correctly uses the apostrophe (')?

A The toys' in the boxes are Kates but the others are mine.

B The toys in the boxes are Kates but the other's are mine.

C The toys in the boxes are Kate's but the others are mine.

D The toys in the boxes' are Kates but the others are mine.

12 Circle two letters to show where the missing speech marks (" and ") should go.

A↓Now, now, **B**↓whispered the driver **C**↓who was filling in a form.**D**↓

Read the text *Homework*. The text has some gaps. Choose the best option to fill each gap.

Homework

Lee gets homework most days of the week.

Text		A	B	C	D
Lee does her homework before ______	13	Dinner	Dinner!	dinner	dinner.
She starts with ______ for Mr Lim.	14	English,	english,	English	english
The new questions are too ______	15	hard!	hard?	hard,	Hard!
______ teacher will not believe her	16	her.	Her	her,	Her,
when she tells him ______ Mr Lim	17	so	so?	so,	so!

will just say, "Work harder, Lee."

18 A word in this sentence should have a capital letter. Write the word in the box.

Kings highway runs right down the main street of the capital city.

Answers and explanations on page 97

PUNCTUATION Intermediate level questions

Mini Test 2

1 This sentence contains at least one word that should start with a capital letter.
even today nomadic shepherds watch over their sheep in many african nations.
Use as many boxes as you need to write the words that should begin with a capital letter.

2 Which of the following best completes the sentence?

What a difference an hour makes ______

A question mark (?) **B** exclamation mark (!)
C comma (,) **D** semicolon (;)

3 How should the sentence *its hers, so leave it there* be written?

A It's her's, so leave it there! **B** Its her's, so leave it there!
C Its hers, so leave it there! **D** It's hers, so leave it there!

4 Circle the letter to show where the missing apostrophe (') should go.

Many pupil (A) s own backpack (B) s to carry their book (C) s to school but all of Tim (D) s are in his desk.

5 Which sentence has the correct punctuation?

A All my brothers, Mark, James and Sean, have joined the Landcare volunteers.
B All my brothers Mark, James and Sean have joined the Landcare volunteers.
C All my brothers Mark, James, and Sean, have joined the Landcare volunteers.
D All my brothers, Mark, James and Sean have joined the Landcare volunteers.

6 Which of the following correctly completes the sentence?

Katie and Sara said it was ______ but the ball really belongs to Lester.

A hers **B** their's **C** theirs **D** her's

7 Which pair of sentences has the correct punctuation?

A Look at that light! Is it a comet! **B** Look at that light? Is it a comet?
C Look at that light! Is it a comet? **D** Look at that light? Is it a comet!

8 Which sentence has the correct punctuation?

A The witness replied softly that, "It was not his car."
B The witness replied, "Softly that it was not his car."
C "The witness replied softly that it was not his car."
D The witness replied softly that it was not his car.

9 Which of the following correctly completes the sentence?

"Do you want an apple with your ______ asked Mum.

A lunch?" **B** lunch," **C** lunch"? **D** lunch.

Answers and explanations on pages 97–98

10 Circle the letter to show where the missing question mark (**?**) should go.

Is that your scooter ↑ on the drive ↑ or is it Ken's ↑ How I wish you would do the right thing ↑

A B C D

11 Which sentence is correctly punctuated?

A A huge, black ugly spider crept out of a dark, hole.

B A huge, black, ugly spider crept out of a dark hole.

C A huge, black, ugly, spider crept out of a dark hole.

D A huge, black, ugly, spider crept out of a dark, hole.

12 Which sentence is correctly punctuated?

A "You can go to bed now" suggested my father.

B "You can go to bed now." suggested my father.

C "You can go to bed now," suggested my father.

D "You can go to bed now?" suggested my father.

Read the text *Instructions*. The text has some gaps. Choose the best option to fill each gap.

Instructions

Our group leader told us to sit down.

Text		A	B	C	D
We ______ He looked very serious.	**13**	did?	Did!	did,	did.
"______ tell you this once and	**14**	I'ill	I'll	Iw'll	i'll
once only. Every hiker ______ including	**15**	(,)	(')	(.)	(?)
those in Mr ______ group, must take a	**16**	Smiths	Smiths'	Smith's	Smithses
turn at the rear. Is that clear ______	**17**	(?")	(.)	(!")	(?)

18 Circle the letter to show which word should not start with a capital letter.

The Play *Hamlet* has been performed in some English theatres since the Middle Ages.

A (Play) B (English) C (Middle) D (Ages)

PUNCTUATION Intermediate level questions

Mini Test 3

1 Which of the following correctly completes the sentence?

Mick said it was someone ______ rubbish and he was not picking it up.

A el'se **B** else's **C** elses' **D** elses's

2 Which of the following correctly completes the sentence?

We have all the teams' results except for those of the last two teams to play and ______ will be here shortly.

A theirs **B** their's **C** their **D** theirs'

3 Which sentence has the correct punctuation?

A Tanya looked at her watch "and exclaimed, It's after ten o'clock!"

B Tanya looked at her watch and exclaimed, It's after ten o'clock!

C "Tanya looked at her watch and "exclaimed", It's after ten o'clock!

D Tanya looked at her watch and exclaimed, "It's after ten o'clock!"

4 Choose the word that is the verb. Write the word in the box.

It happened during the game on Wednesday against the Tasmanian Raiders. [ ]

5 Which sentence is an example of a command sentence?

A May your guardian angel be with you **B** Well done

C Shut the lid before you try to lift the box **D** Don't you ever eat pumpkin

6 Which sentence has the correct punctuation?

A If you, would like a free copy, of the book, call the publisher.

B If, you would like a free copy of the book call the publisher.

C If, you would like a free copy, of the book call the publisher.

D If you would like a free copy of the book, call the publisher.

7 Which of the following correctly completes the sentence?

There was a disaster on the ship, HMAS *Ibis*. All the ______ bags were soaked in a storm.

A crews **B** crew's **C** crews' **D** crews's

8 Which punctuation correctly completes the sentence?

"How long before you get the results ______ asked the patient.

A question mark, closing speech mark (**?"**) **B** comma, closing speech mark (**,"**)

C closing speech mark, question mark (**"?**) **D** comma (**,**)

Answers and explanations on pages 98–99

9 Circle the letter to show where the missing comma (,) should go.

We need bright red (A) pale (B) green (C) and deep blue (D) for the poster.

10 Circle the letter to show where the missing apostrophe (') should go.

After the class (A) test, Kim found her result, but all the other girl (B) s (C) result (D) s were lost.

11 Which sentence has the correct punctuation?

A When I get to Ceduna I will rest?

B When do you have breakfast?

C When Martin finds his bag we can go home?

D When to take pills depends upon when you have meals?

12 Which of the following correctly completes the sentence?

All vehicles in ______ have to have a yearly inspection for roadworthiness.

A N.S.W. **B** nsw **C** N.S.Wales **D** NSW

Read the text *Hospital visit*. The text has some gaps. Choose the best option to fill each gap.

Hospital visit

The only time I've been in hospital was when I was born.

That was nine ______ six months and

13 **A** years. **B** Years, **C** years, **D** years

one week ago but when ______

14 **A** your **B** you're **C** your're **D** you've

a baby you ______ really remember anything.

15 **A** don't **B** dont **C** didn't **D** donnot

"Your nasty appendix has to come ______

16 **A** out." **B** out **C** out" **D** out,"

Dad said softly. ____ are off to hospital."

17 **A** You" **B** "you **C** "You **D** You

18 Which of the following correctly completes the sentence?

By the ______, there was at least one computer in every home.

A 1990s' **B** 1990s **C** 1990's **D** 1990S

Answers and explanations on pages 98–99

PUNCTUATION Advanced level questions

Mini Test 4

1 Which of the following correctly completes the sentence?

Did you want to go rowing ______ There is still time.

A full stop (.)
B comma (,)
C question mark (?)
D exclamation mark (!)

2 This sentence contains at least one more word that should begin with a capital letter.
The chorus singers like asian cooking, but the orchestra prefers continental food.
Use as many boxes as you need to write the words that should begin with a capital letter.

[ ] [ ] [ ]

3 Which sentence has the correct punctuation?

A "That's enough," said the trainer. "You look tired."
B "That's enough, "said the trainer." You look tired.
C That's enough, said the trainer. "you look tired."
D That's enough, said the trainer. "You look tired."

4 The words *Good luck on your trip* are an example of

A a question.
B a command.
C an exclamation.
D a statement.

5 Which of the following correctly completes the sentence?

Kelvin isn't sure what to ______ he really doesn't like his new jeans.

A wear, as
B wear. As
C wear as,
D wear. as

6 Circle the letter to show where the missing comma (,) should go.

Boxes (A) of apples (B) bags of potatoes (C) and trays of strawberries (D) were for sale in the markets.

7 Brackets ( ) are required in this sentence. Which part of the sentence needs brackets?
Enid Mary Blyton 1897–1968 was a British children's writer also known as Mary Pollock.

A Mary
B 1897–1968
C British
D known as Mary Pollock

8 Which sentence has the correct punctuation?

A Dad watches many films, mainly westerns, but I prefer, action movies.
B Dad watches many films, mainly westerns but I prefer, action movies.
C Dad watches many films, mainly westerns but, I prefer action movies.
D Dad watches many films, mainly westerns, but I prefer action movies.

9 Which of the following correctly completes the sentence?

We went to the school's open day. We saw ______ art lesson before lunch.

A Jacks and Marys'
B Jacks and Marys
C Jack's and Mary's
D Jack and Mary's

Answers and explanations on page 99

10 Which option correctly completes the sentence?

There were ______ eyes staring at the hunters.

A dark, beady, evil, looking
B dark beady, evil looking
C dark, beady, evil-looking
D dark, beady evil, looking,

11 Which of the following correctly completes the sentence?

There's a book on the floor. ______ book is it?

A Whose **B** Who's **C** whose **D** who's

12 Where do the two missing speech marks (" and ") go?

While reading the paper (A) Clem looked up and (B) said in a quiet voice, (C) I don't believe it! (D)

Read the text *Choosing pets*. The text has some gaps. Choose the best option to fill each gap.

Choosing pets

Some animals enjoy being stroked or cuddled.

Text		A	B	C	D
Some don't. ______ you want a pet	13	if	if,	If,	If
to cuddle, make sure ______ a pet	14	its	it's	It's	its'
that likes to be touched ______ you will	15	, or	. Or	! Or	or,
both be disappointed. Animals ______	16	are'nt	arn't	aren't	ar'not
toys. They don't belong to ______	17	People.	people.	people,	people?

18 Which of the following correctly completes the sentence?

Where are the ______ followed some hikers into the bush.

A dogs, They **B** dogs. They **C** dogs? they **D** dogs? They

 Answers and explanations on page 99

PUNCTUATION Advanced level questions

Mini Test 5

1 Which sentence is correct?

A Wow! That was an excellent movie.
B Wow, That was an excellent movie.
C Wow! that was an excellent movie
D Wow That was an excellent movie.

2 Which of the following correctly completes the sentence?

The reporter spoke to ______ Isaacs before he left on his flight to Bali.

A captain
B capt.
C Capt.
D CAPT

3 Which of the following correctly completes the sentence?

Those are the Year Six students' ribbons, but these are ______!

A our's
B ours's
C ours'
D ours

4 Which sentence has the correct punctuation?

A "It is not starting before midday," said Ms Glover, "so you will have to wait."
B "It is not starting before midday," said Ms Glover, so you will have to wait.
C "It is not starting before midday, said Ms Glover, so you will have to wait."
D "It is not starting before midday," Said Ms Glover, "So you will have to wait."

5 Which sentence is an example of a question sentence?

A What a fool I've been
B What day is it
C What it is, I don't know
D What Basil did next

6 Which sentence has the correct punctuation?

A You will need sensible clothes, so pack your thongs, board, shorts, cap and, a towel.
B You will need sensible clothes, so pack your thongs, board shorts, cap, and a towel.
C You will need sensible clothes, so pack your thongs, board, shorts, cap and a towel.
D You will need sensible clothes, so pack your thongs, board shorts, cap and a towel.

7 Which of the following correctly completes the sentence?

I ______ got the answer right but I was not listening.

A could'ov
B could've
C could'er
D could'ave

8 Which punctuation best completes the sentence?

"Beat it ______ snapped my father when a magpie landed near the picnic basket.

A full stop, closing speech mark (**."**)
B closing speech mark, exclamation mark (**"!**)
C exclamation mark, closing speech mark (**!"**)
D comma, closing speech mark (**,"**)

9 Circle the letter to show which word should not have a capital letter.

The small town West Wyalong is South of Condobolin.

A (West) B (Wyalong) C (South) D (Condobolin)

Answers and explanations on pages 99–100

10 Circle the letter to show where the missing apostrophe (') should go.

The goat(A)s belonged to two sister(B)s, and the farmer(C)s all knew they had ruined Fay(D)s crop.

11 Which sentence has the correct punctuation?

A Judy Blume, one of the worlds' most popular childrens author's, visited our class.
B Judy Blume, one of the world's most popular children's authors, visited our class.
C Judy Blume, one of the world's most popular childrens' authors, visited our class.
D Judy Blume, one of the world's most popular childrens authors, visited our class.

12 Which of the following correctly completes the sentence?

The last answer in the test paper should have been 10 ______ , not four miles!

A Km. **B** km. **C** km **D** Km **E** kilos

Read the text *Instructions*. The text has some gaps. Choose the best option to fill each gap.

Instructions

The first thing my teacher does is give instructions.

		A	B	C	D
As he enters the room he says, ______	**13**	,"Take	;Take	Take,	"Take
out ______ Maths books now."	**14**	you're	your're	you've	your
Then Tegan calls out, "What ______	**15**	page.	page?	page?"	page"?
The teacher tells her to be ______	**16**	quiet."	quiet.	quiet,	quiet!
______ How about the next page," calls	**17**	"Hey!	Hey!	Hey,	"Hey,

Jodie who likes to joke.

18 Which of the following correctly completes the sentence?

The ______ was fifth in line for the British throne.

A Duke Of Kent **B** duke of Kent
C Duke of Kent **D** Duke of kent

Answers and explanations on pages 99–100

TIPS FOR READING

Here is a list of descriptions of different types of texts in the reading tests. You can refer to this list if you need to when you read the tests. Please note:

- in the Mini Reading Tests you are told what type of text it is
- in the Sample Tests you are not told the type of text, but instead they are listed below.

A narrative
- is a form of prose writing that tells a story
- has entertainment as its main purpose
- uses literary techniques such as figurative language.

Sample Test 1, page 66; Sample Test 2, page 71; Sample Test 3, page 75

A legend
- is a form of narrative and part of an oral storytelling tradition
- is an attempt to explain a significant event or situation
- is presented as history but is unlikely to be true.

Sample Test 1, page 61

A report
- is used to present information about something
- usually focuses on one topic or subject
- begins with an introductory statement introducing the subject which is followed by a series of paragraphs. A concluding paragraph (optional) summarises the information in the report, or provides a personal opinion
- is commonly found in reference books.

Sample Test 1, page 62; Sample Test 2, pages 68, 70, 72; Sample Test 3, page 79

A poem
- can take many forms. It can tell a story (narrative verse), paint a word picture, or be the format for a play
- uses literary techniques, such as figurative language, rhyme and rhythm, to help the poet create experiences that can be shared with the reader
- is written by a poet (author). The person who is telling the story or poem is called the narrator.

Sample Test 1, page 65; Sample Test 2, page 69; Sample Test 3, page 77

A persuasive text
- is a form of prose intended to influence the reader or listener
- is used to 'argue' the case for or against a particular action, plan or point of view
- needs to be well organised and clear with an introduction stating the presenter's point of view, a series of arguments supporting that point of view and a conclusion that sums up the arguments in a positive manner.

Sample Test 2, page 73; Sample Test 3, page 78

Tables and graphs
- are diagrammatic and condensed representations of information
- have as their purpose to provide quick access to information without reading through unnecessary words
- provide and arrange data and information in a format that is easy to find and read.

A comic strip
- is a form of narrative based on a set of sequential drawings
- generally tells an amusing story but may have deeper meanings
- is often organised as a series of individual pictures, called frames.

Sample Test 1, page 63

A review
- is often a form of persuasive writing urging the reader to consider a course of action
- is a formal assessment of something such as a film or book
- may contain information allowing the reader to make an informed decision.

Sample Test 1, page 64

A recount
- is a record of events that happened in sequence
- may include personal or historical writing
- can often take the form of a newspaper report.

Sample Test 1, page 67

A poster/flyer
- tries to capture the reader's attention and provide information with a minimum of reading
- is often displayed or distributed by organisations to advertise coming events.

Sample Test 2, page 74

An explanation
- tells how or why something happens
- can be about natural or scientific phenomena, how things work or events
- often starts with a definition or a question.

Sample Test 3, page 76

A cartoon
- is a simple drawing showing the features of its subjects in a humorously exaggerated way
- often makes a comment about topical issues in a way that highlights a social issue
- can often be found in a newspaper or magazine.

Sample Test 3, page 80

A procedure
- is a set of instructions (often called steps) on how to do something
- will often include a list of materials and tools needed and helpful hints. A common procedure is a recipe.

Sample Test 3, page 81

READING

Standard level questions

Mini Test 1: Narrative

Read the narrative and answer the questions.

Go to page 31 to read about **Narratives**.

Tolly and Emily had to buy some oranges, lemons and apples. As they passed the pet shop they looked in the window. 'What are those pretty fish?' Emily suddenly asked her brother.

'Goldfish,' replied Tolly.

'Some are,' agreed Emily, 'but not all the fish are gold. I can see pink ones, silver ones and white ones. In that tank they are black!'

'They are still goldfish,' said Tolly.

Emily thought that if they were called goldfish they should be gold.

They passed a man walking two very lean dogs.

'What are those dogs?' asked Emily.

Tolly looked at her and said, 'Emily, they are greyhounds.'

Emily looked at the dogs. One was black, one was white.

'No they are not,' corrected Emily. 'They are black and white. Not grey!'

'They are still called greyhounds,' said Tolly.

Emily thought that if they were greyhounds they should be grey.

Next they passed a flower shop. In the window were pots of little flowering plants.

'What pretty flowers!' exclaimed Emily.

'They are violets. African violets,' explained Tolly.

'But they are not all violet,' said Emily. 'I can see pink ones, blue ones and white ones.'

'They are still violets,' sighed Tolly.

Emily thought that if they were violets they should be violet. People had their colours mixed up.

At the fruit shop Tolly asked for some oranges and lemons. 'Mum doesn't want them if they are green,' he said.

'But if they are orange or lemon, how can they be green?' asked Emily.

The greengrocer looked at her and grinned, 'Don't worry Emily,' she said, 'but did you know that blackberries are red when they are green?'

Emily shook her head slowly.

'They can be grown in greenhouses,' smiled the greengrocer.

'And greenhouses aren't green!' nodded Emily.

Tolly laughed, 'That's right. They are glasshouses!'

'And the people who grow them have green thumbs,' grinned Emily.

Then they all laughed.

1 What colour did Emily think the African flowers should be?
A violet **B** white **C** pink **D** green **E** grey

2 Emily and Tolly were going down the street to buy
A fish. **B** flowers. **C** dog food. **D** fruit.

3 When did Tolly and Emily look at the flowers?
A before they saw the goldfish
B while in the fruit shop
C after seeing the greyhounds
D as they were passing a glasshouse

4 Why did Emily think the goldfish were named incorrectly?
A The fish were in the wrong tank.
B They were other colours as well as gold.
C Tolly told her it was the wrong name.
D She couldn't see any gold-coloured fish.

5 When Emily and Tolly spoke to the greengrocer she was
A annoyed. **B** confused. **C** disbelieving. **D** cheerful.

6 The text is intended to
A inform the reader of problems.
B give the reader enjoyment.
C warn the reader about dogs.
D explain things to the reader.

Note: the numbers in the margin are line references to help you use the answer section more effectively.

Answers and explanations on pages 100–101

READING Standard level questions

Mini Test 2: Table

Read the table and answer the questions.

Go to page 31 to read about **Tables**.

Numbers can be described in many ways. They can have several features.
Counting numbers start at one (1).
Odd numbers end with 1, 3, 5, 7 or 9. All other numbers are even numbers.
Factors are two or more numbers which when multiplied create a composite number. Composite numbers have factors but prime numbers have no factors (except for one (1) and the number itself). Factors of 15 are 3 and 5 (3 × 5 = 15). They are prime numbers so they are prime factors.
One (1) is considered neither prime nor composite.
A square number is the number you get when a number is multiplied by itself (2 × 2 = 4).
A cubed number is any number you get when a number is multiplied by itself three times.
The numerals 1 to 9 are called digits or one-digit numbers.
Nought or zero (0) is a place setter. It gives place value to other numbers. Nought (0) is also a digit.

Table of number facts

Number	Odd	Even	Prime	Composite	Square number	Cubed number
0						
1	Y				Y	Y
2		Y	Y			
3	Y		Y			
4		Y		Y	Y (2 × 2)	
5	Y		Y			
6		Y		Y		
7	Y		Y			
8		Y		Y		Y (2 × 2 × 2)
9	Y			Y	Y (3 × 3)	
10		Y		Y		

Key:	Y = Yes	Blank box = No

1 How many digits are needed to write ten as a number? Write your answer in the box.

2 The number one (1) can be described as
A a prime number. **B** a place setter. **C** a composite number. **D** a digit.

3 The counting number one hundred and one (101) is
A a one-digit number.
B a two-digit number.
C an odd number.
D the first three-digit counting number.

4 The counting number nine (9) is
A the largest single-digit number.
B the first odd number.
C a cubed number less than ten.
D the tenth (10th) counting number.

5 According to the table, which statement is correct?
A There are more even numbers, 10 or less, than odd numbers.
B Nought (0) is the first odd number.
C There are more composite numbers, 10 or less, than prime numbers.
D Consecutive odd and consecutive even numbers can be separated by more than one other number.

6 The table would be useful for someone
A learning how to count.
B remembering multiplication facts.
C preparing for a mathematics test.
D wanting to understand features of numbers.

Answers and explanations on page 101

READING

Intermediate level questions

Mini Test 3: Narrative

Read the narrative and answer the questions.

Go to page 31 to read about **Narratives**.

I don't know what happened first, whether I heard this strange 'thlump' against the outside wall or I wanted to go to the loo. I signed the Signing Out Sheet and left the classroom.

Outside the sky was dark and rumbly and it was about to rain. I looked around suspiciously. Then I saw it.

It was lying next to the wall looking quite splattered. I crept over to it. It was most unusual. I didn't know what it was at first. It was a sort of greasy-looking blob of meat. I crept closer, then got down on my hands and knees and peered at it.

It was a sausage. A cooked sausage. It looked as if it had been hit with a softball bat. It was smashed.

Dark stains were seeping onto the concrete. I looked at the wall. There was a messy, fatty mark on the wall that was covered in little bits of sausage mince. Someone's throwing sausages at the school, I thought. I stood and looked around. There were other sausages near another wall. I had better tell Ms Mann.

'Ms Mann,' I called as I barged into the room, 'I just went outside when I heard a noise on the wall and I looked around and I saw this stuff on the ground and meaty bits on the school wall. There was this smashed-up sausage lying on the ground—near where we play handball. It looked awful. Someone threw a sausage at our classroom. I heard it and they must've run away. I didn't see them but …'

I stopped. Everyone was looking at me.

I looked at Ms Mann. 'It's true,' I said in my most honest voice.

Ms Mann just looked at me and raised her fine eyebrows. Then she said, 'So, someone's throwing sausages at the school. Jenny, what will you think of next? Raining sausages?'

'It's true!' Someone laughed, then someone else.

'Yuk. Throwing sausages at the school! Was it cooked?' called Anthony.

'Yes!' I called back but they were all laughing. When the last of them had stopped rolling about their desks I said to Ms Mann again, 'It's true!'

1 Where did Jenny see her first sausage?

A at the base of a brick wall
B a short way up a classroom wall
C on a handball court
D near the school toilets

2 What made Jenny suspicious that something had happened outside?

A A storm was developing.
B She had heard an odd sound.
C The students were laughing.
D Ms Mann had raised her eyebrows.

3 The class were *rolling about their desks* (line 23). This means they

A were upset by Jenny's description.
B had nothing better to do.
C were laughing without control.
D had become sick from the sausages.

4 Write the numbers 1 to 4 in the boxes to show the correct order in which events happened in the text. The first one (1) has been done for you.

☐	Ms Mann didn't believe Jenny's story.	☐	The class started laughing.
☐	Jenny signed the Signing Out sheet.	1	Jenny heard a noise against the outside wall.

5 Which word would best describe Jenny's manner after she returned to the classroom? Choose **two** options.

A insistent
B vague
C confused
D cheeky
E bothered
F positive

6 Jenny says: '*I didn't see them …*' (line 14). What is she referring to when she uses the word *them*?

A handball players
B smashed sausages
C the people who threw sausages
D students from her class

Note: the numbers in the margin are line references to help you use the answer section more effectively.

Answers and explanations on page 101

READING Intermediate level questions

Mini Test 4: Report

Read the report and answer the questions.

Go to page 31 to read about **Reports**.

The Indian word *nimba* means a tree which provides good health. According to Hindu custom, on the Hindu New Year's Day, it is a custom to eat a few tender nimba leaves.

The nimba is also known as the *neem* tree. It has been grown in India for centuries. The neem is an extremely useful tree with small leaves, sweet-smelling flowers and small fruit. It is a fast grower, acts as a windbreak, is resistant to insects and needs little water. It will grow in salty soil and is long living.

That is why in a country like Oman, one of the Arab nations, the neem has been widely planted. Oman is dry and hot. Neem trees line roadways. They add greenery to parks in a land where greenery is not common.

Although the neem tree is deciduous it doesn't lose all its leaves at once. It allows a glow of gold to affect some of the leaves and renews its foliage slowly as summer approaches.

Experiments in Oman have shown that on blistering hot days the temperature under the neem tree can be up to eight degrees lower.

In India, few villages are without a neem tree. It is more or less a backyard chemist shop. Much of the folk medicine has been supported by scientific discoveries: 135 chemical compounds have been isolated. One chemical is an insect repellent, while others stop swelling, fight tuberculosis, or reduce pain. It can be a gargle for sore throats and is used in the treatment of diabetes, leprosy and malaria. Scientists are investigating claims that the tree is an air purifier. Boiled leaves provide a treatment for skin infections. The small, knobbly nuts provide oil for the treatment of head lice.

Many Indians make and eat neem leaf chutney for good health. It seems the neem tree can cure almost any complaint.

Farmers use the trees as a pesticide and to protect their crops from fungus and insect disease. Termites avoid the tree. It is no wonder it is called 'the world in a tree'.

1 Which words best describe the neem tree? Choose **two** options.

A fragile **B** sacred **C** delicate **D** hardy **E** valued

2 What is a feature of the neem tree on very hot days?

A The leaves drop off.
B It provides cooling shade.
C Its fruit ripens.
D Its leaves change from green to gold.

3 Farmers use the neem tree especially

A as protection for their crops.
B for firewood.
C to make a throat gargle.
D as fodder for their farm animals.

4 Why is the neem tree particularly important in Oman and India?

A Both countries have a lot of diseases.
B It can survive in long, hot, dry summers.
C The leaves can be made into chutney.
D The nuts provide a valuable oil.

5 The neem tree is described as *deciduous* (line 9). This means it

A provides delicious fruit.
B is an important shade tree.
C can be used to treat health complaints.
D loses its leaves.

6 The neem tree is most useful

A as an ornamental garden tree.
B for its plentiful supply of fruit.
C as a tree for maintaining health.
D for its shade in parks and along roads.

Answers and explanations on pages 101–102

READING

Intermediate level questions

Mini Test 5: Poster

Read the poster and answer the questions.

Go to page 31 to read about **Posters**.

How to protect your back

Your back, or spine, is one of the most important bone systems in your body.

Before lifting an object make sure:
- you can comfortably lift the object without help
- the object has no sharp edges or loose parts
- where you are going to walk is clear of obstacles.

DO THIS

Lift with your legs.

Use your feet to turn.

Teamwork works best.

DON'T DO THIS

Never lift with your back.

Never twist or overreach.

1. Before lifting a heavy object make sure you have a firm footing, with feet turned out. Bend with your legs NOT your back!

2. When carrying the object turn with your feet. Don't turn by twisting your back.

3. Do not carry oversized objects by yourself. Work with a mate, both lifting at the same time. Keep your load level and walk smoothly.

4. Put the load down at the same time, bending at the knees. Do NOT bend with the load.

Back problems are difficult to put right. Follow these simple guidelines and you will protect your back throughout life.

1 The poster is mainly concerned with
- **A** damaging heavy goods.
- **B** being cooperative.
- **C** saving time.
- **D** workers' safety.

2 To lift a very heavy object to a new position it is best to
- **A** do it as quickly as possible.
- **B** use your back to take the most weight.
- **C** work with another person.
- **D** do it in short, easy-to-manage stages.

3 What is meant by the term *put right* (line 17)?
- **A** correct the problem
- **B** replace when damaged
- **C** put in a certain spot
- **D** return to the original position

4 Where would be the most suitable place to display this notice?
Give a reason for your answer. Write your answer on the line.

____

5 When carrying a large and heavy object workers should make sure they
- **A** warn others to keep clear.
- **B** have a clear path.
- **C** work with enthusiasm.
- **D** do not carry other small objects.

6 The purpose of the diagrams is to
- **A** amuse the reader.
- **B** assist people who have difficulty with the English language.
- **C** make the instructions easy to follow.
- **D** frighten workers into doing the correct thing.

Answers and explanations on page 102

READING Intermediate level questions

Mini Test 6: Poem

Read the poem and answer the questions.

Go to page 31 to read about **Poems**.

Choosing a name

Madeleine Jane had grown tired of her name.
She'd had it for ages, and that seemed a shame.
She had lots of dresses and five pairs of shoes.
Each day when she dressed she could just pick and choose.
And besides, someone else had selected her name.
If she didn't like it, she wasn't to blame!
She thought about Mollie, or Cindy, or Sue;
Now Andrée was pretty, and Sharon was too.
So she stood at the mirror and tried some for size.
Holly meant 'holy' and Bindi meant 'wise'.
She wanted a name that would suit her just right.
Perhaps she'd be Elaine for that meant 'bright light'.
But Sally meant 'princess', Regina 'a queen'.
Or how about Marion? Even Noelene?
She tried being Eleanor, Vicky, and Lou.
Robyn? Fiona? Oh what should she do?
Then she thought of a name that seemed perfectly fine,
And she rolled it around on her tongue for a time.
Then she looked in the mirror and said, 'It is plain,
That the name that best suits me is Madeleine Jane!'

Elaine Horsfield

1 What name did Madeleine think best suited her? Write your answer on the line.

____

2 How did Madeleine react to the names she considered?
- **A** She rejected them.
- **B** She tested them over and over again.
- **C** She thought they were plain.
- **D** She crossed them off her list.

3 According to the poem, the names *Sharon* and *Andrée* were similar. They were both
- **A** popular names.
- **B** foreign names.
- **C** amusing names.
- **D** pretty names.

4 What was Madeleine doing when she settled on a name?
- **A** choosing a dress
- **B** putting on shoes
- **C** looking in a mirror
- **D** speaking to her mother

5 How did Madeleine test the names she was considering?
- **A** She said them aloud.
- **B** She found out what the names meant.
- **C** She looked for names that rhymed.
- **D** She dressed up in her dresses and shoes.

6 Which words best describe how Madeleine felt while thinking of names? Choose **two** options.
- **A** bored
- **B** spiteful
- **C** grateful
- **D** unsure
- **E** disappointed
- **F** doubtful

Answers and explanations on page 103

READING

Advanced level questions

Mini Test 7: Recount

Read the recount and answer the questions.

Go to page 31 to read about **Recounts**.

Robert Maddison, commonly known as Robbie Maddison or 'Maddo', was born on 14 July 1981 and spent his childhood in the town of Kiama, on the NSW south coast. It was here he developed his passion for riding by competing in national motocross events, which led to him becoming a motorbike stunt rider.

He finished school at Kiama High and took up an apprenticeship, but his passion for riding was too strong to spend his life as an electrician.

He improved his skills and techniques over many years of stunt-riding competitions. His idol was Evel Knievel, a world-famous stunt-rider. For forty years Evel Knievel had held most world records for motorcycle jumps and stunts. One of his last feats was a record-breaking jump over the fountains at a casino in Las Vegas. Knievel was often injured doing stunts.

In December 2007 Maddison broke the world motorcycle jumping record, jumping a distance of 98 metres. He repeated the event immediately afterwards, successfully landing the jump, as his girlfriend Amy anxiously watched. His second attempt, however, did not go as far as the first jump. He was not injured in either jump.

On 29 March 2008, he broke his own world record twice during the Crusty Demons Night of World Records show in Melbourne. During his first jump he sailed just over 96 metres and landed on the safety zone, nearly hitting the front of the landing ramp. On his second attempt he broke the world record with a jump of 104 metres. He landed hard on his back tyre and was not satisfied by the jump, so he decided to do another jump. On his third jump he again broke the world record, this time with a jump of almost 107 metres with a perfect landing. This jump was followed by numerous other spectacular stunts across the world. One stunt in 2009 was his jump up the raised ramp of Tower Bridge, London, with a back flip while the drawbridge was open.

Maddison admits people might think he is crazy, but he loves taking on these huge challenges. For him it was an incredible feeling to fly between the two bridge towers and over the famous Thames River. One of Maddison's final jumps was across the Corinth Canal in Greece in 2010.

Sources: <http://en.wikipedia.org/wiki/Robbie_Maddison>, <http://www.kiamaindependent.com.au/.../robbie_maddison_still_calls_kiama_home->.

1 Robbie Maddison could be described as a perfectionist.
Use your own words to give a reason for this opinion. Write your answer on the line.

____

2 Where did Maddison perform his greatest stunt? Write your answer in the box. [ ]

3 What is one indication that Maddison is more than an attention-seeking, cheap show-off?

A He is getting older. **B** His idol is Evel Knievel.
C He didn't finish his apprenticeship. **D** His stunts are becoming more difficult.

4 Write the numbers 1 to 4 in the boxes to show the order of events in Maddison's life.
The first one has been done for you.

1	attends Kiama school		Corinth Canal jump
	Tower Bridge jump		first world record

5 Robbie Maddison could best be described as

A daring. **B** heroic. **C** thoughtless. **D** crazy. **E** irresponsible.

6 Maddison was well prepared to be a stunt rider because of his

A high regard for the skills of Evel Knievel. **B** work as an electrical apprentice.
C achievements while at Kiama High School. **D** early experience in motocross racing.

Note: the numbers in the margin are line references to help you use the answer section more effectively.

Answers and explanations on pages 103–104

READING

Advanced level questions

Mini Test 8: Narrative

Read the narrative and answer the questions.

Go to page 31 to read about **Narratives**.

At the top of the hill the road curved sharply to the right but there was a wide patch of gravel on the side called The Lookout. Here drivers could pull off the road and have a look at the view and take a photo—if they were really impressed.

To the south, straight down the rolling valley, you could see the small town of Willang right at the foot of the hill. It was an old country town with weatherboard cottages and corrugated tin roofs.

The houses struggled out from the main street, which was also the main road through town. There were several two-storey buildings along the street, the most obvious being a corner hotel with a wide balcony over the footpath, and the original bank for the town.

The street was lined with a string of low gums. A number of vehicles angle-parked in their shade. A solitary truck trundled around the corner of the hotel and tooted cheekily before coming to a stop.

A few people wandered or hurried down the street, momentarily lost behind trees, in shop doorways or behind farmers' trucks.

Near the outskirts of town and in a small side street was Willang's only church. On a block further away were two tennis courts and a small clubhouse. Beyond that was the football field with its yellowing grass and the far goal post leaning slightly to one side.

On a small knoll just beyond town were the ruins of an old shearing shed. Between the shed and the town was a small stream. Flashes of light indicated that the summer dry had not yet reduced the stream to a sandy dip. On the bank a windmill was turning lazily. All this was quite peaceful and pleasant.

Looking to the west things got uglier. The limestone quarry was a gash on the grassy landscape. The railway line with its siding was a long, silver and black scar, disappearing behind the hills.

1 The windmill at Willang was situated

A near a church.
B adjacent to a watercourse.
C behind the football field.
D on a railway siding.

2 Write **two** words that would describe life in Willang. Write an answer on each line.

1 ______________________ **2** ______________________

3 The narrator makes a comment in paragraph 1 about taking a photo: *if they were really impressed*. This comment suggests that

A the photo opportunity was not to be missed.
B photos of the Willang valley are difficult to take.
C visitors are more likely to take a photo than local people.
D visitors may decide to take a photo but it would be of little importance.

4 Using the letters N (north), S (south), E (east) or W (west) write the letters in the boxes to show the direction which these points are from The Lookout.

☐ **1** the Willang church ☐ **2** limestone quarry

5 The description of Willang states that: *The houses struggled out from the main street* (line 7). This suggests that the houses were

A not well maintained or cared for.
B in need of repair or completion.
C more spaced out the further one got from the town.
D the houses of the poorer residents of Willang.

6 A suitable title for the text would be

A Train to Willang.
B Summer stream.
C From The Lookout.
D Tennis and football.

Answers and explanations on page 104

READING

Advanced level questions

Mini Test 9: Procedure

Read the procedure and answer the questions.

Go to page 31 to read about **Procedures**.

Using adverbs

Adverbs add meaning to verbs and adjectives. Adverbs very often tell **how** something happened. If the word is answering a **how** or **when** or **where** question, then it is an adverb.

Examples *How* does she sing? She sings *sweetly*. *When* will he arrive? He will arrive *soon*.
Where did the girl sit? She sat *near* the door.

Many **how** adverbs end with ***ly***: *softly*, *angrily*, *heavily*, *really*.
Adverbs of frequency (**when**-type adverbs) include *soon*, *always*, *never*, *often*, *sometimes* and *at night*.
These adverbs usually come before the main verb.
Adverbs of place (**where**-type adverbs) include *there*, *here*, *near* and *on*.

Instructions for learning about adverbs

Step 1. Look in a sentence for words that end in ***ly***. Adverbs are often formed by adding ***ly*** to adjectives (e.g. *hopeful* → *hopefully*). This is only one step in finding an adverb. Some adverbs do not end in ***ly***, and not all words ending in ***ly*** are adverbs (e.g. *silly*, *reply*). Also check to see if any words answer one of the above question types.

Step 2. Practise using adverbs that help the verb. For example: *The rain fell hard*. The adverb *hard* tells how the rain fell. In the sentence *He will leave soon* the adverb *soon* tells when he will leave. Neither of these adverbs end in ***ly***.

Step 3. Look for adverbs that modify adjectives. For example: *She is an extremely excited winner*. *Extremely* modifies the adjective *excited*, which describes *winner*.

Step 4. Take care not to misuse adverbs in speech. People do things *well*, not *good*. Use adverbs to tell how something is done, instead of adjectives. Remember to say *speak slowly* or *come quickly*, rather than *speak slow* or *come quick*. We say *really happy*, not *real happy*.

Be careful! Some adjectives don't change when they become adverbs. The most important of these are *fast* and *hard*. **Examples** a *fast* race (adjective) / the car was stuck *fast* (adverb)
a *hard* test (adjective) / Bill works *hard* (adverb)

1 The text, *Using adverbs*, is mainly an example of a
A narrative. **B** method. **C** report. **D** persuasive text.

2 Step 4 in the Instructions is mainly about
A having fun with adverbs.
B avoiding problems when using adverbs.
C using the correct adverbs in speech.
D changing adjectives to adverbs.

3 Which statement is correct?
A All words ending with ***ly*** are adverbs.
B Adverbs are never placed before verbs.
C Words that are adjectives can never be used as adverbs.
D Some words can be adverbs or adjectives.

4 The tone of the passage suggests that the writer is
A trying to be helpful.
B poking fun at people who make mistakes when speaking.
C tired of people who misuse adverbs.
D showing off how much better he is than most people.

5 To find out if a word is an adverb, a person can ask a
A who-type question. **B** which-type question. **C** how-type question. **D** do/did-type question.

6 This information would be most useful for
A a journalist. **B** a school student. **C** an author. **D** a signwriter.

Answers and explanations on pages 104–105

READING Advanced level questions

Mini Test 10: Explanation

Read the explanation and answer the questions.

Go to page 31 to read about **Explanations**.

Rural bushfire action plan

Many people in country areas feel isolated when it comes to protection from bushfire. There is also the difficult choice: stay and protect property, or leave early to save lives? This is the big question. There is no correct answer. Each situation must be treated in a manner that best suits the individual family and property but there are some strategies that can help.

Leave early or defend?

Each family needs to have a plan prepared well before the summer fire season. A plan means avoiding bad decisions. It saves making on-the-spot decisions based on limited information. Each family should have a list of all the things to be taken. These may include important family documents, jewellery, family photo albums, computers and pets.

Who should leave before fire threatens?

1. Those people with little ability to fight fires or save themselves, e.g. children, the elderly and sick people. The decision as to who stays should be worked out well in advance to save arguments.
2. People who quickly panic. Such people hinder fire-fighting efforts.
3. People who have limited access to water, especially to fight spot fires.
4. People who live in places that are dangerous and difficult to defend, such as isolated forest areas and on steep slopes.
5. People who have not carried out fire prevention maintenance of their homes—or who live next to properties that have a high fire risk.

For those who stay

Those who plan to stay should have a survival kit in a safe place that is easy to get to.

Survival kits should include:

- protective clothing (overalls, sturdy footwear, woollen socks, broad-brim hats, goggles, bandanna/scarf, suitable gloves)
- ample drinking water
- first aid kit, towels, woollen blankets
- fire extinguishers, buckets, backpack sprays
- shovels, metal ladders, mops, hessian* bags (wet)
- battery-operated radio, torch with fresh batteries.

*Hessian is a coarse natural fibre.

Adapted from *Bush FireWise Action Plan*, NSW Rural Fire Service.

1 In a fire emergency situation the first difficult question is
A should families leave or stay?
B who should leave?
C what should be taken?
D where is the survival kit?

2 The text *Rural bushfire action plan* could best be described as
A a recount.
B a recommendation.
C a narrative.
D a description.

3 Why should children, the elderly and sick people leave early if there is a danger from fire?
A They are the least important people in the family.
B They don't understand the dangers of bushfires.
C They are the least able to fight fires.
D They forget to do what they have been told.

4 What is a fire-fighting plan mainly aimed at saving?
Write your answer in the box.

5 A neighbour's property could be a problem for those who decide to stay if the
A neighbour has a different fire plan to other people.
B neighbour lives in an isolated, hilly area.
C neighbour also decides to stay rather than leave.
D neighbour's property is a fire risk.

6 This information would be most suitable for
A fire-fighters.
B children.
C parents.
D schoolteachers.

TIPS FOR WRITING A PERSUASIVE TEXT

Check the Writing section (www.nap.edu.au/naplan/writing) **of the official NAPLAN website for up-to-date and important information on the Writing Test.** Sample Writing Tests and marking guidelines that outline the criteria markers use when assessing your writing are also provided. Please note that, to date in NAPLAN, the types of texts that students have been tested on have been narrative and persuasive writing.

The Australian Curriculum for English requires students to be taught three main types of texts:

- imaginative writing (including narratives and descriptions)
- informative writing (including procedures and reports)
- persuasive writing (expositions).

Informative writing has not yet been tested by NAPLAN. The best preparation for writing is for students to read a range of texts and to get lots of practice in writing different types of texts. We have included information on all types of texts in this book.

Persuasive texts

Persuasive texts (expositions or opinions) are used to 'argue' the case for or against a particular action, plan or point of view—to *persuade* others to see it your way. Persuasive texts need to be well organised and clear so that readers will understand and be convinced of your arguments.

When writing persuasive texts it is best to keep the following points in mind. They will help you get the best possible mark.

Before you start writing

- Read the question carefully. You will probably be asked to write your reaction to a particular question or statement, such as *Dogs should be kept out of parks*. Most of the topics that you will be asked to comment on are very general. This means you will probably be writing about something you know and can draw upon your experience. When writing your personal opinion you may include such phrases as *I think*, *I believe* and *It is important*. Remember to sound confident. Some common ways for the question to be worded are: *Give your opinion on …*; *Do you agree or disagree?*; *What do you think is/are … ?*; *What changes would you like to see … ?*; *Is … a good idea or a bad idea?*
- You will be expected to give your reasons. Sometimes the question may actually ask *Give your reasons*. Remember: the stance taken in a persuasive text is not wrong, as long as the writer has evidence to support his or her opinion. How the opinion is supported is as important as the opinion itself.
- Give yourself a few minutes before you start writing to get your thoughts in order and jot down points.

The introduction

- Right from the beginning it is important to let the reader know what position you have taken or what you believe. You can do this via the title or in the first line or paragraph, which may include a brief preview of the main arguments and some background information.

The body

- **Follow the structure of persuasive texts.** As persuasive texts aim to convince readers, your reasons must be logical and easily understood. You must provide both arguments (points) and evidence to support the arguments.
- **Correctly paragraph your writing.** Use paragraphs with topic sentences to organise your information. Without paragraphs your arguments become confused and difficult to follow. Use one paragraph for each idea or argument. Arguments can be ordered according to your choice. They can be 'numbered', e.g. *firstly, secondly, finally*.
- **Make sure your arguments (or points) are relevant.** They must add to your case. 'Waffle' and unnecessary detail don't improve a persuasive text. It is better to stick to the facts without getting sidetracked. Once you have made a point there is no need to repeat it.
- **Use interesting, precise words.** Include strong persuasive words such as *must*, *believe*, *important* or *certainly*. Avoid common words that carry little or no meaning, such as *good*. You can state your arguments using sentences beginning with words such as *firstly*, *furthermore*, *finally*.
- **Vary the types and lengths of sentences and the words that begin each sentence.** If your writing includes a personal opinion, try to avoid too many sentences starting with *I*.
- **Use impersonal writing**, although personal opinions can be part of the text.

The conclusion

- The final paragraph must restate your position more forcefully and wrap up your case. It can include a recommendation.

When you have finished writing give yourself a few moments to read through your persuasive text. Quickly check spelling and punctuation and insert any words that have been accidentally left out. Direct speech is not a feature of persuasive texts. Indirect speech (reported speech) does not have speech marks (" ").

WRITING

Mini Test 1
Persuasive text

Before you start, make sure you read the Tips for Writing on page 42.

Today you are going to write a persuasive text, often called an exposition.

Mother's Day—a day of celebration

What do you think about this idea? Do you support or reject it?

Write to convince a reader of your opinion.

Before you start writing, give some thought to:

- whether you strongly agree or disagree with the celebration of Mothers' Day
- the way you will present your ideas: clearly list or order your points
- the reasons or evidence for your arguments
- your brief but definite conclusion. In your conclusion list some of your main points—you may add a personal opinion.

Don't forget to:

- plan your writing before you start
- write in correctly formed sentences and take particular care with paragraphing
- choose your words carefully and pay attention to your spelling and punctuation
- write neatly but don't waste time
- quickly check your writing once you have finished. Your position must be clear to your reader.

Remember: The stance taken in a persuasive text is not wrong, as long as the writer has evidence to support their opinion. How the opinion is supported is as important as the opinion itself.

Start writing here or type your answer on a tablet or computer.

☞ Once the student has completed the Writing Test, turn to pages 105–106 and use the Marking checklist to check the student's writing. Also go to pages 124–126 where sample pieces of writing (Standard, Intermediate and Advanced levels) can be used to check at what level the student is writing. These writing samples have been analysed based on the marking criteria used by markers to assess the NAPLAN Writing Test.

TIPS FOR WRITING A NARRATIVE TEXT

Narrative texts

A **narrative** is a form of prose writing that tells a story. Its main purpose is to entertain. Writers of narratives create experiences that are shared with the reader. To do this the writer uses literary techniques. Such techniques include figurative language (similes, metaphors, alliteration, onomatopoeia, rhetorical questions and repetition), variety in sentence length and type, variety in paragraph length, and direct speech.

In narratives, the author is the person who wrote the story. If the story is in the first person (*I*), we call the character who is telling the story the narrator.

Give your story vitality by using a variety of sentence beginnings.

Don't forget that your story can include not only the things you or your character might see, but also what you or your character might feel, hear, smell or taste. Remember: there are five senses.

When writing narratives it is best to keep the following points in mind. They will help you get the best possible mark.

Before you start writing

- Read the question and check the stimulus material carefully. *Stimulus material* means the topic, title, picture, words, phrases or extract of writing you are given to base your writing on.
- Write about something you know. Don't try to write about something way outside your experience.
- Decide if you are going to be writing in the first person (you become a character in your story) or in the third person (about other characters). When writing in the first person be careful not to overuse the pronoun *I* (e.g. *I did this*, *I did that*).
- Take a few moments to jot down your ideas on a piece of paper. Write down the order in which things happen. These could be the points in your story where you start new paragraphs.
- Remember: stories have a beginning, middle and end. It sounds simple but many stories fail because one of these three parts is not well written.

The introduction

- Don't start with *Once upon a time*—this is too clichéd and predictable.
- Don't tell the reader too much in the beginning. Make the reader want to read on to find out more. The beginning should introduce a problem to be solved.

The body

- **In the middle of your story include events that make solving the problem more difficult or doubtful.** This makes the story interesting.
- **Use a setting that you are familiar with**, e.g. home, school, sport, holiday place or shopping centre. You will then be able to describe the setting realistically.
- **Choose characters that are like people you know** because they are easier to imagine. You don't have to use their real names—it's probably best not to!
- **Use your imagination to make the story more interesting,** but don't try to fill it with weird or disgusting events.
- **Enhance your story with the use of literary techniques**, e.g. similes, metaphors, onomatopoeia and alliteration.
- **Make your paragraphing work for you.** New paragraphs are usually needed for new incidents in your story, changes in time or place, descriptions that move from one sense to another, or changes in the character who is speaking.

The conclusion

- The ending is the hardest part to write because it has to have something to do with the beginning.
- Never end your stories with: *and it was just a dream*; *I was saved by a superhero (or by magic)*; *I was dead*; and *they lived happily ever after!* Endings like these just tell the marker that you don't have a creative way to end your story.

When you have finished writing give yourself a few minutes to read through your story. Now is the time to check spelling and punctuation, and to insert words that have been accidentally left out.

There is an old saying: *practice makes perfect*. This applies to writing as much as other skills. Try writing a few short stories before you go into any narrative writing test. Follow these few tips and you will become a better writer.

WRITING

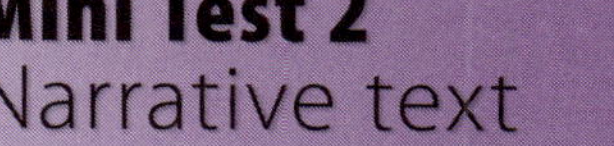

Mini Test 2
Narrative text

Before you start, make sure you read the Tips for Writing on page 44.

Today you are going to write a narrative or story. The idea for your story is **An embarrassing experience**.

Think about some embarrassing experiences you have had or seen. Embarrassing incidents are often of a minor nature. It could be a small mishap. It could be a misunderstanding or doing the wrong thing. It might be making a speech or getting caught out on an April Fools' Day trick. Don't be tempted to make your story about a disgusting event.

It could be a story about you or about someone else. It might include an animal. How did others react to the incident? What finally happened?

Your story might be amusing or it might be serious.

Before you start writing, give some thought to:

- where your story takes place (the setting)
- the characters and what they do in your story
- the events that take place in your story and the problems that have to be resolved
- how your story begins, what happens in your story, and how your story ends.

Don't forget to:

- plan your story before you begin writing
- write in correctly formed sentences and take care with paragraphing
- choose your words carefully and pay attention to your spelling and punctuation
- write neatly but don't waste time
- quickly check your story once you have finished.

Start writing here or type your answer on a tablet or computer.

☞ Once the student has completed the Writing Test, turn to page 106 and use the Marking checklist to check the student's writing. Also go to pages 127–129 where sample pieces of writing (Standard, Intermediate and Advanced levels) can be used to check at what level the student is writing. These writing samples have been analysed based on the marking criteria used by markers to assess the NAPLAN Writing Test.

TIPS FOR WRITING A RECOUNT TEXT

Recount texts

A **recount** tells about events that have happened to you or other people. The purpose of a factual recount is to record a series of events in the order they happened and evaluate their importance in some way. A recount can also be fictitious. Whether the recount is factual or fictitious remember to tell who, what, when, where and why. There are many types of recount—diaries, newspaper reports, letters and biographies. Recounts can be the easiest texts to write if you are given the choice. They don't need much planning or organisation as they are a straightforward record of events.

Add interest to your recount by using a variety of sentence beginnings.

Don't forget that your recount can include not only the things you or your character might see, but also what you or your character might feel, hear, smell or taste. Remember: there are five senses.

When writing recounts it is best to keep these points in mind. They will help you get the best possible mark.

Before you start writing

- Read the question and check the stimulus material carefully. *Stimulus material* means the topic, title, picture, words, phrases or extract of writing you are given to base your writing on.
- Remember that a recount is usually told in the past tense because the events described have already happened.
- Write about something you know. Don't try to write about something way outside your experience.
- Use a setting you are familiar with, e.g. home, school, sport, holiday place or shopping centre.
- When you have chosen your topic it might be helpful to jot down a few ideas quickly on paper so you don't forget them. Make up your mind quickly if you are writing a first-person recount (using *I* as the main character) or a third-person recount. If it is a personal recount, try to avoid too many sentences beginning with *I*.

The introduction

- A striking title gives impact to a recount. Newspaper reports do this well.
- The orientation may provide a brief statement about the who/what/when/where of the recount. This informs the reader quickly and clearly about the content of the recount.

The body

- **Use conjunctions and connectives** e.g. *when*, *then*, *first* or *next*. Because recounts can record either events that happen over a short period or events that happen over a lifetime, you need conjunctions and connectives to link and order the events.
- **Correctly paragraph your writing.** You need a new paragraph when there is a change in time or place or a new idea. You may want to comment on the events as you write about them.
- **Include personal comments**, e.g. about your feelings, your opinions and your reactions but only include comments that add to your recount. 'Waffle' and unnecessary detail don't improve a recount. It is better to stick to the facts without getting sidetracked.
- **Use language imaginatively** so that the recount is interesting, but don't try to fill it with weird or disgusting events.
- **Use figurative language** (similes, metaphors, alliteration, onomatopoeia, rhetorical questions and repetition) when appropriate, but use it in moderation.

The conclusion

- Include a conclusion. This tells how the experience ended. You may give your opinion about what happened and some thoughts you may have had about it. This final comment on the events or experiences is a way to wrap up your recount.

When you have finished writing give yourself a few moments to read through your recount. Quickly check spelling and punctuation, and insert words that have been accidentally left out.

There is an old saying: *practice makes perfect*. This applies to writing as much as other skills. Try writing a few short recounts before you go into any recount writing test. Follow these few tips and you will become a better writer.

WRITING

Mini Test 3
Recount text

Before you start, make sure you read the Tips for Writing on page 46.

A recount (which is a type of informative text) tells about events that have happened to you or other people. It is usually a record of events in the order they happened. If it is a personal recount, you will use the word *I*.

Paragraphs are usually organised by time periods. Sometimes subheadings are used. Jot down events in the order they happened before you start.

Today you are going to write a personal recount about **A new sporting event**. Briefly state what your new sporting event or experience is. It may be going to an important sporting event such as a grand final. It may be joining a new team. It may be trying something totally different, such as kayaking or rock climbing. Where did the event take place? Did anyone go with you? How did you get there? Did anything happen while you were there? What were the conditions like?

Was it a successful experience? What difficulties had to be overcome? Remember to stick to things that could be factual. This is not an opportunity to write a story.

Before you start writing, give some thought to:

- where your recount takes place
- the characters and what they do in your recount
- the events that take place in your recount and the problems that have to be resolved
- how you and others reacted to your sporting event. You may make brief personal comments on events as you write about them.

Don't forget to:

- plan your recount before you begin writing
- write in correctly formed sentences and take care with paragraphing
- choose your words carefully and pay attention to your spelling and punctuation
- write neatly but don't waste time
- quickly check your story once you have finished.

Start writing here or type your answer on a tablet or computer.

☞ **Once the student has completed the Writing Test, turn to page 107 and use the Marking checklist to check the student's writing. Also go to pages 130–132 where sample pieces of writing (Standard, Intermediate and Advanced levels) can be used to check at what level the student is writing. These writing samples have been analysed based on the marking criteria used by markers to assess the NAPLAN Writing Test.**

SAMPLE NAPLAN ONLINE–STYLE LITERACY TESTS

DIFFERENT TEST LEVELS

- There are nine tests for students to complete in this section. These sample tests have been classified as either standard, intermediate or advanced according to the level of the majority of questions. This will broadly reflect the NAPLAN Online tailored testing experience where students are guided into answering questions that match their ability.
- The following tests are included in this section:
  - three Reading Tests at standard, intermediate and advanced levels
  - three Conventions of Language Tests at standard, intermediate and advanced levels
  - three Writing Tests.

CHECKS

- The NAPLAN Online Conventions of Language and Reading tests will be divided into different sections.
- Students will have one last opportunity to check their answers in each section when they have reached the end of that section.
- Once they have moved onto a new section, they will not be able to go back and check their work again.
- We have included reminders for students to check their work at specific points in the Sample Tests so they become familiar with this process before they take the NAPLAN Online tests.

Excel Test Zone

- After students have consolidated their topic knowledge by completing this book, we recommend they practise NAPLAN Online–style questions on our website at www.exceltestzone.com.au.
- Students will be able to gain valuable practice in online skills.
- Students will also become confident in using a computer or tablet to complete NAPLAN Online–style tests so they will be fully prepared for the actual NAPLAN Online tests.

Sample Online-style Test 1

Standard level

1 Which word correctly completes the sentence?

"The money was ______ from my purse," complained Robyn.

A stole **B** stealed **C** stoled **D** stolen

2 Which word correctly completes the sentence?

Melody was so excited. She said, "This was the ______ party I've ever had!"

A bestest **B** best **C** more best **D** most best

3 Which sentence has the correct punctuation?

A Where I go is not your worry?
B Where you go you cause trouble?
C Where is Richmond on this map?
D Where to plant the tulips?

4 Which pronoun can be used instead of the highlighted words?

Dad ordered hot chilli and pumpkin soup at the café. The hot chilli and pumpkin soup came in a large brown bowl.

A Them **B** It **C** They **D** That

5 This sentence contains **at least** one verb.

Angelo was in the park looking for the lost ball.

Use as many boxes as you need to write any verbs included in this sentence.

[ ] [ ] [ ]

Read the text *Stars*. The text has some gaps. Choose the correct word to fill each gap.

Stars

When I went outside I saw stars twinkling **6** in the sky. I called my dad.
He **7** me that most of what I saw were stars but some were planets.
There are very few planets in the night sky but some have a **8** light than stars.

6 **A** brightly **B** brighter **C** bright **D** brightness

7 **A** tell **B** telled **C** tolded **D** told

8 **A** strong **B** stronger **C** strongest **D** strongly

 Answers and explanations on pages 108–110

9 Which sentence has the correct punctuation?

A Gina wondered why her teacher should be so late?
B Gina wondered, "Why her teacher should be so late?"
C Gina wondered why her teacher should be so late.
D Gina wondered why? her teacher should be so late.

10 Which part of speech is *wire* in this sentence?

We got an electrician to wire the shed for lights.

A adjective
B noun
C pronoun
D verb

11 Which word correctly completes the sentence?

There was a disaster for the netballers. All the ______ uniforms were left at the airport.

A clubs
B club's
C Club's
D clubs'

12 Which word correctly completes the sentence?

After running along the beach, Harley had left ______ deep footprints in the wet sand.

A more
B much
C many
D the
E a

13 Which sentence has the correct punctuation?

A "Is cricket a popular game?" asked Shane.
B "Is cricket a popular game, asked Shane?"
C "Is cricket a popular game? asked Shane."
D "Is cricket a popular game," asked Shane.

14 Circle the letter to show where the missing comma (,) should go.

Cars (A) trucks (B) and huge buses (C) were held up in the long (D) traffic jam (E) on the highway.

Answers and explanations on pages 108–110

Year 5 Conventions of Language Sample Online-style Test 1

Read the text *Candlelight*. The text has some gaps. Choose the correct word to fill each gap.

Candlelight

Fran looked at her friend. "You **15** have electricity!" said Fran with a frown.
"No electricity, **16** we have candles. Big candles," stated Bronnie, nodding her head.
"How can you cook with candles?" Fran asked **17**
Bronnie replied, "We do very **18** with our old fuel stove."

15 **A** dont **B** don't **C** doesn't **D** donnot

16 **A** as **B** and **C** but **D** yet

17 **A** question mark (**?**) **B** exclamation mark (**!**) **C** comma (**,**) **D** full stop (**.**)

18 **A** good **B** well **C** all right **D** goodly

19 A punctuation sign has been left out of this sentence.
Put the correct punctuation in the box to complete the sentence.
"How we missed the turn-off I will never really know ☐ " said the driver.

20 Which sentence has the correct punctuation?
A The City of Darwin was struck by cyclone Tracy on Christmas Morning.
B The city of Darwin was struck by cyclone Tracy on Christmas morning.
C The city of Darwin was struck by Cyclone Tracy on Christmas morning.
D The City of Darwin was struck by Cyclone Tracy on Christmas Morning.

Read the text *The report*. The text has some gaps. Choose the correct word to fill each gap.

The report

I looked at the brown envelope in my hand. The **21** was more than 3 **22** from where I stood. I had been ordered to post the envelope before the post office closed. That gave me over half **23** hour to make the journey. I was not sure if **24** Hansen had given me enough time.

21 **A** G.P.O. **B** GPO **C** g.p.o. **D** GPO.

22 **A** kms **B** km. **C** km **D** Km.

23 **A** a **B** the **C** and **D** an

24 **A** Dr **B** Dr. **C** DR. **D** dr

25 Which word in this sentence is a common noun?
Adam is the only boy who works quickly without complaining.
A Adam **B** boy **C** works **D** complaining

It would be a good idea to check your answers to questions 1 to 25 before moving on to the other questions.

Answers and explanations on pages 108–110

Year 5 Conventions of Language Sample Online-style Test 1

To the student

Ask your teacher or parent to read the spelling words for you. The words are listed on page 146. Write the spelling words on the lines below.

26 ______________________ 27 ______________________

28 ______________________ 29 ______________________

30 ______________________ 31 ______________________

32 ______________________ 33 ______________________

34 ______________________ 35 ______________________

36 ______________________ 37 ______________________

38 ______________________ 39 ______________________

40 ______________________

Read the sentences. The spelling mistake in each sentence is underlined. Write the correct spelling of the underlined word in the box.

41 After a hike Olivia had several unnusuall bites on her arms. [ ]

42 Dad put a clear coat of vanish on the antique, wooden table. [ ]

43 Any serious judge could see that the whole message was a faik. [ ]

44 The bomming of the skyscrapers was a terrorist act. [ ]

45 "You don't disserve your allowance this week," commented Dad. [ ]

Read the text *Dunnarts*. Each line has a word that is incorrect.
Write the correct spelling of the word in the box.

Dunnarts

46 Many tiny creatures live in the Australian counteryside. [ ]

47 Dunnarts are small, rarely seen marsuipels. They are numerous [ ]

48 in the Australian bush from the forests to the deserts. In parshed [ ]

49 regians they have survived where medium-sized mammals have [ ]

50 almost disappeared. They are caniverous and mainly eat insects. [ ]

Year 5 Conventions of Language

Sample Online-style Test 2

Intermediate level

1 Which word correctly completes the sentence?

When you ______ I locked the door straight away.

A ringed **B** rang **C** rings **D** ranged

2 Which word correctly completes the sentence?

Martin, I knew you ______ late yesterday and I didn't say anything!

A were **B** is **C** are **D** was **E** will be

3 Which pronoun can be used instead of the highlighted words?

Gina saw books and pencils scattered all over the path. She knew they were the books and pencils she owned.

A hers **B** she's **C** them **D** her's

4 Which sentence has correct punctuation?

A Jock, my brother, was asked where? he found the money?
B Jock, my brother, was asked where he found the money?
C Jock, my brother, was asked where he found the money.
D Jock my brother was asked where he found the money?

5 This sentence contains **at least** one adjective.

James went fishing and caught a bright, yellow fish and a small crab!

Use as many boxes as you need to write any verbs included in this sentence.

Read the text *Hot Water Beach*. The text has some gaps.
Choose the best option to fill each gap.

Hot Water Beach

Hot Water Beach actually **6** hot water. You have to dig a hole in the beach to find it. When the tide is low you take **7** spade and bucket and dig a hole as big as a bathtub. It will fill up with hot water. The hot water **8** from a deep underground basin. It is heated by New Zealand's volcanic landform. Heat forces the water to the surface.

6 **A** have **B** has **C** had **D** having

7 **A** yer **B** you're **C** you'r **D** your

8 **A** coming **B** come **C** came **D** comes

Answers and explanations on pages 110–112

9 Which word can be used instead of the highlighted words?

The school's Under 10 softball team won one match at the carnival. The school's Under 10 softball team's win was for a game against Murdock Public School.

A Their **B** It's **C** They **D** Them

10 In which sentence is *top* used as an adjective?

A If Jane has a good hit she will get the top score.
B Rhett was at the top end of the street when he heard the siren.
C The climbers reached the top of the mountain at dusk.
D A spinning top was a popular child's toy many years ago.

11 Which word can replace the pronoun *each* in this sentence?

Last year, each baker gave a cake to the king and queen for the banquet.

A one **B** the **C** every **D** no

12 Which word correctly completes the sentence?

The temperature was high during the day but it was ______ at night.

A little **B** small **C** low **D** short

13 Which word is unnecessary in this sentence?

For their annual wedding anniversary my parents enjoy the relaxation of a river cruise.

A annual **B** wedding **C** relaxation **D** river

14 Circle the letter to show where the missing full stop (.) should go.

This is Danny's tree (A) house (B) It was built on Sunday (C) just in time (D) for Troy's party.

Read the text *The search*. The text has some gaps. Choose the correct word to fill each gap.

The search

Simon was searching under his bed for **15** latest edition of a magazine. To his surprise he found a library book he **16** was lost. He had even paid the fine for the lost book. He could return the book **17** the library and get his money back. Five dollars **18** the fine—enough for a new magazine!

15 **A** a **B** an **C** these **D** the

16 **A** thought **B** thinks **C** thinked **D** thinking

17 **A** for **B** at **C** to **D** in

18 **A** have been **B** had been **C** has been **D** were

19 Which word correctly completes the sentence?

The ______ tails were neatly brushed before the parade commenced.

A pony's **B** ponys' **C** ponies's **D** ponies'

20 Which sentence has the correct punctuation?

- A Boxes of toys, bags of books, and cartons of comics filled the shelves in the shed.
- B Boxes of toys, bags of books and cartons of comics, filled the shelves in the shed.
- C Boxes of toys, bags of books and cartons of comics filled the shelves in the shed.
- D Boxes, of toys, bags, of books and cartons, of comics filled the shelves in the shed.

Read the text *Dad's advice.* The text has some gaps. Choose the correct word to fill each gap.

Dad's advice

"How do I put batteries in the **21** Bruce asked his father.

"First, you have to turn the clock upside down to find a panel," said his **22** .

"Found it!" said Bruce. "There are little arrows on it. **23** pointing towards the back."

Bruce's father said, "Push the panel **24** with your thumbs and it will slide off."

21 **A** clock" **B** clock?" **C** clock." **D** clock"?

22 **A** father **B** Father **C** FATHER **D** fatheR

23 **A** It is **B** There're **C** they's **D** They're

24 **A** gentle **B** gentlely **C** gently **D** real gently

25 Which word should be omitted from this sentence? Write your answer in the box.

Looking forward to the future, we can all find a little happiness if we work hard.

It would be a good idea to check your answers to questions 1 to 25 before moving on to the other questions.

Answers and explanations on pages 110–112

Year 5 Conventions of Language Sample Online-style Test 2

To the student

Ask your teacher or parent to read the spelling words for you. The words are listed on page 147. Write the spelling words on the lines below.

26 ______________________ 27 ______________________

28 ______________________ 29 ______________________

30 ______________________ 31 ______________________

32 ______________________ 33 ______________________

34 ______________________ 35 ______________________

36 ______________________ 37 ______________________

38 ______________________ 39 ______________________

40 ______________________

Read the sentences. The spelling mistake in each sentence is underlined. Write the correct spelling of the underlined word in the box.

41 The notise warned: *Beware of purse-snatchers and pickpockets*. [ ]

42 Many clients have lost money to dishonest building contracters. [ ]

43 Echidnas can be observed in any area with a plentyfull ant supply. [ ]

44 The small bilby has survived wear other desert dwellers haven't. [ ]

45 "Do you expeck your allowance this week?" queried Dad. [ ]

Read the text *Boabs*. Each line has a word that is incorrect. Write the correct spelling in the box.

Boabs

46 Resent studies of the boab reveal some of its features. [ ]

47 Boabs, or bottle trees, inhabit the tropical, north-west cornor of [ ]

48 Australia. The Aboriginals used the root fibers to make string. [ ]

49 The flesh under the skin of the fruit has a refreshing flavor and the [ ]

50 seeds, which have a kideny shape, are ground into a white paste. [ ]

Answers and explanations on pages 110–112

Year 5 Conventions of Language

Sample Online-style Test 3

Advanced level

1 This sentence contains **at least** one adverb.

Later in the day Enrico was seen walking peacefully through the park.

Use as many boxes as you need to write any adverbs included in this sentence.

[ ] [ ] [ ]

2 Which word correctly completes the sentence?

The prices in the shop ______ going up as we stand here!

A was **B** is **C** were **D** are

3 Which word or words are unnecessary in this sentence?

The cruise ship disappeared from view as the evening fog rolled in.

A cruise **B** from view **C** evening **D** in

4 Which word correctly completes the sentence?

The cups on your shelf are similar ______ the ones we have at home.

A with **B** at **C** to **D** like

5 Which words correctly complete the sentence?

The saleswoman looked at Mum and said, "We have ______ sizes in caps."

A small, medium, and large
B small, medium, and large
C small, medium and, large,
D small, medium and large

Read the limerick *Man from Bengal*. The text has some gaps.
Choose the best option to fill each gap.

Man from Bengal

There was a young man from Bengal,
6 went to a fancy dress ball.
He thought **7** risk it
And went as a biscuit,
And a dog **8** him up in the hall.

6 **A** that **B** Which **C** What **D** Who

7 **A** he'd **B** He'd **C** he'ld **D** hed

8 **A** et **B** eat **C** ate **D** ated

9 Which word correctly completes the sentence?

There wasn't ______ water in the birdbath after the rain.

A many **B** some **C** much **D** no **E** plenty

Read the text *Wake up!* The text has some gaps. Choose the best option to fill each gap.

Wake up!

The magpies warbled in the nearby gum trees.

The sun ______ through the bedroom

	shine	shone	shined	shineded
10	A	B	C	D

window right onto ______ face. She

	Annes	Annes'	Anne's	Anne
11	A	B	C	D

blinked. ______ she was awake.

	Suddenly	sudden	suddenly	Sudden
12	A	B	C	D

Although the night had been ______

	warm.	warm	warm!	warm,
13	A	B	C	D

a shiver ran through her body.

14 Which word correctly completes the sentence?

William Tell's house, ______ is painted cream, has just been sold.

A what **B** which **C** who **D** that

15 In which sentence is *spring* used as an adjective?

A The creek was fed by an underground spring.
B Jump over the log and spring into the creek.
C There was plenty of spring in the jumping castle.
D The spring blossoms made a spectacular display.

16 Which pronoun correctly completes the sentence?

Wade has two spare blankets and he will give them to Bobby and ______ .

A I **B** mine **C** we **D** me

Answers and explanations on pages 112–114

Year 5 Conventions of Language Sample Online-style Test 3

Read the text *Good morning*. The text has some gaps. Choose the correct word to fill each gap.

Good morning

Anne sat up in bed. She had a funny tingling feeling. Why did she feel so **17**

She got dressed and went out to the kitchen. Her mother was **18** the stove, cooking.

"Have you checked the horses?" her mother asked as she lifted a pot off the stove **19**

Anne said **20** She would do it after breakfast.

17 **A** strange? **B** strange. **C** strange, **D** strange

18 **A** in **B** by **C** over **D** to

19 **A** exclamation mark (!) **B** question mark (?) **C** full stop (.) **D** comma (,)

20 **A** she hadn't. **B** She hadn't. **C** "She hadn't." **D** "she hadn't."

21 Which word can be used instead of the highlighted words?

Dad bought a set of garden tools, young plants and plastic pots before he started work. He wanted the garden tools, young plants and plastic pots to make a new garden for Mum.

A that **B** it **C** they **D** them

22 Which word describes how the Fighters played the game?

After many (**A**) tackles and high (**B**) kicks the Fighters struggled bravely (**C**) until (**D**) the final (**E**) bell.

23 Which sentence has the correct punctuation?

A We rented two DVDs for the weekend at the beach.

B We rented two DVD's for the weekend at the beach.

C We rented two D.V.D.s for the weekend at the beach.

D We rented two D.V.D.'s for the weekend at the beach.

24 Which word correctly completes the sentence?

The ______ colour had changed over the years. It was Mum's favourite.

A trays' **B** tray's **C** traies' **D** trays's

25 Which word in this sentence is a pronoun?

The children, without making a mess, completed the painting by themselves.

A children **B** mess **C** completed **D** themselves

It would be a good idea to check your answers to questions 1 to 25 before moving on to the other questions.

Answers and explanations on pages 112–114

Year 5 Conventions of Language Sample Online-style Test 3

To the student

Ask your teacher or parent to read the spelling words for you. The words are listed on page 148. Write the spelling words on the lines below.

26 ______________________ 27 ______________________

28 ______________________ 29 ______________________

30 ______________________ 31 ______________________

32 ______________________ 33 ______________________

34 ______________________ 35 ______________________

36 ______________________ 37 ______________________

38 ______________________ 39 ______________________

40 ______________________

Read the sentences. The spelling mistake in each sentence is underlined. Write the correct spelling of the underlined word in the box.

41 A rust-bucket is the name for a beaten-up, unroadworthy <u>autermobile</u>. [ ]

42 A clear coat of lacquer was <u>requiered</u> on the handrail. [ ]

43 A <u>refridgerator</u> is essential in summer heat. [ ]

44 Calm seas and swaying <u>plams</u> are features of the perfect holiday. [ ]

45 "This present is totally <u>unecessary</u>," remarked Mum. [ ]

Read the text *Blue waterlilies.* Each line has a word that is incorrect. Write the correct spelling of the word in the box.

Blue waterlilies

46 Botanists do not need comparses to find water-loving plants. [ ]

47 Aquatic plants abound in the billerbongs of northern Australia. Many [ ]

48 are submerdged and only seen when their buds poke above the [ ]

49 water's surface and the flowers open. The blue waterlily veries in [ ]

50 colour from white to pale blue, and has numeruos yellow stamens. [ ]

Year 5 Reading

Sample Online-style Test 1

Standard level

Read *A Dreamtime legend* and answer questions 1 to 6.

A Dreamtime legend

This is a legend from the Dreamtime about two young brothers who went up into the Northern Flinders Ranges of South Australia to hunt.

Two young brothers of the tribe were known as very clever hunters. The tribe desperately needed meat so the brothers decided to make a hunting trip up into the mountains that we now call the Flinders Ranges.

Soon after they had begun to climb they spotted an emu hiding among the boulders and they quickly caught and killed it. They carried it with them as they continued on up into the mountains. However, by midday the emu was covered in flies. The brothers tried to drive them away but despite whatever they did the flies kept returning and increasing in numbers. The brothers became worried that the meat would be spoiled so they eventually decided to light a fire, hoping that the flames and smoke would drive the flies away. It did, but a strong wind blew up and fanned the fire so that it quickly began to spread through the dry grass that was all around. In a short time the whole mountainside was on fire and the two young brothers were trapped.

There was no way they could get back down onto the plains so they scrambled onto a rocky ledge and watched terrified as the fire grew stronger and more widespread, the flames coming closer and closer to them. The brothers were frantic, they could barely breathe because of the smoke, and with a great effort they began to climb higher up the cliff until they reached the uppermost tip. Even here they were not safe. The fire reached out to them and the flames burned their skin. There was nothing they could do; there was nowhere else to go. In desperation they began to scream and suddenly they discovered they could fly. They flew up high over the flames and smoke. They went higher and higher into the distant world of the night sky.

The ancestors, who had been watching, had taken pity on them and given them the power of flight to escape the flames. With relief the two men realised they were at last safe and they made their camp in the sky world where they remain till this day. At night their camp fires can still be seen as The Pointers, the two bright stars that point to the Southern Cross.

Source: http://members.optusnet.com.au/virgothomas/space/abobeliefs2.html

1 Complete this sentence. Write your answer on the line.

The brothers climbed to the top of the hill to ______________________________

2 What happened straight after the brothers lit their fire?

A The flies kept away from the dead emu.
B A strong wind caused the fire to spread.
C Both brothers started to panic and scream.
D Two stars appeared pointing to the Southern Cross.

3 The brothers decided to light a fire to

A cook the emu.
B burn the long grass.
C keep flies off the dead emu.
D get warm on the mountain.

4 The ancestors (line 22) in the story are most likely

A stars in the night sky.
B evil spirits.
C the parents of the brothers.
D spirits of a past generation.

5 The story of the two brothers is intended to

A explain a natural fact.
B warn people about the dangers of fires.
C advise people how to hunt.
D criticise those who hunt native animals.

6 At the end of the story, what happened to the brothers?

A They got burnt to death in the fire.
B They became stars in the night sky.
C They returned to their tribe with the emu.
D They screamed and were saved by other hunters.

Read *Wairere Boulders* and answer questions 7 to 12.

Wairere Boulders

The Wairere Boulders are an unusually large, chaotic mass of basalt boulders (black, volcanic rocks) along a small stream in the Hokianga in New Zealand's North Island. It is as if a giant has spilled a handful of boulders down a valley full of rainforest vegetation. The valley is about 2 kilometres long and 350 metres wide.

The boulders in the valley are the eroded remains of a lava flow about three million years ago. The underlying soil is clay. Lava on a clay base is unusual. As the clay washed away, large pieces of the basalt sheet broke off and the boulder valley was formed.

The boulders in the valley have eroded in an unusual way. They have deep channels in them, called flutes or cuts. Some of the flutes are up to a metre deep and 35 centimetres wide.

Early settlers in the region had no explanation for how the hundreds of rocks were formed. It is now understood that the flutes were caused by an unusual form of erosion. Basalt is an extremely hard rock and erosion of basalt is an uncommon and very slow process.

At one time the area was covered in Kauri forests. The rain fell through the Kauri leaves and branches, picking up a weak acid from the trees, which dripped onto the rocks below. Over many centuries the flutes developed. Once the flutes had started, the dripping water tended to follow the same path.

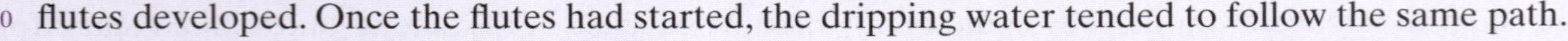

Some of the rocks have horizontal flutes. It is obvious that the narrow horizontal flutes were once vertical. When the softer clay surface underneath washed away, the boulders rolled to one side.

Sources: Printed handout from the site and <http://www.wairereboulders.co.nz/>.

7 Which statement is true?
- **A** The clay lies on top of the basalt rock.
- **B** All the channels in the rock are vertical (run up and down).
- **C** The channels in the rock formed before any volcanic eruption.
- **D** The formation of the valley was not immediately understood.

8 The acid that formed, which caused the boulders to erode, came from
- **A** black, volcanic rock.
- **B** the small stream by the rocks.
- **C** sap from the Kauri trees.
- **D** the clay base under the lava flow.

9 Choose **two** options. Another word for *flutes* would be
- **A** grooves.
- **B** cracks.
- **C** cuts.
- **D** lines.
- **E** holes.
- **F** ridges.

10 Over time the rocks can become unstable because of
- **A** volcanic activity.
- **B** erosion of ground under the boulders.
- **C** erosion of the banks by the stream.
- **D** damage done by rainforest vegetation.

11 The purpose of the illustrations is to show the
- **A** beauty of the stream.
- **B** stream's direction and flow.
- **C** damage done by volcanoes.
- **D** actual size and shape of the rocks.

12 What is the main purpose of the passage? Write your answer on the lines.

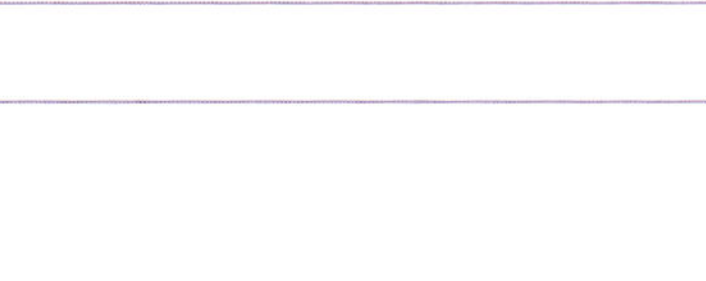

It would be a good idea to check your answers to questions 1 to 12 before moving on to the other questions.

Answers and explanations on pages 114–117

Year 5 Reading Sample Online-style Test 1

Read *School Days* and answer questions 13 to 17.

13 The children feel the money spent on pets is

A unfair.
B necessary.
C careless.
D understandable.

14 Choose **two** options. When Kate was first told the news she was

A amused.
B confused.
C shocked.
D panicky.
E dubious.
F excited.

15 Which of these upset Kate the most?

A She would have to sit next to a dog in class.
B Pets were to be given free bus passes.
C Dogs and cats had better medical care.
D Her allowance seemed very small compared to what was spent on pets.

16 The looks on the pets' faces in frame 6 show they are

A aghast.
B delighted.
C confused.
D disappointed.
E horrified.
F excited.

17 Although the cartoon strip is amusing it is also a serious comment on

A children reading newspapers without fully understanding what they are reading.
B difficulties with pets on buses and in schools.
C the seemingly excessive amount of money spent on pets.
D a problem with school bus passes.

Year 5 Reading Sample Online-style Test 1

Read the *Graphic novel review* and answer questions 18 to 23.

Graphic novel review

Captain Congo and the Maharaja's Monkey by Ruth Starke
Illustrated by Greg Holfeld
Reviewed by Claire Saxby

Captain Congo's new adventure.

'Have more caramel, Monsieur Pug, to build up your strength. Who knows when you and the Captain will be off again.'

'Soon, I hope.'

'There's nothing like the call to adventure, eh Pug?'

Captain Congo, with the help of his not-quite-so-courageous offsider Pug, solves mysteries. Their first adventure was set in Africa and this new call takes the pair to India. They have been asked to investigate the sudden death of the Maharaja. Plans are already underway for the installing of his successor. Although the Maharaja had left information about his successor, not everyone is happy with his choice. Rumours abound. Meanwhile, Captain Congo and Pug (now cunningly—if reluctantly—disguised as a woman) are to infiltrate the palace and see if they can discover what happened to the old Maharaja. They will also investigate the rumours surrounding the succession. *Captain Congo and the Maharaja's Monkey* is a large format, hardback, full-colour graphic novel in the style of *Asterix* and *Tintin*.

It is an adventure in grand style. Captain Congo, a gorilla, Pug, a penguin, and Captain Congo's housekeeper are non-humans acting like humans. The rest of the characters are human. The humans accept Captain Congo as an equal, with the deputy chief minister being beguiled by the in-disguise Pug. There is plenty of humour here, along with the cracking-pace adventure. Captain Congo plays it straight, although if 2D eyes could twinkle, his would! He is very worldly, has many friends and connections and speaks many unexpected languages. Pug is the reluctant sidekick, expected to shine in roles he would not choose. Their combination of detective work, disguises and luck win the day so Captain Congo and Pug can return to their island home. Recommended for mid-primary and beyond.

Captain Congo and the Maharaja's Monkey, Omnibus Books, 2009
Source: http://www.aussiereviews.com/article2975.html

18 Who provided the full-colour graphics for the reviewed book?
Write your answer on the line.

____

19 The paragraph beginning with *Captain Congo, with the help …* (lines 9–17) is mainly about
- **A** the plot.
- **B** *Asterix* and *Tintin*.
- **C** the quality of the writing.
- **D** the characters.

20 Pug and Captain Congo have to go to India to
- **A** find the Maharaja's monkey.
- **B** uncover information about the Maharaja's death.
- **C** release animals from the palace.
- **D** install a new successor to the Maharaja.

21 You are told *Rumours abound* in the palace (line 13). This means
- **A** the palace is full of secret, mysterious talk by the staff.
- **B** palace staff are all busybodies and gossips.
- **C** truthful, private information is being made public.
- **D** there are many stories going around that cannot be supported by facts.

22 What is Pug's relationship with Captain Congo?
- **A** a half-hearted assistant
- **B** a faithful girlfriend
- **C** an ungrateful helper
- **D** a younger brother

23 Which term best describes the reviewer's opinion of the graphic novel?
- **A** cautious approval
- **B** highly favourable
- **C** somewhat unsatisfying
- **D** general disappointment

It would be a good idea to check your answers to questions 13 to 23 before moving on to the other questions.

Year 5 Reading Sample Online-style Test 1

Read *Ducks' Ditty* and answer questions 24 to 28.

Ducks' Ditty

All along the backwater,
Through the rushes tall,
Ducks are a-dabbling,
Up tails all!

Ducks' tails, drakes' tails,
Yellow feet a-quiver,
Yellow bills all out of sight
Busy in the river!

Slushy green undergrowth,
Where the roach* swim,
Here we keep our larder,
Cool and full and dim.

Everyone for what he likes!
We like to be,
Heads down, tails up,
Dabbling free!

High in the blue above,
Swifts† whirl and call—
We are down a-dabbling,
Up tails all!

Kenneth Grahame 1859–1932 (from *Wind in the Willows*)

* Freshwater fish
† Small, high-flying bird

24 In the poem, what are the ducks and drakes doing most of the time?
- **A** making a lot of noise
- **B** watching out for fish
- **C** looking for food under the water
- **D** wishing they could fly like the swifts

25 The poem creates the impression that the ducks are
- **A** carefree.
- **B** wishing they were flying.
- **C** feeling hungry.
- **D** being hassled.

26 The poem suggests that the ducks spend much of their time
- **A** quacking.
- **B** with their heads under water.
- **C** catching fish.
- **D** chasing one another.
- **E** flying with swifts.
- **F** waddling on the bank.

27 The word *We* is in italics in the last two stanzas. This is to
- **A** draw attention to how unfortunate the ducks are in a backwater.
- **B** point out that ducks' lives are not like the lives of other animals.
- **C** highlight similarities between ducks and swifts.
- **D** emphasise that the ducks are happy doing their own thing.

28 What is meant by the term *blue above* (line 17) in the poem?
- **A** the daytime sky
- **B** the colour of the backwater
- **C** the reflection of the sky in the surface of the water
- **D** the colour of the feathers on the ducks' heads

Answers and explanations on pages 114–117

Year 5 Reading Sample Online-style Test 1

Read the extract from *The Night of the Scarecrow* and answer questions 29 to 34.

The Night of the Scarecrow

I went to bed that night a little more relaxed. But I was still tense. I jumped at every little noise even if I recognised it almost immediately. I'd lie still for a while just listening until the silence almost hurt my ears.

It was a still night of bright moonlight. The window was a rectangle of white light. Silver light reflected dully off some of the shinier objects in the room.

I went to sleep before Mum and Dad had switched off the kitchen lights.

Then it happened. *Tap. Tap-tap. Tap*. I awoke abruptly. Fully awake in seconds and lying rigid in my bed.

Nothing for a few minutes. *You're being foolish James*, I thought to myself.

Then *tap. Tap-tap. Tap*.

I twisted my head slowly, ever so slowly, towards the window and stared half hoping, half dreading I'd see something.

Some distance away I heard the familiar *Tap. Tap-tap. Tap*. again.

I guessed it was Jenny's window. I toyed with the idea of calling out. I don't know if I was more scared of being terrified or acting foolishly if it was nothing more than a cricket. I didn't call out. The noise had stopped.

I was just starting to relax when the tapping started again at my window. With a little more courage I turned to see what I could see. If my younger sister had been undisturbed by a little noise then I'd have to be brave.

At first I could see nothing. Then I thought I saw a slight movement. My heart started racing. I strained my eyes trying to make out what had moved.

Then I saw it. Suddenly lit up and in the frame of the window was the face of a scarecrow, the scarecrow I had made, right down to Aunt Monica's hat. The bits of mirror I had used for eyes reflecting a hidden light.

The scarecrow had left the field and was now looking in my window.

I screamed and tumbled out of bed.

From Alan Horsfield, *The Night of the Scarecrow*, Macmillan Education Trekker, 2005

29 You are told that the narrator states that he was fully awake in seconds and lying *rigid* (line 15) in his bed. What would be the reason for the narrator's reaction? Write your answer on the line.

____

30 *Then I saw it* (line 44). The word *it* refers to

A moonlight. **B** the window. **C** a scarecrow. **D** a mirror.

31 Why did the narrator first wake up?

A He heard an unusual tapping sound on a window.
B The moonlight was bright in his bedroom.
C The sound of crickets was loud and close to Jenny's window.
D He heard his parents switching off the kitchen lights.

32 The words *I toyed with the idea* (lines 24–25) suggest the narrator was

A enjoying his thoughts. **B** getting ready for fun and action.
C didn't know which was his best idea. **D** unlikely to act on his idea.

33 Write the numbers 1 to 4 in the boxes to show the order in this story of the following events.

☐ The narrator falls out of bed. ☐ There is a tapping sound on Jenny's window.
☐ The narrator goes to sleep. ☐ The parents switch off the lights.

34 A good alternative title for the passage would be

A Tap. Tap-tap. **B** Moonlit night. **C** Jenny's dream. **D** Face at the window.

Answers and explanations on pages 114–117

Read *Normanby Woman* and answer questions 35 to 39.

Normanby Woman

In the early days of the Queensland settlement, Europeans were occasionally discovered living with Aboriginals. Mystery surrounds the origins of the 'Normanby Woman' of Cooktown.

During the Palmer River gold rush of the 1870s a fair-skinned woman was often seen living with Aboriginals of the Normanby River. All police attempts to contact her failed. She became known as the 'Normanby Woman', and was eventually captured near the goldfield after being enticed from an Aboriginal camp with the promise of food. She apparently knew three English words: *Mary, white* and *potato*.

The woman was washed, dressed and fed before being put on a horse, to take her to a new home in Cooktown. Angry Aboriginals attacked the party, demanding her release. The 'rescue' party fired warning shots. The Aboriginals retreated but in the commotion the woman's horse bolted and she was thrown. She lay unconscious and injured. Two Chinese men were hired to carry her by stretcher on the two-day walk to Cooktown.

She died of her severe head injuries at the hospital on 30 August 1887, the day after she arrived. Interest in the woman was high in Cooktown and locals were charged one shilling (about ten cents) to view the 'Normanby Woman'.

At the inquest, the woman was described 'to be about sixty years of age. She was a skeleton. Her hair was flaxen, about 3 inches [about 7 centimetres] long. Her eyes were brown … she had the appearance of a European'.

Cooktown's doctor agreed with the description but added, 'The formation of her head was that of an Aboriginal woman'. The doctor had no doubt 'that she belonged to an Aboriginal race'.

Fair-skinned Aboriginals were not unknown. It is not surprising she knew three English words. Female Aboriginals often went into miners' camps looking for food. However, many locals claimed she was the sole survivor of a German shipwreck near the Bloomfield River in 1852, and was raised by local Aboriginals.

What was the truth of the 'Normanby Woman'? No one is sure what is fact and what is fiction.

Sources: WT Johnston, *The Normanby Woman*, Historical Society, Cairns, Cooktown Library and http://www.cook.qld.gov.au/visitors/NormanbyWoman.shtml

35 The capture of the Normanby Woman by the white settlers

A was followed by her being thrown from a horse.
B ended when the Aboriginals rescued her.
C was celebrated by the people of Cooktown.
D meant she could rejoin the Germans from the 1852 shipwreck.

36 How long did the Normanby Woman live in Cooktown?

A from 1852 to 1887
B about one day
C two days
D during the gold rush of the 1870s

37 How did the Normanby Woman get to Cooktown? Write your answer on the line.

____

38 The attitude of the local Cooktown inhabitants to the Normanby Woman's hospitalisation could best be described as

A inconsiderate. **B** sensitive. **C** prying. **D** cruel.

39 You are going to compare the texts *The Night of the Scarecrow* (page 66) and *Normanby Woman* (above). What are the features of these texts? Tick **two** options for each text.

	The Night of the Scarecrow	**Normanby Woman**
written for enjoyment	A ☐	A ☐
written as a factual report	B ☐	B ☐
written as a description	C ☐	C ☐
written in the first person	D ☐	D ☐

Answers and explanations on pages 114–117

Sample Online-style Test 2

Intermediate level

Read *The Indian Mynas* and answer questions 1 to 6.

The Indian Mynas

The Indian Myna (or Common Myna) was introduced into Australia in the late 1860s to control insects but has become a huge problem in city suburbs.

Problems with Indian Mynas

Indian Mynas are pest birds. They prefer urban environments where food and nesting sites are plentiful. They eat almost anything. In towns, they congregate around available food scraps, usually near schools, shopping centres and sports fields. The mynas also scavenge unattended pet food from urban backyards.

Mynas can often be seen on powerlines. They gather in large numbers, often more than twenty birds. They roost in trees, making loud chattering noises and leaving droppings everywhere.

Indian Mynas are messy birds and nest in tree hollows, palms and under roofs, in gutters and in sheds. They evict animals and birds from their nests and leave tree hollows that are mite-ridden and unusable by other wildlife. Mynas have adapted to Australian conditions and breed quickly.

The mynas' behaviour is seasonal. They form pairs for breeding from September to March. They have four or five chicks. When the young are ready to fly they travel in small family groups. After March, the mynas join larger groups and move to communal roosts. They split up in the mornings, going off in different directions to find food.

Hundreds of mynas can roost in a single tree or building near a regular food source. When the myna numbers increase and food becomes scarce, a new colony is established.

Black head
Chocolate brown body—Yellow beak and eye patch
White wing patch in flight
Long yellow legs

Stop the invasion

Mynas thrive where food is easy to get.

- Seed for native birds will attract Indian Mynas and they will quickly dominate a garden. If you see mynas at your bird feeder or in your garden, stop putting out birdseed immediately.
- Feed pets inside or, if that is not possible, put pet food inside during the day.
- Feed chickens and ducks in a secure pen so mynas can't get to the food.

Source: <http://www.indianmyna.org/documents/Indian_Myna_Handbookl.pdf>

1 Which word best describes the Indian Myna?
A adaptable **B** secretive **C** charming **D** insignificant

2 What is the main attraction for the mynas to an area?
A suitable shelter
B other birds
C nesting opportunities
D unattended food scraps

3 *Communal roosts* (line 14) are places
A where mynas build their nests.
B where many mynas perch.
C which are suitable areas to raise young mynas.
D that once belonged to other birds.

4 What are **two** ways to discourage mynas from visiting a particular area? Write an answer on each line.
1 ______________________ **2** ______________________

5 Mynas spoil the nests of other animals by
A leaving their droppings in them.
B contaminating them with parasites.
C raising their own young in them.
D creating overcrowded conditions.

6 In the text the subheading *Stop the invasion* gives information about myna
A control. **B** populations. **C** features. **D** behaviour. **E** eradication.

Year 5 Reading Sample Online-style Test 2

Read *Summer fun* and answer questions 7 to 11.

Summer fun

1 The summer's here and we're away
Across the ocean blue
To sail to distant sunny isles
Where people there are few.

2 We'll drop our anchor by the reef,
Make ready for the night,
Then swim on palm-fringed beaches
Where the sand is silver white

3 For dinner we'll eat fish we catch
And pawpaws freshly cut,
Then wash it down with water
From a fresh, green coconut.

4 And when we're tired of swimming
And splashing in the spray,
We'll pull the anchor up and then
We'll gently sail away.

Elaine Horsfield

7 Choose **two** options. The poem creates a feeling of

- **A** exciting adventure.
- **B** relaxed enjoyment.
- **C** frantic action.
- **D** tense excitement.
- **E** listless involvement.
- **F** satisfying leisure.

8 Choose **two** options. *Palm-fringed beaches* (line 7) are ones where palms

- **A** are all the same size.
- **B** completely cover the beach.
- **C** are at either end of the beach.
- **D** grow in a line along the edge of the beach.
- **E** add a border to the shore.
- **F** look like hair on the sand.

9 There are four stanzas in this poem.
Which stanza suggests the enjoyment of the partaking of local produce?
Write a number in the box.

10 What is the main purpose of the poem?

- **A** to inform
- **B** to educate
- **C** to describe
- **D** to entertain

11 A suitable alternative title for the poem would be

- **A** Life at sea.
- **B** Ocean isolation.
- **C** Silver sands.
- **D** Anchors up!

It would be a good idea to check your answers to questions 1 to 11 before moving on to the other questions.

Answers and explanations on pages 117–120

Year 5 Reading Sample Online-style Test 2

Read *The coconut palm* and answer questions 12 to 17.

The coconut palm

When someone says, 'Think South Pacific', most people think of sparkling blue lagoons, deserted beaches—and coconut palms. No picture postcard of the South Pacific is quite complete without a coconut palm somewhere in the scene. Coconut palms are not only found in the South Pacific but in any tropical environment where it is warm and wet. They are found from the beaches of Pacific islands to the flood plains of countries in South East Asia.

But it is the South Pacific where the coconut palm is an important part of daily life and culture. Here the coconut palm is called the Tree of Life. Every part of the tree has a use: leaves, fruit, trunk, bark and roots. They are a source of food and drink, a provider of building materials, and materials for fishing and farming.

Just as with eucalypts or pines, there are different types of coconut palms. The Fijian coconut palm grows up to 40 metres high and towers over its Asian cousin. It has a long slender trunk that bends and sways, without snapping off during most tropical cyclones. A child could reach right around the trunk of a fully-grown tree. The head is made up of fronds of long, spiky leaves and large bundles of coconuts. It can weigh several tonnes. If the head of the coconut palm snaps off in strong winds then the tree dies. Normally, a coconut palm will live around one hundred years. They produce about sixty coconuts every year after about the sixth year. To harvest the coconuts simply walk around a plantation and pick them up off the ground.

Coconuts were once part of the sideshow alley at fairs and shows. Grandparents may remember the coconut shy, a knock-'em-down kind of game. There was even a pop song about playing the game.

The young nuts are green or yellow but turn a greyish-brown just before dropping. A good-sized coconut can be larger than an adult's head and weigh several kilograms. And they float!

Because the nuts float they can drift from one island to another on ocean currents or pushed along by the winds. That is why so many tropical beaches are fringed with coconut palms. The nuts roll up onto the beach, become embedded in the sand and begin to grow.

12 You are going to compare the texts on pages 70 and 71. For what purposes were the texts written? Tick **two** boxes for each text.

	The coconut palm	**Dark rendezvous**
to inform	**A** ☐	**A** ☐
to describe	**B** ☐	**B** ☐
to engage	**C** ☐	**C** ☐
to recount	**D** ☐	**D** ☐

13 What happens if the head of a coconut palm snaps off?

A A new head grows in its place.
B The tree fails to survive the damage.
C There are no coconuts for six years.
D A new coconut grows in its place.

14 The exclamation mark in *And they float!* (line 22) is used to

A make the writing more exciting.
B compare coconuts to other nuts that don't float.
C draw attention to the size of a coconut.
D show that the writer does not believe this fact.

15 The writer of the passage was most interested in the coconut palm because of its

A value as an agricultural crop.
B pleasing photographic appeal.
C ability to withstand cyclones.
D many practical uses.

16 According to the text, which statement is correct?

A In sideshows coconuts are valued for their food.
B There is more than one variety of coconut palm.
C Coconut palms have about six coconuts every year for six years.
D Coconuts cannot survive in salt water.

17 Which word in the text suggests that the coconut palm can withstand high winds?

A *slender* **B** *tropical* **C** *sparkling* **D** *tower*

Answers and explanations on pages 117–120

Year 5 Reading Sample Online-style Test 2

Read *Dark rendezvous* and answer questions 18 to 23.

Dark rendezvous

Brett catches an earlier bus for work. He knows he is being stupid but needs to have a closer look at the mystery site.

He gets off the bus at a stop just before the major intersection with the highway. He crosses briskly as there is no pedestrian crossing and walks along the grassy verge. There is no footpath.

There is a low tide smell stealing up from the bay.

He crosses a wide access ramp with a narrow median strip that has been planted with some sort of native bladed grass. There is a steady stream of traffic.

When he reaches his destination he looks around almost guiltily. He feels like an intruder although it is public space.

The lights turn red and Brett stands awkwardly. There must be a number of drivers and passengers who are wondering what he is up to. It seems to take ages for the lights to turn green. Then they are gone.

Brett looks around. The road sign is larger than he had expected. It looms above his head advising motorists of the correct lane to take for various destinations.

Across the ground is a tangle of struggling vines. Behind the vines are clumps of browning kangaroo paws. Their little paw-like flowers, with torn fingernails, seem to be reaching out desperately for help. He wonders why anyone would plant wilderness flowers alongside a major arterial link.

In the distance he hears goods trains being shunted along lines and over points to new positions. Their crashing makes him shudder.

He looks around expecting to see the lady and relaxes a little, suspecting that she is not there. He wonders if she might be watching him intruding into her special place.

The ground is covered with decaying woodchip and chopped-up leaf litter. In a spot just under the large sign is an area where the surface has been disturbed. It's as if someone had started a garden. Other than that, there is nothing that could be of interest.

18 What was Brett expecting to see at his destination? Write your answer on the line.

____

19 Which pair of words from the text suggests that Brett may be in danger?

A *awkwardly, wondering*
B *struggling, looms*
C *wilderness, decaying*
D *steady, browning*

20 *There is a low tide smell stealing up from the bay* (line 6).
This suggests that the smell is

A distinct. **B** overpowering. **C** foul. **D** sinister.

21 Write the numbers 1 to 4 in the boxes to show the order in this story of the following events.

☐ Brett hears a goods train shunting.
☐ Brett makes his way up an access ramp.
☐ Brett crosses a road near a major intersection.
☐ Brett waits for the lights to turn green.

22 Which word best describes the mood the passage creates?

A foreboding **B** horror **C** despair **D** fear

23 By the end of the extract Brett is feeling

A frightened and lonely.
B suspicious and worried.
C daring but nervous.
D disappointed but relieved.

It would be a good idea to check your answers to questions 12 to 23 before moving on to the other questions.

Answers and explanations on pages 117–120

Year 5 Reading Sample Online-style Test 2

Read *Volcano erupts—Mexicans refuse to budge* and answer questions 24 to 29.

Volcano erupts—Mexicans refuse to budge

San Nicholas, MEXICO December 21, 2000

Knowing that a huge eruption was about to occur, government officials yesterday placed the area around the Popocat volcano on maximum alert.

The volcano, located just 60 kilometres from Mexico City, had been rumbling and spewing smoke for almost 12 hours.

According to a volcano expert this is an indication that the volcano was about to blow.

He said, 'We are in a situation of maximum alert. We are ready for mud slides and lava flows.'

Popocat first erupted briefly late on Tuesday, throwing red-hot rocks into the sky as soldiers patrolled hastily emptied villages nearby to make sure the area had been completely evacuated.

Huge rocks were blasted at least half a kilometre into the air at times.

As many as 56 000 people were warned to leave their homes as experts extended the danger zone from 12 to 24 kilometres around the volcano.

As many as 20 million people could be affected if there is a major eruption.

Two thousand soldiers were called in to control the evacuation of twenty villages in the danger zones.

They are now patrolling ghost-like towns to make sure everyone has left.

Huge traffic jams blocked roads leading out of the danger zone. People have slowly made their way to shelters and camps set up by the government.

One government official said that there were over 21 000 people so far in shelters, or on their way to them.

Though the military have ordered everyone to leave the danger zone many peasant farmers have refused to do so. These people are so poor they are afraid that their homes will be looted and that their basic possessions will take years to replace.

The Red Cross in Mexico City has started a drive for clothing and basic foods.

A spokesman for the Red Cross said that they are having difficulty getting sufficient transport to take what donations they have to the camps.

It is feared that without proper control there could be a major outbreak of disease. Water quality is a major concern.

24 About how many people were warned to leave the danger zone near Popocat?
Write a number in the box.

☐

25 How did authorities know the Popocat volcano was about to erupt?

A Residents from villages near the volcano had been leaving their homes.
B The volcano had been rumbling and billowing smoke for many hours.
C The Red Cross had started a drive for clothing and basic foods.
D Soldiers had warned of the need for extra troops.

26 The Mexican government used its authority to

A bring in clothing for the people forced to move.
B organise transport for donated goods.
C supply sufficient drinking water for the camps.
D call in soldiers to help people move away.

27 Because many people were poor, when the volcano began to erupt they

A decided to stay to protect their few possessions.
B made plans to leave as soon as possible.
C called in the police for protection.
D looted other houses in their villages.

28 The report, as it is written,

A spreads unnecessary fear and warnings.
B is concerned with the facts as they happened.
C is loaded with emotional comments and criticisms.
D is based upon opinion and feelings.

29 The Red Cross feared that the eruption would

A leave many people homeless.
B cause mud slides.
C result in homes being looted.
D end in an outbreak of disease.

Answers and explanations on pages 117–120

Year 5 Reading Sample Online-style Test 2

Read Lisa's essay and answer questions 30 to 35.

Lisa had to write an essay on the topic of *Playtime for primary school students*. This is her essay.

The world is getting busier, yet children nowadays waste far too much time. This is especially so during their time at primary school. Primary school time is not used efficiently.

The times not spent in class at primary school are wasted. In fact, there are times when the breaks distract from the work that goes on in class. In the schoolyard there are times when pupils are bullied, called names or simply ignored. There is a lot of time being bored or waiting for the bell to ring. There are studies that have said that the benefits of playtime are small and that organised outdoor activities are a better way of giving students exercise and a rest from lessons.

Surely disorganised and unruly playground behaviour such as the shouting, racing about and fighting that goes on at break time would be much better for both staff and pupils if it had some purpose? Children have plenty of opportunity to play (or do nothing) outside school hours. During the school day it is vital they are educated for the maximum amount of time they are at school.

Think about the amount of time spent in school. You may need a calculator. Each pupil spends 6.5 hours a day for five days. This makes a total of 32.5 hours per week at school. Of those hours, at least seven are before-school time, recess and lunchtime. Many schools have a 10-minute assembly once a week. This gives children less than 25 hours of education per week of school. Take out at least an hour for organised sport, which is also an out-of-school hour activity for many families. There are 40 weeks in a school year. If we use 23 hours per week as the average, for 40 weeks, pupils are only getting lessons for around 920 hours per year! This does not include school trips, pupil-free days, sports carnivals, getting ready for fetes and time spent settling down in class. There are 8760 hours in a year. About one-eighth of each child's year is spent on real education. Pupils spend a small proportion of their time learning!

School breaks are wasted time, and they should be restricted to necessary activities. Limited drink and lunch breaks, with organised exercise activities, along with longer lessons, are the only ways to stop students wasting time. Their energies need to be on their education.

Lisa Tsang

30 Lisa's essay

A is not to be taken seriously.
B highlights bad school behaviour.
C is well thought out.
D pokes fun at school teachers.

31 What is Lisa proposing instead of long breaks between lessons?

A more time at home
B more physical activity at school
C more weeks of school each year
D longer school lessons

32 Why are the words *or do nothing* in brackets (line 10)?

A to give her meaning of play
B to add an additional example
C to shock the reader
D to suggest that Lisa is an expert

33 What could be the main reason for Lisa suggesting *You may need a calculator* (line 12)?

A to show she has confidence in her logic
B she is not sure her calculations are accurate
C she suspects her readers are poor at calculations
D most readers would doubt her numbers

34 How does Lisa feel about organised school sport? What would be the reason for this opinion? Write your answer on the lines.

____

____

35 What reason does Lisa give to show that breaks at school are not good for class work?

A There is too much anti-social behaviour in the schoolyard.
B Teachers are not interested in organising outdoor activities.
C Only one-eighth of the student's year is spent on school work.
D There is no time for relaxing activities.

Answers and explanations on pages 117–120

Year 5 Reading Sample Online-style Test 2

Read *Council Clean-up Dates 2011* and answer questions 36 to 39.

Council Clean-up Dates 2011

Bagaroo Shire Council has several major Special Clean-Up days each year. These are in addition to the regular, bi-weekly garbage household services offered to residents.

To dispose of unwanted household pesticides, unknown chemicals or unwanted farm chemicals simply bring them to the following collection points:

Bagaroo Landfill	Tuesday, 1 February	9 am–12 noon
Sandy Plains Landfill	Tuesday, 1 February	1 pm–4 pm
Mayville Landfill	Thursday, 3 February	9 am–12 noon
Longton Landfill	Thursday, 3 February	1 pm–4 pm

Not acceptable: medicines (return to your chemist), waste oils, paint, car batteries

Council Zone 1 **Bagaroo township, Sandy Plains, Rowlands Creek, Ibis Lagoon, Mudhurst Road**

Residual and general waste collection —First week in February
Green waste collection —First week in June
Scrap metal and whitegoods collection —First week in October

Council Zone 2 **Mayville township, Longton, Rubys Crossing, First Ridge Roadhouse, West Rocks**

Residual and general waste collection —Third week in February
Green waste collection —Third week in June
Scrap metal and whitegoods collection —Third week in October

Please Note Special Conditions for Residual and General Waste

- Not acceptable: mattresses, floor coverings, furniture, small appliances, engine/car parts, builders' waste, gas bottles, spray cans

Please Note Special Conditions for Green Waste

- Not acceptable: treated timber, grass clippings in plastic bags (use cardboard boxes), branches longer than 1.5 m

Please Note Special Conditions for Scrap Metal and Whitegoods

- Household limits: 2 cubic metres (standard trailer size)
- Scrap metal and whitegoods include lawnmowers, bicycles, small hot water systems, washing machines, microwaves, stoves, fridges (It is a legal requirement that the doors be removed from stoves and fridges.)
- Total weight of any single item **not** to exceed 40 kg
- Unwanted home-office electronic equipment will **not** be collected with whitegoods.

All items must be secured (small loose items will not be collected).
Uncollected items must be removed within two days after collection has been completed.

36 Complete this sentence. Write your answer on the line.

Before a fridge can be collected ______________________________.

37 If the council failed to collect some items for pick-up what must the resident do?

A Advise the council.
B Leave it out for the next bi-weekly service.
C Remove it from the footpath within two days.
D Take it immediately to the closest landfill tip.

38 How many Special Clean-up days did Rowlands Creek have in 2011?
Write a number in the box.

39 What must a resident do with unwanted medicines?

A Return them to a chemist.
B Leave them out for the bi-weekly service.
C Wait for council advice.
D Take them to the nearest landfill site.

Year 5 Reading

Sample Online-style Test 3

Advanced level

Read *The Brazilian cat* and answer questions 1 to 6.

The Brazilian cat

Arthur Conan Doyle (1859–1930) was famous for his Sherlock Holmes stories. This extract comes from one of his *Tales of Terror* (1923), 'The Brazilian Cat'. *Marshall King is visiting Everard King, in rural England. Everard is showing off his menagerie (collection of wild animals) to Marshall. Such collections were popular in the late 1800s.*

The whole afternoon was occupied by an inspection of Everard's menagerie.

Finally, he led me down a corridor, which extended from one wing of the house. We came to a heavy door with a sliding shutter, and beside it there projected from the wall an iron handle attached to a wheel and a drum. A line of stout bars extended across the passage.

'I am about to show you the jewel of my collection,' said Everard. 'There is only one other specimen in Europe, now that the Rotterdam cub is dead. It is a Brazilian cat.'

'But how does that differ from any other cat?'

'You will soon see that,' said he, laughing. 'Kindly draw that shutter and look through.'

I did so, and found that I was gazing into a large, empty room, with stone floor, and small, barred windows on the farther wall. In the centre of the room, lying in the middle of a golden patch of sunlight, there was stretched a huge creature, as large as a tiger, but as black and sleek as ebony. It was an enormous and very well-kept black cat, and it cuddled up and basked in that yellow pool of light exactly as a cat would do. It was so graceful, so sinewy, and so powerful I could not take my eyes off it.

'Isn't he splendid?' said my host, enthusiastically.

'Glorious! I never saw such a noble creature.'

'Some people call it a black puma, but really it is not a puma at all. Four years ago he was a little ball of black fluff, with two yellow eyes staring out of it. He was sold to me as a newborn cub, up in the wild country at the head-waters of the river Rio Negro.'

'They are ferocious, then?'

'The most absolutely treacherous and bloodthirsty creatures upon earth. They prefer humans to game. This fellow has never tasted living blood yet, but when he does he will be a terror. At present he won't stand anyone but me in his den. As to me, I am his mother and father in one.'

As he spoke he suddenly, to my astonishment, opened the door and slipped in, closing it instantly behind him. At the sound of his voice the huge, lithe creature rose, yawned and rubbed its round, black head affectionately against his side, while he patted and fondled it.

1 Everard King's attitude to his animal collection was one of

A pride. **B** indifference. **C** cruelty. **D** fearfulness. **E** contempt.

2 Why was the Brazilian cat particularly special for Everard? Write two reasons on the lines.

1 ______________________________

2 ______________________________

3 To Marshall King (narrator), the black animal in the room was behaving like a

A trapped, caged creature.
B tame, domestic cat.
C starved, wild captive.
D bloodthirsty man-killer.

4 Which term suggests that the Brazilian cat could be dangerous?

A *the Rotterdam cub is dead*
B *lying in the middle of a golden patch of sunlight*
C *stout bars extended across the passage*
D *such a noble creature*

5 Marshall is astonished when Everard enters the room with the Brazilian cat because

A the cat could be thirsty for human blood.
B of the size of the cat compared to Everard.
C the cat's behaviour was not predictable.
D of the speed at which Everard opened the door.

6 What does Everard mean when he says that the Brazilian cat is the *jewel of my collection*?

A It is a sparkling example.
B It is his most precious specimen.
C It is small but valuable.
D It is rare and difficult to replace.

Answers and explanations on pages 120–123

Year 5 Reading Sample Online-style Test 3

Read *Hibiscus facts* and answer questions 7 to 12.

Hibiscus facts

Hibiscuses are garden plants from the tropics, grown in gardens for their large colourful flowers. They are famous throughout the Pacific islands where it is common to see young people wearing a flower behind an ear or in their hair.

Hibiscus facts

1. The largest hibiscus flower measured was 30 centimetres in diameter (across the centre).
2. The oldest hibiscus growing in Australia is known to have been planted in Camden Gardens in 1880.
3. The hibiscus is the fifth most popular garden plant in the world today. It comes after roses, azaleas, carnations and orchids, in that order.
4. In Asia the hibiscus is called the 'shoeshine' plant because the flower can be rubbed over leather to shine or blacken it.
5. The purplish-black juice from crushed red flowers has been used as a dye, as an ink, and as colouring for alcoholic drinks. It has been used by women for tinting hair and eyebrows.
6. Recently, the flower has become more important in Asia as an ingredient in herbal medicine. Australia recently exported 25 tonnes to China.
7. The fruit of one hibiscus is often eaten as a 'vegetable'—okra.
8. The Chinese pickle flowers for eating and sometimes use them as a tea. Hawaiians eat them raw to control digestion.
9. In the Pacific wearing a hibiscus behind the right or left ear indicates if the wearer is married or not.
10. Flowers picked from a bush last the same length of time whether in or out of water.
11. Hibiscus bark has been used to make fibre for weaving and for making cords and ropes.
12. One of the most important pollinators of the hibiscus is the hummingbird.
13. Hibiscus fruit can be used to make jam.

Source: *Hibiscus* by J Walker, Firefly Books, 2001

7 Which statement is correct?

A Hibiscus plants have no food value for humans.
B Red is the only colour for hibiscus flowers.
C The hibiscus plant can be pollinated by birds.
D Picked hibiscus flowers last longer in water than out of water.

8 Write the numbers 1 to 4 in the boxes to show the popularity of these garden flowers. Use 1 for most popular and 4 for least popular.

☐ azalea ☐ hibiscus ☐ orchid ☐ carnation

9 Which part of the hibiscus plant is used to make rope? Write your answer on the line.

____

10 Australia exported 25 tonnes of hibiscus flowers to China. What were they used for? Write your answer on the line. ______________________________

11 Which part of the plant is used as a shoe polish? Write your answer on the line.

____

12 According to the text, the hibiscus plant

A has no commercial value.
B has many functional applications.
C has not been cultivated in Australia.
D does not grow well outside Asia.

It would be a good idea to check your answers to questions 1 to 12 before moving on to the other questions.

Answers and explanations on pages 120–123

Year 5 Reading Sample Online-style Test 3

Read *The dust elf* and answer questions 13 to 17.

The dust elf

There's a dust elf lives at our house,
And you know just where he's been,
For he leaves a trail of dust around the place.
He runs across the furniture,
And on the polished floor.
His behaviour is an absolute disgrace!

He likes to climb on bookshelves,
And he loves the picture frames,
And the way he treats our TV is a crime!
But I think the thing he likes best
Is to come into my room
And sprinkle my belongings with his grime.

He curls up in the corner,
Right underneath my bed,
And lays in wait until I've lost a shoe.
Then when I crawl beneath the bed
The dust gets up my nose,
And I have to scramble out with a 'Kerchoo!'

There's a dust elf lives at our house
As an uninvited guest,
And I wish that he would leave and go away,
For he really isn't welcome here—
We'd much prefer he left.
But I fear that this dust elf is here to stay!

Elaine Horsfield

13 The poet regards the dust elf as mischievous. Using information in the poem, give a reason for this opinion. Write your answer on the lines.

____

____

14 There is dust in the poet's home. She believes it is carried in

A on her clothes.
B on her shoes.
C by an imaginary creature.
D by an uninvited visitor.

15 What is the poet doing that makes her sneeze?

A She is cleaning the house of dust.
B She is watching a dusty TV.
C She is shaking dust from her clothes.
D She is getting shoes from under her bed.

16 Choose **two** options. For the poet, the dust throughout the house could best be described as part of a

A small mishap.
B spiteful scheme.
C deliberate act.
D cheeky prank.
E sudden occurrence.
F frivolous ploy.

17 The poet

A reluctantly accepts the dust elf's presence.
B has plans to rid her house of the dust elf.
C intends to trap the dust elf under her bed.
D believes that the dust elf will get tired of spreading dust.

Answers and explanations on pages 120–123

Year 5 Reading Sample Online-style Test 3

Read Raymond's speech and answer questions 18 to 23.

Raymond gave a class talk on the value of having school on Saturday. This is his speech.

Good morning students.

Many people think students should go to school on Saturday. These people believe that the extra day would raise the standard of education in Australia closer to those of other advanced nations.

Many private schools have Saturday activities for students, but these are mostly sporting, and sometimes cultural. However, as a student, I disagree with any form of Saturday school.

What are the benefits for a family? Saturday classes would definitely reduce family time to do things together. This is sometimes called quality time, but there is no quality time if family members are at different places! For others, Saturday is the one time they can see family for more than just a few minutes at night. This would be true for students whose parents are separated or who both work unusual hours. School years run on four ten-week terms.

The extra day of classes would cut down on competitive sports days for students. I don't mean interschool sport but local community sport.

Some students enjoy paid work on Saturday. This may be their only source of pocket money. These students are learning to be independent.

Saturday classes would also mean one less day of rest when students can complete assignments or be involved in their own special interests. It would be one less day for teachers who often use weekends for lesson preparation and book marking. The extra day of work will create less efficient and less prepared teachers—and disgruntled students. Then Sunday would not be a day of rest and a time to recharge batteries. A recharged student will learn better than a tired, stressed-out student. The same goes for teachers. A rested, relaxed teacher can prepare better and teach more confidently than a stressed-out teacher. Classes will be calmer and more organised.

Just one day may not sound like a lot; but it adds up to forty days each year. A lot can be done—and earned—in forty days. Who are these people that want Saturday school? They are not parents and certainly not students. And certainly not me!

Thank you for listening.

Raymond Wolloch (Year 6)

18 How does Raymond feel about the idea of school on Saturday?

A He is entranced by the concept.
B He believes it's best for private schools.
C He considers the idea may have merit.
D He is hostile to the innovation.

19 Why does Raymond comment on a period of *forty days*? (line 42)

A It is a long time for students to have to work.
B A lot of pocket money can be earned in that time.
C It is unfair to expect students to work that long.
D It is the amount of sport provided by private schools.

20 *For others, Saturday is the one time they can see family* (lines 14–15). The word *others* refers to

A parents.
B teachers.
C students.
D families.
E relatives.

21 The term *recharge batteries* (line 34) is used to imply

A feeling refreshed after a demanding work period.
B regaining control over a stressful situation.
C waking up and feeling less tired.
D becoming more aggressive.

22 Raymond's speech is intended to

A entertain.
B persuade.
C ridicule.
D educate.

23 The term *and earned* in the last paragraph, is a reference to

A students working part-time.
B parents who work unusual hours.
C school teachers.
D parents who are separated.

It would be a good idea to check your answers to questions 13 to 23 before moving on to the other questions.

Answers and explanations on pages 120–123

Year 5 Reading Sample Online-style Test 3

Read *Black Mountain* and answer questions 24 to 29.

Black Mountain

Known as 'Kalkajaka' (place of spear or place of death), Black Mountain was an important meeting place for clans of the Kuku Yalanji Aboriginal people and is the source of many Dreaming stories.

Black Mountain is in North Queensland and is an imposing short range of massive, black granite boulders. The boulders look as if they have been roughly stacked on one another. Some are the size of houses, and many appear to be dangerously balanced as if defying gravity. This range of jumbled rocks is the home of frogs, wallabies, gigantic pythons and a strange beast some call the Queensland Tiger. There have been many reported sightings of the 'Tiger' which, it is said, has mauled and killed cattle in the Cooktown area. The Tiger is described as a large striped cat somewhat like the marsupial lion, which lived in Queensland until 20 000 years ago, when it became extinct.

The granite rock is actually a drab pinkish colour. Black Mountain's dramatic, sinister black appearance is due to a film of microscopic blue-green algae growing on the surface. Grey patches on the mountain indicate a continuing break-up of the rocks. The blistering, hot rocks will often crack and split with explosive results when hit by the cold rain of a summer storm.

Huge holes are abundant over the surface of the mountain, representing space between groups of boulders leaning against each other. The outstanding feature of the area, which is made up of a number of peaks, is the entire absence of soil on the surface. A number of hikers into the area have had accidents, died or simply disappeared.

Black Mountain's structure resulted from slow geological processes. Some 260 million years ago, a mass of molten rock (magma) from volcanic action slowly solidified deep below the Earth's surface, forming a layer of hard granite rock. As softer land surfaces above eroded away, the cracked top of granite layer was slowly exposed. Softer granite readily cracked while the harder rock remained as large rectangular blocks. Over the centuries wind, rain and heat rounded off the corners, turning them into boulders. The surrounding countryside eroded faster than granite, thereby creating Black Mountain as a small range. The solid core of the ancient volcanic site now lies beneath the jumbled cover of boulders.

Sources: http://www.derm.qld.gov.au/parks/black-mountain/culture.html, http://www.cook.qld.gov.au/visitors/BlackMtn.shtml, http://www.derm.qld.gov.au/parks/black-mountain/about.html

24 Black Mountain's reputation and history could best be described as

- **A** mysterious.
- **B** unbelievable.
- **C** solemn.
- **D** magical.

25 *[M]any reported sightings of the 'Tiger' which, it is said, has mauled and killed cattle.* (lines 9–10)
This sentence suggests that the writer

- **A** believes the information is reliable.
- **B** cannot make up his mind about the truth of the matter.
- **C** is not really interested in the stories of the Tiger.
- **D** is not convinced of the existence of the Tiger.

26 Which feature of Black Mountain does the writer find impressive? Write your answer on the line.

____

27 The original volcanic core

- **A** was crushed by the weight of the rocks.
- **B** was cracked by heat and rain.
- **C** lies under the black rocks.
- **D** has been eroded away.

28 What is the real colour of the rock on Black Mountain?
Write your answer in the box.

[ ]

29 Why are there very few green plants on Black Mountain?

- **A** There is an evil presence in the area.
- **B** There is an absence of surface organic material.
- **C** The heat generated by the rocks prevents germination.
- **D** Most plants cannot co-exist with algae.

Answers and explanations on pages 120–123

Read the cartoon and answer questions 30 to 34.

30 What is most likely shocking the lady with the cup?

A The rats have read the paper.
B Rats are taking over the house.
C The drink in her cup tasted awful.
D the FOR SALE sign on the rat hole

31 The cartoon is amusing because

A the rats have very human qualities.
B the cartoonist has made the characters' expressions funny.
C the articles in the paper are true in an unexpected way.
D the older couple are not sure how to cope with the situation.

32 The look on the real estate agent rat's face suggests he is

A trying to please the two smaller rats.
B involved in something not quite honest.
C about to evict the two smaller rats from their home.
D worried that the older couple will hear him.

33 If one of the characters said 'We can soon get rid of the present residents' who would it most likely be?

A either of the pair of rats near the hole
B the old man sitting down
C the old woman with the cup of tea
D the fat real estate agent rat

34 A good caption for the cartoon would be

A Unexpected residents.
B The rat plague.
C Look at that!
D Rats can talk.

 Answers and explanations on pages 120–123

Read *How to change a light bulb* and answer questions 35 to 39.

How to change a light bulb

There is an ever-circulating light bulb joke.

The joke asks how many people of a certain group are needed to change a light bulb. The punchline answer usually pokes fun at, or insults, a particular group of people.

Q. *How many students (or any other group) does it take to change a light bulb?*

A. *Three—one to hold the light bulb and two to turn the ladder!*

Changing a light bulb can be dangerous. With some lights you cannot be sure whether the power is on or off. Before changing a light bulb, follow these tips.

You will need: • A replacement light bulb. Know beforehand if the fitting needs a screw-mount or a bayonet-mount bulb. • A ladder or stable object to stand on, such as a milk crate, if the bulb is in a high ceiling. • An assistant, if the light bulb has to be removed from a high-ceiling fitting.

Note: Change the bulb during daylight so that you can clearly see what you are doing.

Step 1 Make sure to turn off the light or lamp at the wall. You then know that the light will not be switched on—it can be surprising and dangerous if the light comes on in your hands as you plug the new bulb in!

Step 2 If you are replacing a working bulb with another type of bulb, allow a hot bulb to cool before touching it.

Step 3 If you have to use a ladder for an overhead light, have an assistant hold the ladder steady. The assistant can take the removed bulb and pass up the replacement bulb, which saves unnecessary fiddling while on the ladder.

Step 4 *For bayonet-fitting bulbs*: using your hand, put a little upward pressure on the glass bulb, and rotate it anticlockwise (as you look up at it). It will unlock the bulb shank from the metal frame. The bulb will come out downwards.

For screw-fitting bulbs: grasp the bulb firmly and turn anticlockwise until it is freed from the socket.

Step 5 Insert a replacement bulb lightly and firmly into the socket, and turn it clockwise until it's snug. It is the reverse process to removing a bulb.

Step 6 Turn the light on to check that the bulb works and it has been correctly installed.

Step 7 Dispose of the used bulb properly. Old bulbs are not recycled with other glass.

35 What is the main reason for following these instructions?

A safety **B** convenience **C** speed **D** to save money

36 The writing in these instructions is

A obvious and unnecessary. **B** complicated and serious.
C daunting but important. **D** light but practical.

37 To change a light bulb in a high ceiling, a second person is required to

A ensure the power is switched off before starting.
B test the new bulb after the old bulb has been replaced.
C make the task safer and more efficient for the person up the ladder.
D get medical help in case of an accident or emergency.

38 To remove a bayonet-type light bulb you first have to

A unlock the bulb shank from the metal frame. **B** apply upward pressure on the bulb.
C rotate the bulb in an anticlockwise direction. **D** twist the bulb firmly in a clockwise direction.

39 You are going to compare the texts on pages 78 and 79. For what purposes were the texts written? Tick **two** boxes for each text.

	Raymond's speech	Black Mountain
to inform	A ☐	A ☐
to describe	B ☐	B ☐
to persuade	C ☐	C ☐
to explain	D ☐	D ☐

Answers and explanations on pages 120–123

Year 5 **Writing**

Sample Online-style Test 1

Before you start, make sure you read the Tips for Writing on page 43.

Today you are going to write a persuasive text, often called an exposition.

Testing in schools

Schools have many types of tests. Are there too many tests? Do test results really matter?

What do you think about tests at school?

Write to convince a reader of your opinion.

Before you start writing, give some thought to:
- whether you strongly agree or disagree with testing in schools
- the way you will present your ideas—clearly list or order your points
- the reasons or evidence for your arguments
- your brief but definite conclusion. In your conclusion list some of your main points. You may add a personal opinion.

Don't forget to:
- plan your story before you begin writing
- write in correctly formed sentences and take particular care with paragraphing
- choose your words carefully and pay attention to your spelling and punctuation
- write neatly but don't waste time
- quickly check your writing once you have finished. Your position must be clear to your reader.

Remember: The stance taken in a persuasive text is not wrong, as long as the writer has evidence to support his or her opinion. How the opinion is supported is as important as the opinion itself.

Start writing here or type your answer on a computer or tablet.

☞Turn to pages 105–106 and use the Marking checklist to check the student's writing. Also go to pages 133–135 where the sample pieces of writing (Standard, Intermediate and Advanced levels) can be used to check at what level the student is writing.

Year 5 Writing

Sample Online-style Test 2

Before you start, make sure you read the Tips for Writing on page 45.

Today you are going to write a narrative or story.

Your story will be about a **Night camp-out**.

The picture on the right may give you some ideas.

You might want to describe the campsite. Were you alone, with other campers or with your family? How did you set up the camp? What events took place to make your night camping interesting? Was there anything special about the morning after? You could include some information about other sensory experiences, such as smells, sounds and any physical feelings.

Your story may be serious or humorous but keep it realistic.

Your writing will be judged on expression and the structure of your story.

Before you start writing, give some thought to:

- where your story takes place (the setting)
- the characters and what they do in the story
- the events that take place in the story and the problems that have to be resolved
- how your story begins, what happens in your story, and how your story ends.

Don't forget to:

- plan your story before you start
- write in correctly formed sentences and take care with paragraphing
- choose your words carefully and pay attention to your spelling and punctuation
- write neatly but don't waste time
- quickly check your story once you have finished.

Start writing here or type your answer on a computer or tablet.

☞Turn to page 106 and use the Marking checklist to check the student's writing. Also go to pages 136–138 where the sample pieces of writing (Standard, Intermediate and Advanced levels) can be used to check at what level the student is writing.

Year 5 **Writing**

Sample Online-style Test 3

Before you start, make sure you read the Tips for Writing on page 47.

A recount (which is a type of informative text) tells about events that have happened to you or other people. It is usually a record of events in the order they happened. If it is a personal recount, you will use the word *I*.
A recount can conclude with a personal opinion of the event.
Paragraphs are usually organised by time periods. Sometimes subheadings are used.
Jot down events in the order they happened before you start.

Today you are going to write a personal recount called **My holiday**.

Think about the holidays you have experienced. They can be school holidays at home. The holiday might be short or long. It might be nearby, say, to a relative's place or somewhere a long way from home. How did you get there? Who did you go with? Were there any interesting events during your holiday? Was there a special reason for the holiday? How did you feel at the end of the holiday?

Before you start writing, give some thought to:

- where your recount takes place
- the characters and what they do in your recount
- the events that take place in your recount and the problems that have to be resolved
- how you and others reacted to your holiday. You may make brief personal comments on events as you write about them.

Don't forget to:

- plan your story before you start writing
- write in correctly formed sentences and take care with paragraphing
- choose your words carefully and pay attention to your spelling and punctuation
- write neatly but don't waste time
- quickly check your story once you have finished.

Start writing here or type your answer on a computer or tablet.

☞ **Turn to page 107 and use the Marking checklist to check the student's writing. Also go to pages 139–141 where the sample pieces of writing (Standard, Intermediate and Advanced levels) can be used to check at what level the student is writing.**

Standard level questions

SPELLING Mini Test 1

Page 1

1 hungry **2** city **3** forget **4** answer **5** cruise **6** flashes **7** diaries **8** tadpoles **9** envelope **10** address **11** postcode **12** truly **13** through **14** solar **15** volcanoes **16** breathe **17** Luckily **18** happens

1 Make sure you pronounce the word correctly: 'hun + gry', not 'hun + ery'. If you are *hun**gry***, you might get *an**gry***.

2 *City* is a very common word. *City* only has one ***t***. The ***y*** is not a suffix. There are only a few short words with a similar spelling pattern (e.g. *pity*, *duty*). *City* is a word you must learn and remember how to spell.

3 *Forget* is a compound word: *for* + *get*. *Four* (4), *fore* (in front of) and *for* are homonyms—words that sound the same but which are spelt differently.

4 *Answer* is a very common word. Watch for the silent ***w*** in *answer*. A silent ***w*** also follows an *s* in the word *sword*.

5 *Cruise* and *crews* are homonyms—words that sound the same but which are spelt differently. A *cruise* is a voyage on a ship. *Crews* are the people who work on ships.

6 *Flash* can be either a noun or a verb. The plural noun or the singular verb is made by adding ***s***. If a word, such as *flash*, ends in ***sh*** then the correct change is to add ***es*** to make the new form. Other examples include *crashes*, *pushes* and *dashes*.

7 To make plurals from words that end with a consonant then ***y***, it is common practice to change the ***y*** to ***i*** before adding ***es*** (e.g. *pony—ponies*).

8 *Tadpoles* is a double-syllable word. Both ***oal*** and ***ole*** can represent the same sound as in *sole* and *coal*. You should recognise and remember when to use the different spellings. Get to know groups of words with ***ole*** spellings (e.g. *role*, *dole*).

9 *Envelope* is a tricky word. Different people may have different pronunciations. *Envelope* is a word you must learn and remember how to spell.

10 Double letters can cause a few spelling problems. There is a double ***d*** (***dd***) and a double ***s*** (***ss***) in *address*.

11 Both ***ode*** and ***oad*** can represent the same sound as in *rode* and *road*. You should recognise and remember when to use the different spellings. Get to know groups of words with the ***oad*** spelling (e.g. *toad*, *load*) and ***ode*** spelling (e.g. *rode*, *bode*, *mode*).

12 *Truly* is a tricky word. It is *true* + ***ly***. Before adding the suffix ***ly*** you must drop the ***e***. *Truly* is a word you must learn and remember how to spell.

13 *Through* and *threw* are homonyms—words that sound the same but which are spelt differently. *Through* refers to a movement from one position to another. *Threw* is the past tense of *throw*. Learn to spell and use each word correctly.

14 *Solar* is an adjective describing objects that relate to the sun. It comes from the word *sol*, a word from Roman mythology describing the god of the sun, with the ***ar*** suffix.

15 Remember: *one volcano*, *many volcanoes*. To make plurals from many common words that end with ***o***, you add ***es***. Examples are *potatoes*, *heroes*. There are many words ending in ***o*** where you simply add an ***s*** (e.g. *kangaroo*). You need to learn the difference.

16 *Breathe* (verb) comes from the word *breath* (noun). Both words are tricky to spell. They are words you must learn and remember how to spell. *Clothe* and *cloth* follow a similar pattern.

17 *Luckily* is *lucky* + ***ly***. When a word ends with a consonant then ***y*** it is common practice to change the ***y*** to ***i*** before adding the suffix ***ly***. Examples are *happy* + ***ly***—*happily*, *merry* + ***ly***—*merrily*.

18 Double letters can cause a few spelling problems. *Happens* is a common word. It has a double ***p*** (***pp***). It is a word you must learn and remember how to spell.

Standard level questions

SPELLING Mini Test 2

Page 2

1 trail **2** different **3** dreadful **4** birthday **5** animals **6** string **7** cheese **8** happiness **9** flooring **10** worst **11** sorry **12** groom **13** witches **14** riches **15** source **16** everything **17** types **18** temperatures

1 Both ***ale*** and ***ail*** can represent the same sound as in *male* and *mail*. There are quite a few ***ail/ale*** words that are homonyms. You should recognise

Year 5 Literacy Mini Test Answers

and remember when to use the different spellings. Get to know groups of words with ***ail*** spellings (e.g. *frail*, *tail*).

2 Make sure you pronounce *different* correctly. It has three syllables: ***diff*** + ***er*** + ***ent***.

3 When adding the suffix ***ful*** to a word it is spelt with a single ***l***. Examples are *useful*, *wasteful* and *hopeful*.

4 The letters ***er***, ***or***, ***ur*** and ***ir*** can sound the same. You should recognise and remember when to use the different spellings (e.g. *were*, *work*, *fur*). It is easy to confuse ***er*** and ***ir*** in words. *Birthday* is a compound word: *birth* + *day*.

5 Look at the word closely when you write it, as ***m*** and ***n*** have a similar appearance.

6 Get to know groups of words with similar spellings (e.g. *ring*, *thing*). Remember: *Bri**ng** the stri**ng***.

7 Both ***ea*** and ***ee*** can represent the same sound. You should recognise and remember when to use the different spellings (e.g. *reach*, *screech*).The ***eese*** ending is uncommon.

8 *Happiness* is *happy* with the suffix ***ness***: *happy* + ***ness***. When a word ends with a consonant then ***y*** it is common practice to change the ***y*** to ***i*** before adding a suffix.

9 *Floor* has two vowels before the final consonant. You do not double the final consonant when adding the suffix ***ing***.

10 In words beginning with ***w*** a silent ***h*** often follows the ***w***, however *worst* is not one of these words.

11 *Sorry* is a common word. It has a double ***r*** (***rr***). There are only a few words with a similar spelling (e.g. *lorry*). *Sorry* is a word you must learn and remember how to spell.

12 Both ***oom*** and ***ume*** can represent the same sound. You should recognise and remember when to use the different spellings (e.g. *fume*, *room*).The ***ume*** word ending is uncommon.

13 When making a plural of words ending with ***tch*** add ***es*** (not just an ***s***). Examples are *matches*, *batches* and *pitches*. If you say *witches* you will hear a definite ***es*** sound at the end of the word.

14 When making a plural of words ending with ***ch*** and ***sh*** add ***es*** (not just an ***s***). Examples are *latches*, *inches* and *pushes*. If you say *riches* you will hear a definite ***es*** sound at the end of the word.

15 *Source* and *sauce* are homonyms—words that sound the same but which are spelt differently. *Source* refers to the place where something starts. *Sauce* is a liquid added to food to change its flavour. Learn to spell and use each word correctly.

16 Make sure you pronounce the word correctly. *Everything* is a compound word: *every* + *thing*.

17 Both the ***y*** and ***i*** following the letter ***t*** can make the same sound (e.g. *tyre* and *tire*). You should recognise and remember when to use the different spellings.

18 Make sure you pronounce the word correctly. *Temperatures* has four syllables: ***tem*** + ***per*** + ***a*** + ***tures***.

Intermediate level questions

SPELLING Mini Test 3

Page 3

1 health **2** reach **3** canary **4** decide **5** evening **6** hollow **7** knives **8** learning **9** mean **10** piece **11** figure **12** smiling **13** skinny **14** vacant **15** deserted **16** other **17** person **18** private

1 The ***eal*** in *health* has a similar sound to ***ell*** in *well*. *Health* also rhymes with *wealth*. *Health* and *wealth* are something everyone would like!

2 Both ***ea*** and ***ee*** can represent the same sound. You should recognise and remember when to use the different spellings (e.g. *teach*, *screech*). Get to know the group of words with the ***each*** spelling (e.g. *beach*, *peach*).

3 It's easy to confuse *cannery* (a factory for filling food cans) and *canary* (a yellow whistling bird). Make sure you pronounce each word correctly. *Cannery* is a word built on *can* and has a double ***n*** (***nn***).

4 Make sure you pronounce *decide* correctly. It has two syllables: ***de*** + ***cide***.

5 *Evening* is a common word you must learn and remember how to spell. Do not confuse it with *beginning*, a common word of three syllables with a double ***n***.

6 Make sure you pronounce *hollow* correctly. It has both the short and long 'o' sounds. *Hallow* refers to things that are holy.

7 Learn to recognise words with a silent ***k*** (e.g. *knot*, *knew*, *knight*). The ***k*** is not pronounced before an ***n*** at the beginning of a word. Remember: *one knife* but *many knives*. Make sure you pronounce *knives* correctly.

8 *Learning* is *learn* + ***ing***. Get to know groups of words with each spelling (e.g. *burn*, *churn* and *learn*, *yearn*).

9 Both ***ene*** and ***ean*** can represent the same sound. Compare *scene* and *bean*. You should recognise and remember when to use the different spellings. The ***ene*** ending is less common.

Year 5 Literacy Mini Test Answers

10 *Piece* and *peace* are homonyms—words that sound the same but which are spelt differently. *Peace* is that time between wars. Remember: You can have a ***pie****ce* of ***pie***.

11 The ***ure*** and ***uer*** endings can sound much the same. The ***uer*** ending is much less common.

12 *Smiling* is *smile* + ***ing***. To add ***ing*** to words ending with a consonant and ***e***, simply drop the ***e*** and add ***ing***. Examples are *race—racing*, *hope—hoping*.

13 For short words that end with a single vowel followed by a single consonant, in most cases you have to double the final letter when you add a suffix. Examples are *run—running*, *skip—skipping*.

14 Make sure you pronounce *vacant* correctly. It ends with an ***ant*** sound and not an ***ent*** sound.

15 *Desert* can be either a noun (a dry land) or a verb (leave without permission). *Dessert* is a sweet food dish. Make sure you use the words correctly.

16 Make sure you pronounce *other* correctly. Think of *other* rhyming with *mother* and *brother*.

17 The letters ***er***, ***ur*** and ***ir*** can sound the same. You should recognise and remember when to use the different spellings (e.g. *sir*, *serve*, *fur*). Get to know the group of words with the ***er*** spelling (e.g. *perhaps*, *permit*).

18 Make sure you pronounce *private* correctly: ***pri*** + ***vate***. *Private* is an important word that you should learn and remember how to spell.

Intermediate level questions

SPELLING Mini Test 4

Page 4

1 flavour **2** agents **3** amateur **4** flooded **5** kangaroo **6** reindeer **7** varnish **8** volume **9** weather **10** wallaby **11** kennel **12** rainy **13** entrance **14** attract **15** holds **16** invisible **17** towards **18** metals

1 The US spelling is *flavor*. The Australian spelling is the traditional spelling of *flavour* using ***our***, as in *favour*, *harbour*, *humour* and many other ***our*** words.

2 There are times when ***j*** and ***g*** can make the same sound. Think of *agents* as being gentle. Take time to learn to spell *agents* correctly.

3 *Amateur* is a tricky word. It came into English from the French language. Make sure you pronounce it correctly: ***am*** + ***a*** + ***teur***. Take time to learn the correct spelling.

4 *Flood* rhymes with *blood*. As *flood* has two vowels before the final consonant (***d***) the ***d*** is not doubled.

5 Make sure you pronounce *kangaroo* correctly: ***kan*** + ***ga*** + ***roo***.

6 *Reindeer* is a two-syllable word: *rein* + *deer*. Notice the correct spelling of *rein* is as in the strap a horse rider uses to control a horse. *Deer* and *dear* are homonyms—words that sound the same but which are spelt differently. *Deer* is both singular and plural for the Arctic animal.

7 Make sure you pronounce *varnish* correctly. It is a two-syllable word: ***var*** + ***nish***. In the word *varnish*, the ***ish*** is not a suffix.

8 Take care not to add a silent ***n*** to *volume*; *volume* is not spelt like *column* and *autumn*, two common words that end with a similar sound.

9 *Weather*, *whether* and *wether* are homonyms—words that sound the same but which are spelt differently. *Weather* refers to the climate. There is no silent ***h*** in *weather*. *Whether* indicates an alternative. *Wether* refers to a particular type of male sheep.

10 The word *wallaby* is spelt with the letters ***by*** at the end of the word rhyming with *baby*.

11 *Kennel* does not end with a double ***l*** (***ll***). The double ***l*** ending in two-syllable words is uncommon. *Travel*, *cancel*, *marvel* and *petrol* all end with a single ***l***.

12 *Rain* (wet weather), *rein* (a strap used to control a horse) and *reign* (rule over) are homonyms—words sounding the same but having different meanings. *Rainy* is *rain* + ***y***. The ***y*** suffix changes the noun (*rain*) into an adjective.

13 Make sure you pronounce *entrance* correctly: 'en + trance'. It is not 'enter + ance'. *Hindrance* follows the same spelling pattern.

14 Make sure you pronounce *attract* correctly: 'a + ttract'. Words with the same ***tract*** ending include *detract*, *contract*, *extract* and *subtract*.

15 Make sure you pronounce *holds* carefully. *Holes* is a plural noun meaning 'empty spaces'. *Holds* is a singular verb meaning 'takes something firmly'.

16 Make sure you pronounce *invisible* correctly: ***in*** + ***vis*** + ***i*** + ***ble***. ***In*** is a prefix meaning 'not'. Think of *vision* and *visible* with similar beginnings.

17 *Towards* is a compound word: ***to*** + ***wards***. *To*, *too* and *two* (2) are homonyms—words that sound the same but which have different spellings. *To* refers to the direction of something. *Too* can mean 'more' or 'also'.

18 *Mettle* and *metal* sound very similar. *Mettle* refers to courage. *Metal* refers to such substances as iron, gold and copper. *Metal* does not end with a double ***l*** (***ll***). The double ***l*** ending in two-syllable words is uncommon. *Travel*, *cancel*, *marvel* and *petrol* all end with a single ***l***.

Intermediate level questions

SPELLING Mini Test 5

Page 5

1 elastic **2** handwritten **3** delayed **4** orchids **5** galah **6** janitor **7** sandals **8** cherries **9** porridge **10** potatoes **11** raised **12** presents **13** smooth **14** dangerously **15** wharf **16** repairing **17** pelican **18** morning

1 Make sure you pronounce *elastic* carefully. *Elastic* has three syllables: ***e*** + ***las*** + ***tic***. The suffix ***ic*** forms adjectives. Other examples of ***ic*** words include *periodic*, *allergic*, *aquatic* and *electric*.

2 *Handwritten* is a compound word: *hand* + *written*. *Writ* is the old-fashioned, past-tense word for *wrote* or *written*. The ***en*** suffix is still used to make the past tense in a number of words (e.g. *broken*). When a suffix such as ***en*** is added to a word that ends with a single vowel followed by a single consonant you double the last letter before adding the suffix. Examples are *bit—bitten*, *flat—flatten*.

3 To turn most verbs that end with a vowel followed by a ***y*** into the past tense you simply add the suffix ***ed***. Examples are *play—played*, *destroy—destroyed*.

4 Make sure you pronounce *orchid* correctly with the ***ch*** having a ***k*** sound. Simply add an ***s*** to make the plural.

5 The word is ***ga*** + ***lah***. It does not have a double ***l*** (***ll***) and is one of those words you simply have to remember how to spell.

6 For many descriptions of people, the ***or*** ending is common, especially following a ***t*** (e.g. *actor*, *traitor*, *visitor*).

7 Make sure you pronounce *sandals* carefully. The ***le*** and ***al*** endings can sound very similar. Simply add an ***s*** to make the plural.

8 Remember: one *cherry* and *many cherries*. To make plurals from words that end with a consonant then ***y*** it is common practice to change the ***y*** to ***i*** before adding ***es***. Examples are *pony—ponies*, *fairy—fairies*, *berry—berries*.

9 The ***d*** in *porridge* can create spelling problems. Learn to recognise word groups with ***dge*** spellings (e.g. *ridge*, *edge*, *hedge*, *fridge*).

10 Remember: *one potato* and *many potatoes*. Words that end with a single ***o*** are often made into plurals by adding ***es*** (e.g. *tomatoes*, *canoes*, *echoes*). In English spelling there are often exceptions to the rule.

11 'Raysed' is not a word. *Raised* and *razed* are homonyms—words that sound the same but which are spelt differently. *Raised* refers to lifting. *Razed* means 'burning something to ground level'.

12 *Presents* and *presence* are homonyms—words that sound the same but which are spelt differently. *Present* is a common noun referring to a gift. Simply add an ***s*** to make the plural of *present*. *Presence* is an incorrect word in this sentence. It means 'the existence of something or someone close by'.

13 'Smoove' is not a word. Make sure you pronounce *smooth* correctly.

14 Make sure you pronounce *dangerously* correctly. *Dangerously* has three parts (the noun and two suffixes): *danger* + ***ous*** + ***ly***. It has four syllables: ***dan*** + ***ger*** + ***ous*** + ***ly***.

15 *Wharf* has a silent ***h***. There are a number of common words that have a silent ***h*** after a ***w***. Learn to recognise and spell these words. Examples include *who*, *where*, *what* and *when*.

16 *Repair* is *re* + *pair*. ***Re*** is a prefix meaning 'do again'. *Pair* and *pare* are homonyms—words that sound the same but which are spelt differently. *Pare* is a verb meaning 'remove the skin from something, such as a piece of fruit'. *Pairing* indicates the bringing together of two parts, such as forming pairs.

17 *Pelican* does not have a double ***l*** (***ll***). It is one of those words you have to remember how to spell.

18 *Morning* is *morn* + ***ing***. *Morning* and *mourning* are homonyms—words that sound the same but which are spelt differently. *Mourning* means 'showing sadness for someone who has died'. *Morning* is a noun for the name of the start of the day.

Year 5 Literacy Mini Test Answers

Intermediate level questions

SPELLING Mini Test 6

Page 6

1 driveway **2** orbits **3** graphs **4** parcels **5** innocent **6** attic **7** necessary **8** eventually **9** weary **10** truth **11** knuckle **12** blanket **13** plentiful **14** assignments **15** forgotten **16** seen **17** huge **18** kindergarten

1 *Driveway* is a compound word: *drive* + *way*. 'Driveaway' is not a word. Make sure you pronounce *driveway* correctly.

2 Make sure you pronounce *orbits* correctly. *Orbit* ends with ***it*** and not ***et***. To make the singular verb simply add ***s***. *Orbits* is one of those words you have to remember how to spell.

3 In many words ***ph*** has an 'f' sound (e.g. *nymph* and *oomph*). To make the plural noun from *graph* simply add ***s***. *Graphs* is one of those words you have to remember how to spell.

4 Make sure you pronounce *parcels* correctly: ***par*** + ***cels***. Note: The last syllable is ***cels*** not ***cles***. To make the plural noun from *parcel* simply add ***s***. *Parcels* is a common word and one you need to learn and remember how to spell.

5 The last syllable (***cent***) can be tricky as *cent* can be spelt three different ways (*cent*, *sent*, *scent*). Make sure you use a double ***n*** (***nn***) when spelling *innocent*. Think of the word as *in* + *no* + *cent*.

6 Make sure you pronounce *attic* correctly: ***at*** + ***tic***. There is no ***ck*** at the end of *attic*. It is one of those nouns you have to remember how to spell.

7 You only double the ***s*** (***ss***). Think of the word as four syllables: ***nec*** + ***es*** + ***sar*** + ***y***.

8 *Eventually* is ***event*** + ***ual*** + ***ly***. The ***ly*** is an additional suffix to ***ual***. Think of the word as an adverb: *eventual* + ***ly***.

9 Take care to listen to the word carefully. It has nothing to do with *weir* or *wear*. Don't be tempted to add a silent ***h*** after the ***w***.

10 *Truth* is a tricky word. It is one of those words you have to remember how to spell.

11 *Knuckle* begins with a silent ***k***. Learn to recognise words with a silent ***k*** (e.g. *knot*, *knew*, *knight*). The ***k*** is not pronounced before an ***n*** at the beginning of a word.

12 The ***c*** is unnecessary in *blanket*. Think of similar words to *blanket* that do not have the ***c*** (e.g. *frank*, *bank*, *prank*).

13 There are two mistakes in 'plentyfull'. When adding the suffix ***ful*** to a word it is spelt with a single ***l***. If a word (e.g. *plenty*) ends with a consonant and ***y***, you must change the ***y*** to ***i*** before adding the suffix ***ful***.

14 *Assignments* has a silent ***g***. There are a few common words that have a silent ***g*** before an ***n*** (e.g. *align*, *gnome*, *reign*, *foreign*). *Sign* is part of a number of common words (e.g. *design*, *resign*).

15 *Forgotten* is a compound word: *for* + *gotten*. When a suffix, such as ***en***, is added to a word that ends with a single vowel followed by a single consonant you double the last letter before adding the suffix. Examples are *bit—bitten* and *flat—flatten*.

16 *Seen* and *scene* are homonyms—words that sound the same but which are spelt differently. *Seen* is the past tense of *see*. *Scene* refers to a view. Remember to use the words correctly.

17 There are very few short ***uge*** words. *Huge* is one of those words you have to remember how to spell.

18 Make sure you pronounce *kindergarten* correctly: ***kin*** + ***der*** + ***gar*** + ***ten***. You will notice the word ends with *garten*, not *garden*. *Kindergarten* came into the English language unchanged from the German spelling.

Advanced level questions

SPELLING Mini Test 7

Page 7

1 easily **2** performed **3** torpedoes **4** unnoticed **5** vanishes **6** eclipse **7** ascended **8** information **9** lottery **10** nocturnal **11** yacht **12** sailing **13** bow **14** cough **15** tonsils **16** magazines **17** specialist **18** operation

1 *Easily* is *easy* + ***ly***. Because *easy* ends with a consonant and ***y***, you must change the ***y*** to an ***i*** before adding the suffix ***ly***. Make sure you pronounce the word correctly: ***eas*** + ***i*** + ***ly***.

2 It is easy to confuse the prefixes ***pre*** and ***pro***. ***Pre*** generally refers to things that happened before something else. Make sure you pronounce *performed* correctly: ***per*** + ***formed***.

3 Remember: *one torpedo*, *many torpedoes*. Make plurals from many common words that end with ***o*** by adding ***es***. Examples are *potatoes*, *heroes* and *volcanoes*. There are also many words that end in ***o*** where you simply add an ***s*** (e.g. *photos*).

4 *Unnoticed* is ***un*** + *noticed*. The prefix ***un*** means 'not'.

5 If a word, such as *vanish*, ends in ***sh*** then the correct change is to add ***es*** to make the new form. Other examples include *crashes*, *pushes*

Year 5 Literacy Mini Test Answers

and *dashes*. If you say the word you will hear a definite ***es*** sound at the end of the word.

6 Make sure you pronounce *eclipse* correctly and take time to learn to spell it.

7 *Ascended* is a tricky word. Make sure you pronounce it correctly. Both the ***s*** and the ***c*** are sounded: ***as*** + ***cen*** + ***ded***.

8 It is *information*, not 'imformation'.

9 Make sure you pronounce *lottery* correctly. It has three syllables: ***lot*** + ***ter*** + ***y***.

10 There is no silent ***k*** before the ***n*** in *nocturnal*. The first syllable has nothing to do with *knock*. The second ***k*** is not necessary.

11 *Yacht* is a tricky word. Take time to learn to spell it correctly.

12 *Sale* and *sail* are homonyms—words that sound the same but which are spelt differently. *Sale* refers to selling and *sail* to boating.

13 *Bow* and *bough* are homonyms—words that sound the same but which are spelt differently. *Bow* (rhymes with *how*) refers to the front of a boat. *Bough* refers to a large tree branch. Remember when to use each word correctly.

14 *Cough* is not a regular word. The letter combination ***ough*** has the same sound as 'off'. Sometimes a word has a spelling that doesn't follow the 'sound' rules (e.g. *said*). Try to remember and recognise such words. Get to know groups of words with ***ough*** spellings (e.g. *tough*, *enough*). These words do not always rhyme with *cough*.

15 The word *tonsils* does not end with a double ***l*** (***ll***). The double ***l*** ending in two-syllable words is uncommon. *Travel*, *cancel*, *camel* and *petrol* all end with a single ***l***.

16 Make sure you pronounce *magazines* correctly: ***mag*** + ***a*** + ***zines***. Take time to learn its spelling.

17 *Specialist* is *special* + ***ist***. The ***ist*** suffix often refers to a type of person (e.g. *dentist*, *violinist*, *racist*). As a suffix, ***est*** usually creates superlative adjectives (e.g. *best*, *biggest*, *greatest*).

18 The ***tion*** ending may be pronounced as 'shun' but it is spelt ***tion*** (e.g. *nation*, *subtraction*, *invitation*).

Advanced level questions

SPELLING Mini Test 8

Page 8

1 blossom **2** shoulder **3** surfacing **4** ostrich **5** naughty **6** foul **7** odours **8** products **9** favouritism **10** astronaut **11** rectangular **12** hexagon **13** border **14** harvesters **15** produce **16** storage **17** overseas **18** manufacture

1 *Blossom* is a tricky word. Remember: A *blossom* is a *bloom*. The letter ***o*** occurs twice in each word.

2 Often two vowels together can make different sounds in different words. The ***ou*** in *shoulder* sounds like the ***oa*** in *shoal* (large group of fish). It is not like the ***ou*** in *should*. *Shoulder* is a common word that you should take time to learn to spell correctly.

3 The letters ***er***, ***or***, ***ur*** and ***ir*** can sound the same. You should recognise and remember when to use the different spellings (e.g. *were*, *work*, *fur*). Get to know groups of words with ***ur*** spellings (e.g. *surplus*, *burp*, *furnace*). Remember: To add ***ing*** to words ending with a consonant and ***e***, simply drop the ***e*** and add ***ing***. Examples are *face—facing*, *hope—hoping*.

4 Make sure you pronounce *ostrich* correctly: ***os*** + ***trich***. *Ostrich* ends with a ***h*** and not a ***t***.

5 *Naughty* is a tricky word. The number *nought* is spelt with ***ought***. Remember: If you are *naughty*, don't get *caught*.

6 *Fowl* and *foul* are homonyms—words that sound the same but which are spelt differently. *Fowl* are birds. *Foul* is an adjective often describing a disgusting smell. Remember when to use each word correctly.

7 The US spelling is *odor*. The Australian spelling is the traditional spelling of *odour* using ***our***, as in *favour*, *harbour*, *humour* and many other ***our*** words.

8 Make sure you pronounce *products* correctly: ***prod*** + ***ucts***. Notice that it ends with a ***t*** and not a ***k***. Take time to learn to spell it.

9 The US spelling is *favoritism*. The Australian spelling is the traditional spelling of *favouritism* using ***our***, as in *favour*, *harbour*, *humour* and many other ***our*** words. *Favouritism* is *favourite* + ***ism***. When adding the suffix ***ism*** to a word that ends with a consonant + ***e***, you drop the ***e*** before adding the suffix (e.g. *race—racism*, *cube—cubism*).

10 *Astronaut* is *astro* + *naut*. *Astro* refers to space. *Naut* comes from the word 'nautes' meaning 'sailor' or 'traveller'. An *astronaut* is a space traveller. The Russians use the word *cosmonaut*.

11 There are three mistakes in the spelling 'reckangeler'. Make sure you pronounce the word correctly: ***rec*** + ***tan*** + ***gu*** + ***lar***. It starts with ***rect***, not 'reck'. *Rectangular* is an adjective from *rectangle*. It is a common word. Take time to learn to spell it correctly.

12 ***Hexa*** refers to six. ***Gon*** is a common suffix in words used to refer to two-dimensional shapes (e.g. *pentagon*).

Year 5 Literacy Mini Test Answers

13 *Border* and *boarder* are homonyms—words sounding the same but having different meanings. *Border* means 'an edge or margin'. *Boarder* means 'a person who rents a room or pays board'. Remember when to use each word correctly.

14 Both ***er*** and ***or*** are used to make nouns to describe people or objects (e.g. *teacher* and *builder*, or *sponsor* and *tailor*). You should recognise and remember when to use the different suffixes.

15 Make sure you pronounce *produce* carefully: ***pro*** + ***duce***. ***Duce*** is a common suffix for a number of words (e.g. *reduce*, *induce*). It is not spelt to rhyme with *juice*.

16 *Storage* is *store* + *age*. When adding the suffix ***age*** to a word that ends with a consonant and ***e***, you drop the ***e*** (e.g. *plumage*, *dosage*).

17 *Overseas* is a compound word: *over* + *seas*.

18 Make sure you pronounce *manufacture* correctly: ***man*** + ***u*** + ***fact*** + ***ure***. It has four syllables. The ***ure*** and the ***eur*** endings can sound much the same. The ***eur*** ending is much less common.

Advanced level questions

SPELLING Mini Test 9

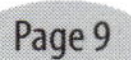
Page 9

1 burglar **2** disappear **3** delighted **4** neighbourhood **5** film **6** famous **7** midday **8** author **9** parsley **10** discussing **11** almonds **12** kiosks **13** pyjamas **14** necklace **15** thought **16** delivery **17** younger **18** check

1 Make sure you pronounce *burglar* carefully. *Burglar* has only two syllables: ***bur*** + ***glar***.

2 *Disappear* is ***dis*** + *appear*. The prefix ***dis*** in *disappear* makes the word mean 'no longer appearing'. *Disappear* has only one ***s*** (as in ***dis***), but a double ***p*** (***pp***).

3 *Delighted* is ***de*** + ***light*** + ***ed***. The letter combination ***ight*** has the same sound as ***ite***. Get to know groups of words with ***ight*** spellings (e.g. *right*, *sight*, *might*). Sometimes a word has a spelling that doesn't follow the 'sound' rules (e.g. *said*). Try to remember and recognise such words.

4 The US spelling is *neighborhood*. The Australian spelling is the traditional spelling of *neighbourhood* using ***our***, as in *favour*, *harbour*, *humour* and many other ***our*** words. The ***i*** and ***e*** have also been reversed. The ***ei*** makes an 'ay' sound in *neighbourhood*. The ***ie*** combination often makes an ***ee*** sound (e.g. *thief*).

5 Make sure you pronounce *film* correctly. *Film* is a one-syllable word. Avoid the common mistake of placing the ***l*** after the ***f*** (***fl***).

6 Avoid adding an ***e*** to words where it is not required.

7 *Midday* is a compound word: *mid* + *day*. It has a double ***d*** (***dd***). It is *midday* and *midnight*.

8 The letter combinations ***or*** and ***au*** can both make the same sound. Both ***er*** and ***or*** are used to make nouns to describe people or objects (e.g. *teacher* or *tailor*). You should recognise and remember when to use the different suffixes. The ***ur*** ending is uncommon.

9 Make sure you pronounce *parsley* carefully: ***pars*** + ***ley***. It is a common word and one which you should remember how to spell.

10 *Discussing* is *discuss* + ***ing***. It has three syllables and is a common word which you should remember how to spell.

11 *Almonds* has a silent ***l***. A silent ***l*** often occurs after an ***a*** (e.g. *walk*, *calm*, *salmon*, *could*). It is often between an ***a*** and an ***m***.

12 Remember: *one kiosk*, *many kiosks*. You do not add ***es*** to make the plural of words that end with ***sk***. You simply add ***s*** (e.g. *flasks*, *desks*). *Kiosk* is of French origin.

13 Make sure you pronounce *pyjamas* correctly. It is a common word and one you should learn to spell.

14 Make sure you pronounce *necklace* correctly. It is a compound word: *neck* + *lace*.

15 Make sure you write the complete word *thought*. It is easy to leave letters off words, especially when the word without the letter still forms a word; in this case *though*.

16 *Delivery* is *deliver* + ***y***. The suffix is ***y***, not ***ey***. The suffix ***y*** in *delivery* has the meaning of suggesting an activity (e.g. *flattery*, *robbery*, *bakery*).

17 *Younger* is *young* + ***er***. Sometimes a word has a spelling that doesn't follow the 'sound' rules (e.g. *said*). Try to remember and recognise such words. *Younger* is one of those words you have to remember how to spell.

18 *Check* and *cheque* are homonyms—words that sound the same but which are spelt differently. *Check* means 'inspect something'. A *cheque* is a bank form for a payment. Remember when to use each word correctly.

Year 5 Literacy Mini Test Answers

Advanced level questions

SPELLING Mini Test 10

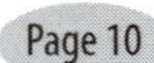

1 probably **2** propeller **3** barrel **4** athletics **5** queried **6** lagoon **7** relief **8** eaves **9** gardener **10** intersection **11** scalp **12** molluscs **13** muesli **14** fifteen **15** existed **16** later **17** method **18** urgency

1 *Probably* is *probable* + ***ly***. When adding ***ly*** to words that end with ***able*** the ***e*** is usually dropped before adding ***ly*** (e.g. *reliable—reliably*, *notable—notably*). Make sure you pronounce the word correctly.

2 *Propeller* is a tricky word. It is *propel* + ***er***. To add the suffix ***er*** you double the ***l*** (***ll***). Both ***er*** and ***ar*** can be used to make nouns to describe people or objects (e.g. *teacher* and *beggar*). You should recognise and remember when to use the different suffixes. Make sure you pronounce *propeller* correctly. It is one of those words you have to remember how to spell.

3 *Barrel* does not end with a double ***l*** (***ll***). The double ***l*** ending in two-syllable words is uncommon. *Travel*, *cymbal*, *marvel* and *petrol* all end with a single ***l***.

4 Make sure you pronounce *athletics* correctly. It has three syllables: ***ath*** + ***let*** + ***ics***. *Athletics* is a common word and one you need to learn and remember how to spell.

5 *Queried* is *query* + ***ed***. To add ***ed*** to a word ending with a consonant and ***y***, you change the ***y*** to ***i***, then add ***ed***. There is no need to double the ***r*** (***rr***).

6 Make sure you pronounce *lagoon* correctly: ***la*** + ***goon***. There is no need to double the ***g*** (***gg***).

7 The basic general rule is ***i*** before ***e*** except after ***c***. It means that, in words where ***i*** and ***e*** fall together, the order is ***ie***, except directly following ***c***, when it is ***ei***. Examples are *friend*, *thief*, *ceiling* and *receive*. Beware: There are a number of exceptions to this rule.

8 *Eve* and *eave* are homonyms—words that sound the same but which are spelt differently. *Eaves* refers to part of a roof that extends beyond the walls. *Eve* refers to the day or a time just before a certain event. *Eve* is rarely used as a plural. Remember when to use each word correctly.

9 *Gardener* is *garden* + ***er***. Make sure you pronounce it correctly: ***gar*** + ***den*** + ***er***. The ***er*** suffix is often used to make nouns to describe people (e.g. *teacher* and *builder*).

10 The ***tion*** ending may be pronounced 'shun' but it is spelt ***tion*** (e.g. *nation*, *subtraction*, *invitation*). The ***k*** (*seck*) is not required.

11 There is no ***e*** on *scalp*. There are a number of words that end with ***lp*** without an ***e*** (e.g. *help*, *pulp*). Take time to learn to spell *scalp* correctly.

12 Remember: *one mollusc*, *many molluscs*. *Mollusc* is a tricky word. You do not add ***es*** to make the plural of words that end with ***sc***. You simply add ***s*** (e.g. *discs*). There are very few common words that end with ***sc***.

13 Make sure you pronounce *muesli* correctly. It has two syllables: ***mues*** + ***li***. *Muesli* came into English from Switzerland.

14 *Fifteen*, more or less, spells as it sounds: ***fif*** + ***teen***. It is not to be confused with the spelling of *fifth*. Make sure you pronounce *fifteen* correctly.

15 Make sure you pronounce *existed* carefully: ***ex*** + ***ist*** + ***ed***. The middle syllable is ***ist***, not ***cist***.

16 *Later* is a comparative adverb (*late*, *later*, *latest*). It refers to a time after a given time. *Latter* refers to the second of two things that have been mentioned. Take time to learn to spell and use each word correctly.

17 Make sure you pronounce *method* correctly: ***meth*** + ***od***.

18 *Urgent* is an adjective. *Urgency* is the noun formed from *urgent*. The final ***t*** becomes ***cy***. This occurs in a number of words, such as *vacant—vacancy* and *truant—truancy*.

Standard level questions

GRAMMAR Mini Test 1

Pages 11–12

1 C **2** D **3** C **4** B **5** C **6** B **7** D **8** A **9** B **10** D **11** A **12** C **13** D **14** B **15** D **16** A **17** C **18** B

1 *A* and *an* are articles. *A* comes before words (nouns and adjectives) that start with a consonant sound. All options begin with a vowel letter but only *useful* begins with a consonant sound. You say ***a*** *useful present*.

2 *An*, *a* and *the* are articles. *The* is a definite article. The writer is referring to a particular knife, not just any knife. It is ***the*** *new knife*.

3 Think of the sentence as two separate sentences. *My mates will always be friends,* and *I will always be friends [with my mates]*. You don't say *Me will always be friends*.

4 *On* is a preposition—***on*** *an ocean liner*. Certain prepositions tend to go with particular situations (e.g. *in winter* but *on weekends*). They have to be learnt and remembered.

Year 5 Grammar Mini Test Answers

5 *Quickly* is an adverb. It tells how fast some typists type. Many adverbs end in ***ly***. Adverbs ending in ***er*** are used to compare two people, while adverbs ending in ***est*** are used to compare many people. *Quick* is an adjective.

6 *Better* is an adverb. It tells how good something is. Think *good*, *better*, *best* and *one*, *two*, *three*. *Good* is used when referring to one person's ability. Adverbs ending in ***er*** are used to compare two people or things, while adverbs ending in ***est*** are used to compare many people or things. 'Gooder' is not a word.

7 *They* is a pronoun referring to *typists*. *She* is incorrect as it is a singular pronoun. *Them* is used in the object form.

8 *And* is a conjunction. It joins ideas and is used to indicate additional things. Not only do typists type but, in addition, they file papers and take messages.

9 *To* is a preposition—you speak to people. Certain prepositions tend to go with particular situations (e.g. *smiled at* but *listened to*). They have to be learnt and remembered.

10 *Them* is a pronoun used to refer to a group of things or people. It saves repeating a series of words. *Them* is used as the object of a statement, not the subject (e.g. *He put them …*).

11 *Scent*, *cent* and *sent* are homonyms—words that sound the same but which are spelt differently. *Scent* is correct. It refers to a smell. *Sense* is pronounced differently and refers to our ability to understand our world in a physical way (e.g. sense of touch).

12 *Had seen* is a past participle. With *seen* you need a 'helper'—another verb to 'help' it. In this case the helper is *had*. *Have* and *has* can also be helping verbs.

13 *Can* and *may* are often confused. *Can* is correct because the narrator (*I*) is *able* (*can*) to reach the switch. *May* would be used if the narrator needed permission to reach it (e.g. *Mum said I may touch the switch*). This is an example of correct usage.

14 The rule is: Plural subjects (nouns) need plural verbs; singular subjects (nouns) need singular verbs. In this case, *play* must be used because there are a *number of kids* (kids play).

15 *An*, *a* and *the* are articles. *The* is a definite article. The writer is referring to particular open spaces, not just any open spaces, but *the open grassy spaces*. *The* can be used with singular or plural nouns. The indefinite articles (*a* and *an*) are only used with singular nouns.

16 The rule is: Plural subjects (nouns) need plural verbs; singular subjects (nouns) need singular verbs. In this case, *train* must be used because there are a *number of joggers* (joggers train).

17 *Among* and *between* are often confused. *Among* is used in situations where there are more than two things involved. *Between* is used when just two things are involved. *Among* is correct because visitors can stroll *among the many gardens*. This is an example of correct usage.

18 *Feed* is present tense. The writer is referring to things that can be done now. *Fed* is past tense.

Intermediate level questions

GRAMMAR Mini Test 2

Pages 13–14

1 D **2** C **3** B **4** A **5** B **6** A **7** D **8** B **9** C **10** A
11 D **12** C **13** team **14** D **15** B **16** C **17** A **18** D

1 *On* is a preposition which is used to designate days and dates. You use *in* for non-specific times during a day, a month, a season or a year. Certain prepositions tend to go with particular situations. These have to be learnt and remembered.

2 *Eat* is an irregular verb. Most verbs in English form their past tenses by adding ***ed*** (e.g. *he walked*). There are a number of irregular verbs when this doesn't happen. So the past of *eat* is *eaten* instead of 'eated'. With the verb *eaten* you need a 'helper'—another verb to 'help' it. *Were* and *was* can be helping verbs.

3 *Who* is a personal pronoun used to refer to people. *Which* is used to refer to animals or things. *What* is most often used to ask a question. *That* is used to refer to, or point out, a particular thing.

4 *Many* is used when the amount or number can be counted. *Much* is used when the quantity cannot be counted, such as sand. *Is* is the correct verb. *Are* is used when talking about more than one person or thing. *Grass* is treated as a singular noun.

5 The rule is: Singular subjects (nouns) need singular verbs; plural subjects (nouns) need plural verbs. In this case *are* must be used because the subject is *boys* (in the rock band). The verb refers to the *boys*, not the singular (one) *band*.

6 The rule is: Singular subjects (nouns) need singular verbs; plural subjects (nouns) need plural verbs. In this case *are* must be used because the subject is *macropods*. *Are* is used when talking about more than one person or thing.

Year 5 Literacy Mini Test Answers

7 *But* is a joining word (conjunction). *And* joins things that are similar. *But* is used to introduce an example that differs from the main idea.

8 *Smaller* is a comparative adjective. Adjectives can be used to compare. *Small* is used to describe one person or thing. *Smaller* is used to compare two people or things. *Smallest* is used when comparing three or more people or things. Only kangaroos and wallabies are being compared in size.

9 *The* is a definite article and can be used with singular or plural nouns: *the open plains*. *A* and *an* are indefinite articles and are used with singular nouns.

10 *See* is an irregular verb. Most verbs in English form their past tenses by adding ***ed*** (e.g. *he walked*). There are a number of irregular verbs when this doesn't happen. So the past of *see* is *seen* instead of 'seed'.

11 *Its* is a possessive pronoun and stands in place of the noun, *the merry-go-round's*. *Its* is used to save repeating *the merry-go-round's* which could sound clumsy. *Them* refers to more than one person or thing. *It's* is a contraction for *It is*.

12 *How* is most often used to ask a question, but it can also be used in an exclamation or as part of an instruction. As a question it will indicate that an answer is required.

13 There are four types of nouns. Collective nouns are the names given to a group or collection of things or people. *Team* is a singular collective noun even though it is made up of many children. *Children* is the plural form of *child* and is a common noun.

14 *Had been* is past tense which is consistent with *avoided* in the first part of the sentence.

15 *Know* is an irregular verb. Most verbs in English form their past tenses by adding ***ed*** (e.g. *he walked*). There are a number of irregular verbs when this doesn't happen, so the past of *know* is *knew* instead of 'knowed'.

16 The rule is: singular subjects (nouns) need singular verbs; plural subjects (nouns) need plural verbs. In this case *was* must be used because the subject is *Sasha* (*she*). *Were* is used when talking about more than one person or thing. *Was* is past tense.

17 *Nor* is a conjunction. Some conjunctions are consistently used in pairs: *neither—nor* and *either—or*.

18 *Think* is an irregular verb. Most verbs in English form their past tenses by adding ***ed*** (e.g. *he walked*). There are a number of irregular verbs when this doesn't happen. So the past of *think* is *thought* instead of 'thinked'.

Intermediate level questions

GRAMMAR Mini Test 3

Pages 15–16

1 C **2** D **3** B **4** A **5** C **6** D **7** B **8** B **9** A **10** A
11 C **12** D **13** A **14** C **15** A **16** D **17** B **18** C

1 *The* is a definite article and can be used with singular or plural nouns—*the old shoes*. *A* and *an* are indefinite articles and are used with singular nouns in specific circumstances.

2 The unnecessary figure is *100%*. If an article is not 100%, then it is not pure. The explanation of *100%* is superfluous. No meaning is lost by omitting *100%*.

3 *Or* is a conjunction which links alternatives. Some conjunctions are consistently used in pairs: *either—or* and *neither—nor*.

4 The rule is: singular subjects (nouns) need singular verbs; plural subjects (nouns) need plural verbs. In this case *was* must be used because the subject is *hiking party*. There is just one hiking party. *Were* is used when talking about more than one person or thing. The event is reported in past tense.

5 The most appropriate word is *long*. *Long* is usually restricted to a situation to do with distance or time. *Big* and *large* refer to great size, amount or number.

6 *It* is a pronoun used to refer to a single item or group of objects, in this case the bag of objects. *It* saves repeating a series of objects. *They* is usually limited to people or animals. *Them* is used as the object of a statement, not the subject (e.g. *Dad spoke to them*).

7 Nouns are naming words for people, places and things. *Wisdom* is an abstract noun. *Coles* is a proper noun. *Breeze* is a common noun. *Gang* is a collective noun.

8 In English the word *not* (*don't* is short for *do not*; *can't* is short for *cannot*) is rarely used in the same part of the sentence as *no*. It is called using a double negative. *But* is incorrect as it is used to introduce an example that differs from the main idea.

9 The rule is: singular subjects (nouns) need singular verbs; plural subjects (nouns) need plural verbs. In this case *are* must be used because the subject is *questions*. *Are* is present tense.

Year 5 Literacy Mini Test Answers

10 *Buy* is an irregular verb. Most verbs in English form their past tenses by adding ***ed*** (e.g. *he walked*). There are a number of irregular verbs when this doesn't happen, so the past of *buy* is *bought* instead of 'buyed'.

11 *Cost* is an irregular verb. Most verbs in English form their past tenses by adding ***ed*** (e.g. *he walked*). There are a number of irregular verbs when this doesn't happen, so the past of *cost* is *cost* instead of 'costed'.

12 *But* is a joining word (conjunction). *But* is used to connect two ideas with the meaning of 'with the exception of'. *And* joins things that are similar.

13 *Do* is correct. It is present tense and relates to more than one person. *Does* is used with a singular subject.

14 *By*, *buy* and *bye* are homonyms—words that sound the same but which are spelt differently. *Bye* can be used to refer to a missed match. *By* is a preposition which refers to a place. *Buy* has to do with money and purchasing goods. ***Bi*** is generally regarded as a prefix.

15 The rule is: singular subjects (nouns) need singular verbs; plural subjects (nouns) need plural verbs. In this case *have* must be used because the subject is *points*. *Have* is present tense.

16 *Win* is an irregular verb. Most verbs in English form their past tenses by adding ***ed*** (e.g. *he walked*). There are a number of irregular verbs when this doesn't happen, so the past of *win* is *won* instead of 'winned'.

17 Adjectives can be used to compare. *Good* is used to describe one result. *Better* is used to compare two possible wins—the result compared to the expectation. *Best* is used when comparing three or more people or things. Remember: good, better, best / 1, 2, 3 (or more).

18 *They* is a pronoun referring to a number of people in another team. *Those* is used before a noun (e.g. *those players*). *It* refers to inanimate objects. *She* is a singular pronoun.

Advanced level questions

GRAMMAR Mini Test 4

Pages 17–18

1 softly **2** A **3** B **4** B **5** D **6** B **7** A **8** A **9** B **10** C **11** D **12** B **13** A **14** C **15** B **16** D **17** A **18** D

1 *Softly* is an adverb. Adverbs add meaning to a verb: *the crowd hissed* (verb) *softly* (adverb).

2 For correct usage you should say *different from*. *To* is used to compare things that are similar: *similar to*. *Than* is often used after comparative adjectives (e.g. *more than*). *Then* is used to indicate time.

3 *Beautiful* describes things that can be seen. *Charming* describes things that delight or attract people. *Remarkable* describes something worth noting or commenting on.

4 Some conjunctions are often used as paired conjunctions. *Not only—but also* is an example. Other examples are *either—or* and *neither—nor*.

5 *Because* is a conjunction joining two clauses. Each part of the sentence can stand on its own: *I have the money* and *I will pay*. *Because* is one of the conjunctions that can begin a sentence.

6 In English the word *not* (*don't* is short for *do not* and *can't* is short for *cannot*) and *no* are rarely used in the same part of a sentence. It is called using a double negative.

7 When adverbs are used to compare two things the words *more* or *less* are also used. *Tightest* and *tighter* are adjectives.

8 *Me* is used as an object in a sentence. Think of the sentence as two separate sentences or parts: *Jan saw herself in the club news./Jan saw me in the club news*. We don't say: *Jan saw I in the club news*.

9 *Tell* is present tense. *Told* is past tense. *Tolled* is not correct. It relates to the ringing of bells.

10 *Write* is present tense. *Wrote* is past tense. *Writ* is rarely used any more.

11 *Write* is an irregular verb. Most verbs in English form their past tenses by adding ***ed*** (e.g. *he walked*). There are a number of irregular verbs when this doesn't happen. So the past of *write* is *written* (or *wrote*) instead of 'writed'. *Written* usually needs another verb to help it, such as *have* or *had*.

12 *But* is a conjunction used to connect two ideas with the meaning 'with the exception of'. *The prince was brave but he had to run away. He had lost his sword.*

13 *Lose* is an irregular verb. Most verbs in English form their past tenses by adding ***ed*** (e.g. *he walked*). There are a number of irregular verbs when this doesn't happen. So the past of *lose* is *lost* instead of 'losed'.

14 *Go* is an irregular verb. Most verbs in English form their past tenses by adding ***ed*** (e.g. *he walked*). There are a number of irregular verbs when this doesn't happen. So the past of *go* is *gone* instead of 'goed'. *Gone* usually needs another verb to help it, such as *have* or *had*.

15 Singular subjects (nouns) need singular verbs;

plural subjects (nouns) need plural verbs. In this case *sail* must be used because there are several yachts: *yachts sail* and *a yacht sails*.

16 *As* is used to connect two ideas. It indicates that one situation depends upon a certain condition.

17 *Board* and *bored* are homonyms—words that sound the same but which are spelt differently. Incorrectly used they can change the meaning of a sentence. *Bored* means 'the feeling when you have nothing to do'. 'Bord' is not a word.

18 *Of* is most often used between two nouns. In this case *the end* and *the wharf*. It shows a relationship between the whole wharf and part of the wharf.

Advanced level questions

GRAMMAR Mini Test 5

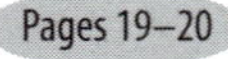

1 C **2** D **3** organisers, decision, squads, sunset **4** A **5** D **6** B **7** A **8** A **9** C **10** A **11** D **12** B **13** C **14** D **15** C **16** A **17** B **18** C

1 *A* and *an* are indefinite articles and are used with singular nouns in specific circumstances. They may precede both nouns and adjectives but *a* goes before a word beginning with a consonant sound and *an* before a word beginning with a vowel sound. *European* may start with a vowel but the ***Eu*** makes a consonant sound. *The* is a definite article and can be used with singular or plural nouns (e.g. *the old shoes*).

2 It is easy to confuse *its* and *it's*. *Its* is a possessive pronoun and does not require an apostrophe ***s*** (a bit like *his*). *It's* is the shortened form (or contraction) of *it is*. A capital letter is needed as it is the beginning of a sentence.

3 Nouns are words for the names of people, places or things. There are four nouns in the sentence: *organisers*, *decision*, *squads* and *sunset*.

4 *Some* on its own is a determiner meaning 'an unknown number'. In this sentence it means 'an unknown *way*'. *Someway* is a compound word. It works as an adverb meaning 'in a way not yet known'. The hyphen is not necessary.

5 *In* is a preposition indicating a place. Prepositions tell about position. Certain prepositions tend to go with particular situations (e.g. *in the park* but *on the beach*). They have to be learnt and remembered.

6 Some conjunctions are often paired with particular other conjunctions. *As—as* is an example. Other examples are *either—or* and *neither—nor*.

7 *They* is a pronoun referring to a number of people. *They* saves repeating the names of the groups (*the girls in the class and the boys*), which could sound clumsy. *It* is used to refer to single, inanimate things.

8 Amounts, such as *five dollars*, are treated as singular amounts. So the correct expression is *five dollars is*.

9 *If* is a conjunction used to indicate a situation that would have existed in order that something else will happen.

10 The rule is: singular subjects (nouns) need singular verbs; plural subjects (nouns) need plural verbs. In this case *are* must be used because the subject is *more cars*. *Are* is present tense.

11 *Drive* is an irregular verb. Most verbs in English form their past tenses by adding ***ed*** (e.g. *he walked*). There are a number of irregular verbs when this doesn't happen. So the past of *drive* is *driven* instead of 'drived'. *Driven* usually needs another verb to help it, such as *being*, *are* or *is*.

12 *Than* is a conjunction used to compare things. *Then* is an adverb used to indicate a time. Make sure you pronounce the words correctly.

13 The rule is: singular subjects (nouns) need singular verbs; plural subjects (nouns) need plural verbs. In this case *has* must be used because the subject is singular (*population*). There is just one population (even if it is made up of many people).

14 *I* is a personal pronoun. *Me* is incorrect as it cannot be used as the subject in a sentence. Think of the first sentence as two sentences: *Grant and Jason want to play guitars./I want to play a guitar.*

15 The rule is: Singular subjects (nouns) need singular verbs; plural subjects (nouns) need plural verbs. In this case *has* must be used because the subject *band* is singular. *Have* would be used with *bands*. *Has* is present tense.

16 The preposition *for* is used to indicate a reason why something happens or is done. Certain prepositions tend to go with particular situations. They have to be learnt and remembered. *With* is incorrect as it carries the idea of things or people already being together.

17 *And* is a conjunction and is used to join words or ideas. *And* joins the two positions available in the band.

18 *Speak* is an irregular verb. Most verbs in English form their past tenses by adding ***ed*** (e.g. *he walked*). There are a number of irregular verbs when this doesn't happen. So the past of *speak* is

Year 5 Literacy Mini Test Answers

spoken instead of 'speaked'. *Spoken* usually needs another verb to help it, such as *have* or *has*.

Standard level questions

PUNCTUATION Mini Test 1

Pages 21–22

1 B **2** D **3** A **4** C **5** B, C **6** A **7** C **8** D **9** B **10** A **11** C **12** A, B **13** D **14** C **15** A **16** B **17** D **18** Highway

1 In shortened words the full stop is not required if the shortened word has the last letter of the complete word. Examples are *Mister—Mr*, *Road—Rd*.

2 The introductory sentence states that the speaker *was stunned*. The second sentence is an exclamation: *It wasn't right!* Exclamations start with capital letters and end with exclamation marks (**!**).

3 Capital letters are required on all proper nouns. The proper nouns in the sentence are the children's names and *Christmas*. All other nouns are common nouns.

4 There is only one question in the options. It is the only choice that you could give an answer to. *When* can be a question starter or an adverb of time.

5 In this sentence a comma is used between the actual words spoken and the speech marks. A comma is also used where a natural pause occurs.

6 There is only one capital city. To show ownership you simply add an apostrophe ***s*** (***'s***). *Cities* is the spelling for more than one *city*.

7 Commas are used to indicate a pause. In this sentence it separates a descriptor (*my cousin*) from the proper noun (*Julie*).

8 *Can't* is a shortened word or contraction. It is short for *cannot*. The apostrophe shows that letters (***no***) have been left out.

9 The question starts with *Where and when*. The question mark goes after the word *week*. *When* has a capital letter and is the beginning of the next sentence, which is a statement about time. It ends with a full stop. *When* is an adverb of time in this sentence.

10 *Captain Smith lost his ship in the Pacific Ocean* is a statement. It records a fact and should end with a full stop.

11 *Kate* is the only word that requires an apostrophe ***s*** (***'s***). She owns the toys. There is no need for an apostrophe ***s*** on any of the nouns. They are simply plurals.

12 Speech marks (inverted commas) are only used to enclose the actual words spoken and the comma.

13 The sentence is a simple statement and ends with a full stop. The next word in the text has a capital letter (*She*) and is the beginning of a new sentence. The word *dinner* is a common noun and does not require a capital letter.

14 *English* is a proper noun. It is the name of a subject.

15 *Hard* is the last word in an exclamation sentence. The next word is *Her*, which is the start of a statement.

16 The word *Her* is the beginning of a new sentence starting after an exclamation mark (*hard!*). It must have a capital letter and is not followed by any punctuation mark.

17 The word *so* is used to add emphasis. Lee is quite upset. The best choice from the options is *so* with an exclamation mark.

18 Capital letters are required for proper nouns, the given names of people, places and things. *Highway* is part of the official name for the road. Other nouns in the sentence are common nouns.

Intermediate level questions

PUNCTUATION Mini Test 2

Pages 23–24

1 Even, African **2** B **3** D **4** D **5** A **6** C **7** C **8** D **9** A **10** C **11** B **12** C **13** D **14** B **15** A **16** C **17** A **18** A

1 *Even* should have a capital letter as it is the first word in a sentence. *African* has a capital because it is a proper adjective from the proper noun *Africa*.

2 There are only four options. The sentence is not a question. The comma and semicolon indicate that a sentence has more to come. It would be incomplete with these punctuation marks. The sentence best performs as an exclamation.

3 *It's* is a shortened word. It is short for *It is*. The apostrophe shows that a letter (***i***) has been left out. *Hers* is a possessive pronoun and does not require an apostrophe.

4 *Tim* is the only name that requires an apostrophe to indicate ownership: *Tim's books*. All other options are simple plural nouns.

5 A comma is required after *brothers* to separate the phrase (*Mark, James and Sean*) from the rest of the sentence; commas are used in this way when referring to people being talked about. The phrase *Mark, James and Sean* is a series of names, and a comma is inserted between the first two names and an *and* between the second and last names. A comma is not necessary before *and*.

6 *Theirs* is a possessive pronoun for two or more people and does not require an apostrophe to indicate ownership.

7 Exclamations are most often short sentences. Questions often begin with *is*. Questions imply that an answer is required.

8 This is an example of indirect or reported speech. The actual words spoken are not quoted. No speech marks are required.

9 *Lunch* is the last word in a quoted question. The question mark goes inside the speech mark.

10 The text is a question followed by a statement. The question actually has two parts. The statement begins with the word *How*.

11 Adjectives in a series (just like nouns) need commas to separate each word. No comma is required between the last adjective and the noun.

12 Only the actual words spoken are in speech marks. The spoken words are: *"You can go to bed now,"* Notice that the comma is after *now*, inside the speech marks.

13 *We did* is a very short statement. The next statement begins with a capital letter (*H*).

14 *I'll* is the first word spoken by the group leader. *I'll* is a shortened word. It is short for *I will*. The apostrophe shows that letters (***wi***) have been left out. The personal pronoun *I* is always a capital letter.

15 Commas are used to show a pause in a sentence. The next word is *including*, without a capital letter. It is not the beginning of a new sentence. A comma is required after *hiker* to separate the phrase (*including those in Mr Smith's group*) from the rest of the sentence when referring to the people being talked about.

16 The apostrophe goes before the ***s*** (***'s***). The group belongs to Mr Smith. There is only one Mr Smith.

17 The last sentence is a question, which starts with a capital letter (***I***) and ends with a question mark. The question mark goes inside the speech marks.

18 The word *play* should not have a capital letter. It is a common noun. All other options are proper nouns.

Intermediate level questions

PUNCTUATION Mini Test 3

Pages 25–26

1 B **2** A **3** D **4** happened **5** C **6** D **7** B **8** A **9** A **10** C **11** B **12** D **13** C **14** B **15** A **16** D **17** C **18** B

1 *Else* is a pronoun representing another person. It requires an apostrophe ***s*** (***'s***). The rubbish belongs to someone else.

2 *Theirs* is a possessive pronoun and does not require an apostrophe to indicate ownership.

3 Only the actual words spoken are in speech marks. The spoken words are: *"It's after ten o'clock!"* which includes the exclamation mark.

4 Verbs express actions, thoughts, feelings and states of being (e.g. *am*, *are*).

5 This is an example of a command sentence. Someone is being told, or commanded, to do something.

6 Commas are used to indicate a natural pause in a sentence.

7 For singular nouns, possession (or ownership) is indicated with an apostrophe ***s*** (***'s***). Although there are many sailors on HMAS *Ibis*, there is only *one crew*. *Crew* is a collective noun.

8 The patient is asking a question. In direct speech the question mark goes between the last word spoken and the closing speech mark.

9 Commas are used in lists of nouns or adjectives where there are more than two items or people. Items in a list can comprise more than one word (e.g. *bright red*). The comma separates the colours *bright red* and *pale green*. *And* is used between the last two colours (*pale green and deep blue*) in the list. A comma is not necessary.

10 As there are many girls the apostrophe goes after the ***s*** (***s'***). *Class* and *results* do not involve the concept of ownership.

11 In this sentence *when* is an adverb used to start a question. All other sentences use *when* as a conjunction.

12 Abbreviations that consist of more than one capital letter or of capital letters only do not require a full stop (e.g. *HMAS*, *GB*).

13 Commas are used in lists of nouns or adjectives where there are more than two items or people. Items in a list can comprise of more than one word (e.g. *nine years*). The comma separates *nine years* and *six months*. *And* is used between the last two time periods (*six months and one week*) in the list. A comma is not necessary.

Year 5 Literacy Mini Test Answers

14 *You're* is a shortened word. It is short for *you are*. The apostrophe shows that a letter (***a***) has been left out.

15 *Don't* is a shortened word. It is short for *do not*. The apostrophe shows a letter (***o***) has been left out. 'Donnot' is not a word.

16 *Out* is at the end of the actual words that Dad said. It is followed by a comma inside the speech marks.

17 *You* begins a new sentence after the full stop. Dad has continued to speak. The actual words must be enclosed in speech marks.

18 *1990s* is a plural form. No ownership or abbreviation is involved. No apostrophe is required.

Advanced level questions

PUNCTUATION Mini Test 4

Pages 27–28

1 C **2** Asian **3** A **4** C **5** A **6** B **7** B **8** D **9** D **10** C **11** A **12** C, D **13** D **14** B **15** A **16** C **17** B **18** D

1 There are two sentences: a question beginning with *Did*, followed by a statement.

2 Proper adjectives made from proper nouns begin with capital letters.

3 Only the actual words spoken are in speech marks. The spoken words are: "*That's enough*" and "*You look tired*". There is a full stop after *trainer* so the next sentence must start with a capital letter (*You*). Notice that the comma and the final full stop are inside the speech marks.

4 Exclamation sentences are used to express feelings and end with an exclamation mark (**!**).

5 *As* is a conjunction joining two ideas. It is preceded by a comma to indicate a pause. The phrase *as he really doesn't like his new jeans* is not a complete sentence. A capital letter is not required.

6 Commas are used in lists where there are more than two items or people. (They are also used in series of adjectives.) In this sentence the comma separates the items *boxes of apples* and *bags of potatoes*. *And* is used between the last two items (*bags of potatoes and trays of strawberries*). A comma is not necessary.

7 Brackets are used to include additional information that may be useful. The years of Enid Blyton's life are additional information that the writer may feel the reader would appreciate.

8 Commas come after *films* and after *westerns*. The commas separate a short explanation (*mainly westerns*) from the rest of the sentence and also introduce a slight pause.

9 *Jack and Mary* are treated as a single unit or a pair. The apostrophe is applied to the last word of the pair. An ***s*** sound is not pronounced after *Jack*.

10 Commas are used to separate adjectives in a series. *Evil-looking* acts as a single adjective.

11 There are two sentences in this text. The first statement ends with a full stop. *Whose* is used to ask the following question. It requires a capital letter. *Who's* is an abbreviation for *who is*.

12 There is a long introduction to the few actual words spoken: *I don't believe it!*

13 The short sentence *Some don't* ends with a full stop. *If* is the first word in the next sentence and doesn't need a comma after it.

14 *It's* is a shortened word which is short for *it is*. The apostrophe shows that a letter (***i***) has been left out. It is not the beginning of a new sentence. *Its* is a possessive pronoun.

15 The comma indicates a pause. *Or* with a capital letter is not the start of a new sentence.

16 *Aren't* is a shortened word. It is short for *are not*. The apostrophe shows that the letter ***o*** has been left out.

17 *People* is the last word in the text. It does not have a capital letter and should be followed by a full stop.

18 The text is made up of a question followed by a statement. The question ends with a question mark and the statement begins with a capital letter.

Advanced level questions

PUNCTUATION Mini Test 5

Pages 29–30

1 A **2** C **3** D **4** A **5** B **6** D **7** B **8** C **9** C **10** D **11** B **12** C **13** D **14** D **15** C **16** B **17** A **18** C

1 There are two sentences in the short text. The first one-word sentence is an exclamation. It is followed by a statement that must start with a capital letter.

2 *Capt.* is part of a proper noun (title). It is an abbreviation for *Captain*. In its shortened form it has a full stop after the ***t*** as this is not the final letter in the title (contrast *Capt.* with *Mr*).

3 *Ours* is a possessive pronoun and does not require an apostrophe to indicate ownership.

4 Only the actual words spoken are in speech marks. The spoken words are in two parts: "*It is not starting before midday*" and "*so you will have to wait*", which is one sentence. There is no need

Year 5 Reading Mini Test Answers

for a capital letter to begin *so*. Take note of the punctuation that is included with the quotation marks.

5 In this sentence *what* is a pronoun used to start a question. A question implies the need for an answer.

6 Commas are used in lists where there are more than two items. (They are also used in a series of adjectives.) Commas separate the items *thongs*, *board shorts* and *cap*. *And* is used between the last two items (*cap and a towel*) in the list. A comma is not necessary. *Board shorts* represents one item.

7 Make sure you pronounce *could've* correctly. *Could've* is a shortened word. It is short for *could have*. The apostrophe shows letters (***ha***) have been left out.

8 The sentence is: *"Beat it!" snapped my father when a magpie landed near the picnic basket.* In direct speech the exclamation mark goes between the last word spoken and the closing speech mark.

9 *West Wyalong* and *Condobolin* are both proper nouns and so need to begin with a capital letter. The word *south* is a common noun and so does not begin with a capital letter.

10 As *Fay* is the owner of the crop, the apostrophe goes before the ***s*** (***'s***). The word *belonged* is sufficient to indicate the sisters own the goats. *Farmers* is a plural form of *farmer*.

11 There is only one *world*. The apostrophe goes before the ***s*** (***'s***). Because the word *children* is a plural noun the apostrophe goes before the ***s*** (***'s***).

12 For measurements in their abbreviated form, there is no full stop, even if the last letter is not part of the abbreviation (e.g. *m* for *metre*, *mg* for *milligram*). The abbreviations are also not capitalised.

13 The correct word is *Take*, after opening the speech marks (*"Take*) for direct speech. The clue to the actual words spoken are the words he says following the comma. The words spoken conclude with *now* (*now.*"). The words the teacher says are the beginning of a sentence and must have a capital letter (*Take*).

14 *Your* is a possessive pronoun showing ownership. *You're* is a shortened word. It is an abbreviation for *you are*. The apostrophe shows that a letter (***a***) has been left out.

15 *Page* is the end of a sentence. The next word, *The*, begins with a capital letter and is on a new line. *What* is the beginning of a question asked by Tegan. A question mark and closing speech mark follow *page*.

16 This is the end of a statement in reported or indirect speech. Speech marks are not required but a full stop is.

17 *Hey* is an exclamation spoken by Jodie. It is her opening word and must follow the speech marks (or inverted commas). *Hey* is followed by an exclamation mark (**!**).

18 *Duke of Kent* is a title. It is a proper noun. Capital letters are used for the individual nouns. Small words, such as *of*, do not require a capital letter.

Standard level questions

READING Mini Test 1: Narrative

Page 32

Go to **inside back cover** for a guide to question types.

1 A **2** D **3** C **4** B **5** D **6** B

1 This is a **fact-finding type of question**. The answer is a fact in the text. You read that *Emily thought that if they were violets they should be violet (see lines 35–37).*

2 This is a **fact-finding type of question**. The answer is a fact in the text. You read that *Tolly and Emily had to buy some oranges, lemons and apples (see lines 1–2).*

3 This is a **fact-finding type of question**. The answer is a fact in the text. You read that *Emily thought that if they were greyhounds they should be grey. Next they passed a flower shop (see lines 22–24).*

4 This is a **fact-finding type of question**. The answer is a fact in the text. You read that *Emily thought that if they were called goldfish they should be gold (see lines 10–11).*

5 This is an **inferring type of question**. To find the answer you have to 'read between the lines'. You read *The greengrocer looked at her [Emily] and grinned (see line 43)* and then the three of them joked about colours. Combine this with your own knowledge of how people behave and you can work out the final answer. The greengrocer was cheerful when talking to Tolly and Emily.

6 This is a **synthesis type of question**. To find the answer you have to read the whole text. The text is a short narrative about two children walking down the street and talking about why the names of the things they pass don't match their colour.

Its tone is lighthearted. For example, you read *The greengrocer looked at her and grinned, 'Don't worry Emily,' she said, 'but did you know that blackberries are red when they are green?'* (see lines 43–45). This short story is meant to entertain and give enjoyment to the reader.

Standard level questions

READING Mini Test 2: Table

Page 33

1 2 (two) **2** D **3** C **4** A **5** C **6** D

1 This is a **fact-finding type of question**. The answer is a fact in the text. You read *The numerals 1 to 9 are called digits or one-digit numbers* (see line 10) and *Nought (0) is also a digit* (see line 11). To write the number ten (10) a person has to use two digits: 1 and 0.

2 This is a **fact-finding type of question**. The answer is a fact in the text. You read *The numerals 1 to 9 are called digits* (see line 10).

3 This is a **fact-finding type of question**. The answer is a fact in the text. You read *Odd numbers end with 1, 3, 5, 7 or 9* (see line 3). So as 101 ends in 1 you know that it is an odd number. You also read *The numerals 1 to 9 are called digits or one-digit numbers* (see line 10) so you can work out that 101 must be a three-digit number. But it is not the first three-digit number: one hundred (100) is the first three-digit number.

4 This is a **fact-finding type of question**. The answer is a fact in the text. You read *The numerals 1 to 9 are called digits or one-digit numbers* (see line 10). The counting number nine (9) is the largest single-digit number. After nine the next numbers are two-digit numbers (10 to 99).

5 This is a **fact-finding type of question**. The answer is a fact in the table. You need to count the number of Ys in each column. There are five composite numbers, 10 or less, and only four prime numbers.

6 This is a **judgement type of question**. You read *Numbers can be described in many ways. They can have several features* (see line 1). This gives you a clue as to what the table is about. Then if you look at the table you will see that it has all the features of the numbers 0 to 10. The best answer is that this table would be useful to anyone who wanted to understand the features of numbers. The table wouldn't help you much with remembering multiplication facts and it may not help you prepare for a mathematics test.

Intermediate level questions

READING Mini Test 3: Narrative

Page 34

1 A **2** B **3** C **4** 3, 2, 4, 1 **5** A, F **6** C

1 This is a **fact-finding type of question**. The answer is a fact in the text. You read that *It was lying next to the wall looking quite splattered* (see line 4).

2 This is a **fact-finding type of question**. The answer is a fact in the text. You read that *'I just went outside when I heard a noise on the wall'* (see line 12).

3 This is an **inferring type of question**. To find the answer you have to 'read between the lines'. You read *they were all laughing. When the last of them had stopped rolling about their desks* (see lines 24–25). Combine this with your own knowledge of how people react to things that are very silly and you can work out the final answer. The class was laughing uncontrollably.

4 This is a **sequencing/fact-finding type of question**. You can find the answer because it is a fact in the text. By reading the text carefully you can identify the correct order of events: 1) Jenny heard a noise against the outside wall. 2) Jenny signed the Signing Out sheet. 3) Ms Mann didn't believe Jenny's story. 4) The class started laughing.

5 This is an **inferring type of question**. To find the answer you have to 'read between the lines'. You read *'It's true,' I said in my most honest voice* (see line 17). Jenny repeated *'It's true'* twice more (see lines 21 and 25). Combine this with your own knowledge of how people react when they are trying to convince someone they are right and you can work out the final answer. Jenny is being insistent and she is positive.

6 This is a **language type of question**. To find the answer you have to read the text carefully, especially the section that is quoted: *'Someone threw a sausage at our classroom. I heard it and they must've run away. I didn't see them'* (see lines 14–15). Combine this with your own knowledge of how language is used in the text to come to a final answer. The pronoun *them* refers to the people who Jenny thought had thrown the sausages and run off.

Intermediate level questions

READING Mini Test 4: Report

Page 35

1 D, E **2** B **3** A **4** B **5** D **6** C

Year 5 Reading Mini Test Answers

1 This is an **inferring type of question**. To find the answer you have to 'read between the lines'. You read *[the neem tree] is a fast grower, acts as a windbreak, is resistant to insects and needs little water. It will grow in salty soil and is long living (see lines 4–5)*. You also read that one of the countries in which it grows (Oman) *is dry and hot (see line 7)*. Combine this with your own knowledge that *hardy* means 'able to survive extreme conditions' to work out that the neem tree is a hardy tree. It is valued for the contribution it makes to the comfort of daily life, as a windbreak *(line 5)*, and for its insecticide quality *(line 5)*.

2 This is a **fact-finding type of question**. The answer is a fact in the text. You read that *Experiments in Oman have shown that on blistering hot days the temperature under the neem tree can be up to eight degrees lower (see lines 12–13)*. The neem tree provides cooling shade.

3 This is a **fact-finding type of question**. The answer is a fact in the text. You read that *Farmers use the trees as a pesticide and to protect their crops from fungus and insect disease (see line 23)*.

4 This is an **inferring type of question**. To find the answer you have to 'read between the lines'. You read *Oman is dry and hot (see line 7)*. Many parts of India are also hot and dry. This is implied in the second paragraph. Combine this with your own knowledge and you can work out the final answer. The neem tree is a hardy tree that can survive long, hot, dry summers.

5 This is a **language type of question**. To find the answer you have to read the text carefully, especially the section that is quoted: *Although the neem tree is deciduous it doesn't lose all its leaves at once (see line 9)*. Combine this with your knowledge of the meaning of the word *deciduous*, which generally refers to trees that lose their leaves in autumn, to work out that the neem tree loses its leaves.

6 This is a **judgement type of question**. You read *The Indian word nimba means a tree which provides good health (see line 1)*. You also read *In India, few villages are without a neem tree. It is more or less a backyard chemist shop. Much of the folk medicine has been supported by scientific discoveries (see lines 14–16)* and *Many Indians make and eat neem leaf chutney for good health. It seems the neem tree can cure almost any complaint (see lines 21–22)*. The neem tree has many uses but it is most useful for maintaining good health.

Intermediate level questions

READING Mini Test 5: Poster

Page 36

1 D **2** C **3** A **4** Suggested answer: a factory. A lot of heavy lifting is done in factories. **5** B **6** C

1 This is a **fact-finding type of question**. The answer is a fact in the text. You read the title of the poster is *How to protect your back*. You also read *Follow these simple guidelines and you will protect your back throughout life (see lines 18–19)*. The poster is mainly concerned with workers' safety. The illustration supports this answer.

2 This is a **fact-finding type of question**. The answer is a fact in the text. You read *Do not carry oversized objects by yourself. Work with a mate (see lines 10–11)*.

3 This is a **language type of question**. To find the answer you have to read the text carefully, especially the section that is quoted: *Back problems are difficult to* ***put right*** *(see line 17)*. Combine this with your own knowledge of how language is used in the text to come to a final answer. The sentence is an expression people use meaning 'to fix something that is broken or not working as well as it should be'. *Put right* means 'correct a problem'.

4 This is a **judgement type of question**. The poster is entitled *How to protect your back*. You are told the best actions to take when lifting heavy objects. You read *Lift with your legs (see lines 6–7)* and *Teamwork works best (see line 17)*. Combine this with your own knowledge and you can work out the final answer, which is that the information would be most useful in a factory or any situation where lifting heavy objects was part of the work environment. Other options include building sites and road transport depots (furniture removalists). The workers' clothes in the illustrations suggest this is a factory environment.

5 This is a **fact-finding type of question**. The answer is a fact in the text. You read that *Before lifting an object make sure … where you are going to walk is clear of obstacles (see lines 2 and 4)*.

6 This is a **judgement type of question**. You can see the diagrams show the right and wrong way to lift heavy objects. These add meaning to the written text. Combine this with your own knowledge and you can work out the final answer, which is that the diagrams make the information easy to follow or understand.

Year 5 Reading Mini Test Answers

Intermediate level questions

READING Mini Test 6: Poem

Page 37

1 Madeleine (or Madeleine Jane) **2** A **3** D **4** C **5** A **6** D, F

1 This is a **fact-finding type of question**. The answer is a fact in the text. You read *Then she looked in the mirror and said, 'It is plain, That the name that best suits me is Madeleine Jane!'* (see lines 19–20).

2 This is a **judgement type of question**. You read *She wanted a name that would suit her just right. Perhaps she'd be Elaine for that meant 'bright light'* (see lines 11–12). You also read *She tried being Eleanor, Vicky, and Lou. Robyn? Fiona? Oh what should she do?* (see lines 15–16) and *Then she looked in the mirror and said, 'It is plain, That the name that best suits me is Madeleine Jane!'* (see lines 19–20). Madeleine considered many names but finally rejected all the names because she was happy with the name she had been given.

3 This is a **fact-finding type of question**. The answer is a fact in the text. You read *Now Andrée was pretty, and Sharon was too* (see line 8).

4 This is a **fact-finding type of question**. The answer is a fact in the text. You read *Then she looked in the mirror and said, 'It is plain, That the name that best suits me is Madeleine Jane!'* (see lines 19–20).

5 This is an **inferring type of question**. To find the answer you have to 'read between the lines'. You read *So she stood at the mirror and tried some for size* (see line 9). You also read *And she rolled it around on her tongue for a time* (see line 18). Combine this with your own knowledge and understanding of language to come up with the answer. If you roll words around your tongue, you are testing how they sound. Madeleine was saying the names aloud.

6 This is a **judgement type of question**. You read *She thought about Mollie* (see line 7) and she *tried some [names] for size* (see line 9). You also read *She wanted a name that would suit her just right. Perhaps she'd be Elaine* (see lines 11–12) and *Or how about Marion?* (see line 14). She doesn't know what name to choose and exclaims *Oh what should she do?* (see line 16). Throughout the poem Madeleine is unsure and doubtful about which name would suit her.

Advanced level questions

READING Mini Test 7: Recount

Page 38

1 A *perfectionist* is a person who demands perfection, especially in his or her own work. Robbie Maddison kept doing jumps until they were perfect. **2** London **3** D **4** 1, 3, 4, 2 **5** A **6** D

1 This is an **inferring type of question**. To find the answer you have to 'read between the lines'. You read *In December 2007 Maddison broke the world motorcycle jumping record, jumping a distance of 98 metres. He repeated the event immediately afterwards* (see lines 10–11). You also read *On 29 March 2008, he broke his own world record twice during the Crusty Demons Night of World Records show in Melbourne … He landed hard on his back tyre and was not satisfied by the jump, so he decided to do another jump* (see lines 14–18). Even when Maddison had completed a successful record attempt, if he wasn't happy with the actual jump he would repeat it. Combine this with your own knowledge that a *perfectionist* is someone who always wants to do everything perfectly.

2 This is a **fact-finding type of question**. The answer is a fact in the text. You read *One stunt in 2009 was his jump up the raised ramp of Tower Bridge, London, with a back flip while the drawbridge was open* (see lines 21–22).

3 This is a **judgement type of question**. You read *Maddison admits people might think he is crazy, but he loves taking on these huge challenges* (see lines 23–24). You also read *He landed hard on his back tyre and was not satisfied by the jump, so he decided to do another jump* (see lines 17–18). Maddison was a stunt rider but his stunts only became more difficult with experience. He took years to develop his skills. He always tried to be successful and professional and would repeat a jump until it was perfect. If he was only interested in attention, he wouldn't worry about how well he jumped or try to take on more challenging and difficult jumps.

4 This is a **sequencing type of question**. You have to find the order in which things were done. The correct order for Maddison is: 1 goes to Kiama High School *(see line 4)*; 2 broke the world record *(see line 10)*; 3 jumps Tower Bridge *(see line 21)*; 4 jumps the Corinth Canal in Greece *(see line 26)*.

5 This is an **inferring type of question**. To find the answer you have to 'read between the lines'. You read *Maddison admits people might think he is crazy, but he loves taking on these huge challenges* (see lines 23–24). You also read *He was not injured in either jump* (see lines 12–13). Maddison was daring but he rarely got injured. He wasn't thoughtless and never underestimated the risks. Combine this with your own knowledge of record-breakers to work out that Maddison was a daring stunt rider.

6 This is a **fact-finding type of question**. The answer is a fact in the text. You read *It was here he developed his passion for riding by competing in national motocross events, which led to him becoming a motorbike stunt rider* (see lines 2–3).

Advanced level questions

READING Mini Test 8: Narrative

Page 39

1 B **2** Suggested answers: unhurried, peaceful or quiet **3** D **4** 1S, 2W **5** A **6** C

1 This is a **fact-finding type of question**. The answer is a fact in the text. You read *Between the shed and the town was a small stream. Flashes of light indicated that the summer dry had not yet reduced the stream to a sandy dip. On the bank a windmill was turning lazily* (see lines 18–20). The word *adjacent* means 'near or close by'. A stream is a watercourse.

2 This is a **judgement type of question**. You read *A solitary truck trundled around the corner of the hotel* (see line 11). You also read *A few people wandered or hurried down the street* (see line 13) and *All this was quite peaceful and pleasant* (see lines 20–21). There is not much happening in town. Combine this information with your own knowledge of small country towns to work out that life in Willang could be described as unhurried, simple, uncrowded or peaceful.

3 This is a **judgement type of question**. You read *Here drivers could pull off the road and have a look at the view and take a photo—if they were really impressed* (see lines 2–3). You also read *A few people wandered or hurried down the street* (see line 13) and *All this was quite peaceful and pleasant* (see lines 20–21). There is not much happening in town and the scene is fairly ordinary. The tone of the comments suggests that the scene was not all that exciting—the words *if they were really impressed* and *quite … pleasant* indicates this. Visitors might consider taking a photo—but they might give it a miss.

4 This is a **fact-finding type of question**. The answer is a fact in the text. The church is in the small town of Willang which is to the south (line 4) of The Lookout. The limestone quarry is to the west (line 22).

5 This is a **language type of question**. To find the answer you have to read the text carefully, especially the section that is quoted: *The houses struggled out from the main street* (see line 7). The word *struggled* is a metaphor which suggests the houses had a tired, possibly run-down look about them the further the houses were from the main street. It was difficult for them to survive.

6 This is a **synthesis type of question**. To find the answer you have to read the whole text. The text is mainly about the different views from The Lookout. You read *At the top of the hill the road curved sharply to the right but there was a wide patch of gravel on the side called The Lookout. Here drivers could pull off the road and have a look at the view* (see lines 1–2). You also read *To the south, straight down the rolling valley, you could see the small town of Willang right at the foot of the hill. It was an old country town with weatherboard cottages and corrugated tin roofs* (see lines 4–6). A suitable title would be: From The Lookout. The other options focus on less important detail.

Advanced level questions

READING Mini Test 9: Procedure

Page 40

1 B **2** C **3** D **4** A **5** C **6** B

1 This is a **synthesis type of question**. To find the answer you have to read the whole text. You read *Instructions for learning about adverbs* (see line 9) and then the different steps to work out whether a word is an adverb. The text is an example of a method. It makes clear the method to use to identify and use adverbs.

2 This is an **inferring type of question**. To find the answer you have to 'read between the lines'. You read *Step 4 Take care not to misuse adverbs in speech* (see line 19). If you have to take care then you will want to avoid having problems when using adverbs. Some of the problems are specifically listed.

3 This is a **fact-finding type of question**. The answer is a fact in the text. You read *Some adjectives don't change when they become adverbs* (see line 22). Some words can be both adjectives and adverbs.

4 This is a **judgement type of question**. You read *Adverbs add meaning to verbs and adjectives*

(see line 1). You also read *Look in a sentence for words that end in **ly** (see line 10)* and *Be careful! (see line 22)*. The tone used is matter-of-fact with explanations about adverbs and many examples, suggesting the author is trying to be helpful.

5 This is a **fact-finding type of question**. The answer is a fact in the text. You read *If the word is answering a **how** or **when** or **where** question, then it is an adverb (see lines 1–2)*.

6 This is a **judgement type of question**. You read the title is *Using adverbs* and it contains *Instructions for learning about adverbs (see line 9)*. You would expect a journalist or author to have this knowledge about adverbs. A signwriter mainly writes or produces what he or she is given. The information would be most useful to a school student.

Advanced level questions

READING Mini Test 10: Explanation

Page 41

1 A 2 B 3 C 4 lives 5 D 6 C

1 This is a **fact-finding type of question**. The answer is a fact in the text. You read *There is also the difficult choice: stay and protect property, or leave early to save lives? This is the big question (see lines 1–2)*.

2 This is a **synthesis type of question**. To find the answer you have to read the whole text. You read *Each situation must be treated in a manner that best suits the individual family and property but there are some strategies that can help (see lines 3–4)*.The text is an example of an explanation or a recommended plan. It is an explanation of what to do in times of bushfire emergencies. Readers are told what to do before a bushfire approaches and what to do to protect property.

3 This is a **fact-finding type of question**. The answer is a fact in the text. You read *Who should leave before fire threatens? 1. Those people with little ability to fight fires or save themselves, e.g. children, the elderly and sick people (see lines 10–12)*.

4 This is an **inferring type of question**. To find the answer you have to 'read between the lines'. You read *Who should leave before fire threatens?*
1. Those people with little ability to fight fires or save themselves, e.g. children, the elderly and sick people (see lines 10–12). As the first step in the plan is about saving the lives of those who can't fight the fire, it implies that the fire-fighting plan is mainly about saving lives first and property second. Any fire-fighting plan must include an understanding of who should leave before it gets too dangerous. You also read *Those who plan to stay should have a survival kit (see line 21)*.

5 This is a **fact-finding type of question**. The answer is a fact in the text. You read *Who should leave before fire threatens? ... 5. People who have not carried out fire prevention maintenance of their homes—or who live next to properties that have a high fire risk (see lines 10–19)*. A neighbour's property could be a problem in a fire situation if the property is one with a high fire risk.

6 This is a **judgement type of question**. You read *Each family needs to have a plan prepared well before the summer fire season (see line 6)*. You also read *Each family should have a list of all the things to be taken. These may include important family documents, jewellery, family photo albums, computers and pets (see lines 7–9)*. The plan is mainly giving information to families. The situation is too dangerous for children to be making decisions. The information would be most useful to parents.

WRITING Mini Test 1: Persuasive text

Page 43

Marking checklist for a persuasive text

Tick each correct point. Read the student's work through once to get an overall view of their response.

Focus on general points

- ☐ Did it make sense?
- ☐ Did it flow? Were the points logical and relevant?
- ☐ Did the points arouse any reactions?
- ☐ Was the body of the writing mainly in third person?
- ☐ Did you want to read on?
- ☐ Were the arguments convincing?
- ☐ Has the writer been assertive (e.g. *is* is used rather than a less definite term)?
- ☐ Was the handwriting readable?
- ☐ Was the writing style suitable (i.e. objective, and not casual or dismissive) for a persuasive text?

Now focus on the detail. Read each of the following points and find out whether the student's work has these features.

Focus on content

- ☐ Did the opening sentence(s) focus on the topic?
- ☐ Was the writer's point of view established early in the writing?
- ☐ Did the writer include any evidence to support his or her opinion?
- ☐ Did the writer include information relevant to his or her experiences?

Year 5 Writing Mini Test Answers

- ☐ Were the points/arguments raised by the writer easy to follow?
- ☐ Did the writing follow the format with an introduction, the body of the text and a conclusion?
- ☐ Were personal opinions included?
- ☐ Was the concluding paragraph relevant to the topic?

Focus on structure, vocabulary, grammar, spelling, punctuation

- ☐ Was there a variety of sentence lengths, types and beginnings?
- ☐ Was a new paragraph started for each additional argument or point?
- ☐ Has the writer used any similes (e.g. *as clear as crystal*) to stress a point raised?
- ☐ Did the writer avoid approximations such as *probably, perhaps* and *maybe*?
- ☐ Did the writer use such phrases as *I know* and *It is important to*?
- ☐ Did the writer refer to the question in the points raised? (A good way to do this is to use the keywords from the question or the introduction.)
- ☐ Has the writer used any less common words correctly?
- ☐ Was indirect speech used correctly?
- ☐ Were adjectives used to improve descriptions (e.g. *expensive buildings*)?
- ☐ Were adverbs used effectively (e.g. *firstly*)?
- ☐ Were capital letters used where they should have been?
- ☐ Was punctuation correct?
- ☐ Was the spelling of words correct?

Writing samples

Go to **pages 124–126** for Standard, Intermediate and Advanced Writing samples for Mini Test 1.

WRITING Mini Test 2: Narrative text

Page 45

Marking checklist for a narrative text

Tick each correct point. Read the student's work through once to get an overall view of their response.

Focus on general points

- ☐ Did it make sense?
- ☐ Did it flow?
- ☐ Did the story arouse any feeling?
- ☐ Did you want to read on?
- ☐ Did the story create suspense?
- ☐ Was the handwriting readable?

Now focus on the detail. Read each of the following points and find out whether the student's work has these features.

Focus on content

- ☐ Did the opening sentence(s) 'grab' the reader's interest?
- ☐ Was the setting established (i.e. where the action takes place)?
- ☐ Was the reader told when the action takes place?
- ☐ Was it clear who the main character(s) is/are? (The story can be in first person using *I*.)
- ☐ Was there a 'problem' to be solved early on in the writing?
- ☐ Was a complication or unusual event introduced?
- ☐ Did descriptions refer to any of the senses (e.g. *cold air, strange smell*)?
- ☐ Was there a climax (a more exciting part near the end)?
- ☐ Was the conclusion (resolution of the problem) believable?

Focus on structure, vocabulary, grammar, spelling, punctuation

- ☐ Was there a variety of sentence types, lengths and beginnings?
- ☐ Was a new paragraph begun for each change in time, place or action?
- ☐ Were conversations or direct speech in separate paragraphs for each change of speaker?
- ☐ Was a range of *said* words used for speech?
- ☐ Were any similes used (e.g. *as clear as glass*)?
- ☐ Were less common words used correctly?
- ☐ Were adjectives used to improve descriptions (e.g. *careful steps*)?
- ☐ Were adverbs used to make actions more interesting (e.g. *shook his head sadly*)?
- ☐ Were capital letters used where they should have been?
- ☐ Was punctuation correct?
- ☐ Was the spelling correct?

Writing samples

Go to **pages 127–129** for Standard, Intermediate and Advanced Writing samples for Mini Test 2.

Year 5 Writing Mini Test Answers

WRITING Mini Test 3: Recount text

Page 47

Marking checklist for a recount text

Tick each correct point. Read the student's work through once to get an overall view of their response.

Focus on general points

- ☐ Did it make sense?
- ☐ Did it flow?
- ☐ Did the story arouse any feeling?
- ☐ Did you want to read on? (Were the events interesting?)
- ☐ Was the handwriting readable?

Now focus on the detail. Read each of the following points and find out whether the student's work has these features.

Focus on content

- ☐ Did the opening sentence(s) introduce the subject of the recount?
- ☐ Was the setting established (i.e. where the action takes place)?
- ☐ Was the reader told when the action took place?
- ☐ Was it clear who the main character(s) was/were?
- ☐ Were personal pronouns used (e.g. *I, we, our*)?
- ☐ Were the events recorded in chronological (time) order?
- ☐ Was the recount in the past tense?
- ☐ Did the writing include some personal comments on the events (e.g. *feeling cold, disappointed*)?
- ☐ Did descriptions make any reference to any of the senses (e.g. *loud commentary, salty air*)?
- ☐ Were interesting details included?
- ☐ Was the conclusion satisfactory?

Focus on structure, vocabulary, grammar, spelling, punctuation

- ☐ Was there a variety of sentence lengths and beginnings?
- ☐ Did a new paragraph begin with every change in time, place or action?
- ☐ Were subheadings used (optional)?
- ☐ Were adjectives used to improve descriptions (e.g. *frozen ground*)?
- ☐ Were adverbs used to make actions more interesting (e.g. *swam strongly*)?
- ☐ Were adverbs used for time changes (e.g. *later, soon, then*)?
- ☐ Were similes used (e.g. *as clear as glass*)?
- ☐ Were less common words used correctly?
- ☐ Was direct and indirect speech used appropriately?
- ☐ Were capital letters used where they should have been?
- ☐ Was the punctuation correct?
- ☐ Was the spelling correct?

Writing samples

Go to **pages 130–132** for Standard, Intermediate and Advanced Writing samples for Mini Test 3.

Year 5 Literacy Sample Test Answers

Standard level

CONVENTIONS OF LANGUAGE

Sample Test 1

Pages 49–52

1 D (Standard level) **2 B** (Standard level) **3 C** (Standard level) **4 B** (Intermediate level) **5 was, looking** (Standard level) **6 A** (Standard level) **7 D** (Standard level) **8 B** (Standard level) **9 C** (Intermediate level) **10 D** (Intermediate level) **11 B** (Advanced level) **12 C** (Standard level) **13 A** (Intermediate level) **14 A** (Intermediate level) **15 B** (Standard level) **16 C** (Intermediate level) **17 D** (Intermediate level) **18 B** (Intermediate level) **19 , (comma)** (Standard level) **20 C** (Standard level) **21 B** (Advanced level) **22 C** (Intermediate level) **23 D** (Advanced level) **24 A** (Standard level) **25 B** (Intermediate level) **26 born** (Standard level) **27 because** (Standard level) **28 coming** (Standard level) **29 enemies** (Intermediate level) **30 blossom** (Standard level) **31 vacant** (Standard level) **32 beautiful** (Intermediate level) **33 rattling** (Standard level) **34 speeding** (Standard level) **35 quitting** (Standard level) **36 broken** (Standard level) **37 clubs** (Standard level) **38 diamonds** (Intermediate level) **39 hearts** (Standard level) **40 spades** (Standard level) **41 unusual** (Intermediate level) **42 varnish** (Intermediate level) **43 fake** (Standard level) **44 bombing** (Standard level) **45 deserve** (Advanced level) **46 countryside** (Standard level) **47 marsupials** (Intermediate level) **48 parched** (Intermediate level) **49 regions** (Standard level) **50 carnivorous** (Advanced level)

1 *Steal* is an irregular verb. Most verbs in English form their past tenses by adding ***ed*** (e.g. *he walked*). There are a number of irregular verbs when this doesn't happen, so the past of *steal* is *stolen* instead of 'stealed'. With the verb *stolen* you need a 'helper'—another verb to 'help' it. *Were* and *was* can be helping verbs.

2 Adjectives can be used to compare. *Good* is used to describe one party. *Better* is used to compare two parties. *Best* is used when comparing three or more parties. Remember: *good, better, best*. 'Bestest' is not a word. It is a double use of ***est***.

3 *Where* can be used to ask a question about time. The word *where* can also be used as a conjunction (joining word) or an adverb (helping a verb). The correct option is a question which needs to end with a question mark. The other options are not question sentences.

4 *It* is a singular pronoun used to refer to objects or things. There was only one bowl. The soup was a combination of chilli and pumpkin. Using *it* saves repeating the full name of the soup, which could sound awkward. *They* is generally used to refer to people or animals.

5 There are two verbs in the sentence. Verbs can be action words or the verb *to be*. *Looking* is an action verb (doing something). *Was* is a form of the verb *to be*.

6 *Brightly* is an adverb adding meaning to the verb *twinkling*. Many adverbs end in ***ly***. *Bright* and *brighter* are adjectives. *Brightness* is a noun.

7 *Tell* is an irregular verb. Most verbs in English form their past tenses by adding ***ed*** (e.g. *he walked*). There are a number of irregular verbs when this doesn't happen, so the past of *tell* is *told* instead of 'telled'.

8 Adjectives can be used to compare. *Strong* is used to describe one light. *Stronger* is used to compare two lights: the light from stars and planets. *Strongest* is used when comparing three or more different strengths. *Strongly* is an adverb.

9 This is a sentence using indirect (or reported) speech. The actual words spoken are not recorded. A question is not asked; instead the reader is told that Gina had thought about a certain question.

10 *Wire* is used as a verb. It is the action undertaken by the electrician.

11 There is only one club. The apostrophe goes before the ***s*** (***'s***). Don't be distracted by the fact that a club is made up of many members.

12 When talking about things that can be counted the word *many* should be used. When talking about uncountable nouns, such as sand or grass or air, the correct word is *much*.

13 Only the actual words spoken must be in speech marks: *"Is cricket a popular game?"* Notice that the question mark is also included.

14 Commas are used in lists where there are more than two items (*Cars, trucks*). *And* is used between the last two items (*trucks and huge buses*) in the series or list. There is no comma between *huge* and *buses* as the combined words refer to one type of vehicle.

15 *Don't* is a shortened word for *do not*. An apostrophe is used to indicate a letter (***o***) has been left out.

Year 5 Literacy Sample Online-style Test Answers

16 *But* is a conjunction or joining word. It is used to join two separate ideas with the intention of introducing an idea that is contrary to what has been already said: *Fran's friend has no electricity (for lights) but instead has candles*.

17 The full stop is used to complete a statement that includes direct speech when the statement begins with the words spoken and concludes with a statement on who spoke the words (*Fran asked*).

18 *Well* carries the meaning of being satisfactory or sufficient. *Good* is an adjective often misused for *well*. *All right* cannot follow *very*.

19 Although the sentence begins with *how* it is not a question. The speaker is making a statement. The actual words spoken conclude with a comma before adding the phrase *said the driver*.

20 The proper nouns include *Darwin*, *Cyclone Tracy* and *Christmas*. *City* and *morning* are common nouns.

21 Abbreviations that consist of more than one capital letter or of capital letters only do not require a full stop (e.g. *HMAS*, *GB*). *GPO* stands for *General Post Office*.

22 For measurements in their abbreviated form there is no full stop, even if the last letter is not part of the abbreviation (e.g. *m* represents *metre* and *mg* represents *milligram*).

23 *An* is used before nouns or adjectives (describing words) that begin with a vowel sound. *Hour* begins with a silent ***h*** and follows *an*.

24 In most shortened words the full stop is not required if the shortened word has the last letter of the word (e.g. *Mister—Mr*, *Street—St*). A capital letter is required for a title.

25 Common nouns are the general names for things, e.g. *boy*. Proper nouns are the names for specific things and have a capital letter, e.g. *Adam*.

26 The letter combinations ***or*** and ***our*** can make the same sound. The ***ourn*** combination is much less common than ***orn***. Learn to recognise groups of words that fit into each group (e.g. *born*, *corn*, *horn* and *mourn*). The final ***e*** is unnecessary.

27 *Because* is a compound word: *be* + *cause*. The letters ***au*** and ***or*** can make the same sound. Learn to recognise groups of words that fit into each group (e.g. *clause*, *pause* and *horse*, *Morse*).

28 When words end with a consonant and ***e***, you should drop the ***e*** before adding ***ing***. Although *coming* sounds like it is spelt with a ***u*** it is actually an ***o***.

29 You can have *one enemy* but *many enemies*. When making plurals of words that end with a consonant and ***y***, you should change the ***y*** to ***i*** before adding ***es*** (e.g. *pony—ponies*, *fairy—fairies*, *family—families*).

30 Make sure you spell *blossom* carefully. Remember: *blossom* has two ***o***s, as does *bloom*.

31 Make sure you pronounce *vacant* carefully: ***va*** + ***cant***. There are quite a few words that begin with ***vac*** (e.g. *vacuum*, *vacation*). A double ***cc*** after ***va*** is uncommon.

32 *Beauty* + *full* should be spelt *beautiful*. When adding the suffix ***ful*** to a word it is spelt with a single ***l***. If the word (*beauty*) ends with a consonant and ***y***, you must change the ***y*** to ***i*** before adding the suffix ***ful***.

33 Remember: When adding ***ing*** to words ending with a consonant + ***e***, simply drop the ***e*** and add ***ing***. Examples are *hobble—hobbling*, *face—facing* and *hope—hoping*.

34 Because *speeding* has two vowels before the final consonant, the final consonant (***d***) is not doubled when the suffix ***ing*** is added.

35 Because *quitting* has only one vowel before the final consonant (***t***) the rule is to double the final consonant when the suffix ***ing*** is added.

36 Both ***oke*** and ***oak*** can represent the same sound, as in *joke* and *soak*. You should recognise and remember when to use the different spellings. Get to know the group of words with the ***oke*** spelling (e.g. *poke*, *yoke*).

37 *Clubs* is a common word especially in card games. To make the plural of *club* simply add an ***s***.

38 Make sure you pronounce *diamonds* carefully: ***dia*** + ***monds***.

39 *Hart* and *heart* are homonyms: words that sound the same but which are spelt differently. *Hart* refers to a male deer. *Heart* is the organ that pumps blood through the body. Remember when to use each word correctly. The ***e*** before the ***s*** is unnecessary.

40 The letter combination ***ade*** can have the same sound as ***aid***. Get to know groups of words with each spelling (e.g. *paid*, *raid* and *made*, *grade*).

41 *Unusual* is the word *usual* with a prefix: ***un*** + *usual*. There is no double ***n*** (***nn***) or double ***l*** (***ll***).

42 Make sure you pronounce *varnish* correctly: ***varn*** + ***ish***.

43 Both ***ake*** and ***aik*** can represent the same sound as in *bake* and *haiku*. (Note: ***aik*** is an uncommon letter combination.) Get to know groups of words with ***ake*** spellings (e.g. *lake*, *drake*).

44 There is a silent ***b*** in *bomb*. When adding the suffix ***ing*** there is no need for a double letter.

45 Make sure you pronounce *deserve* correctly: ***de*** + ***serve***. *Disserve* means to cause someone harm.

46 *Countryside* is a compound word: *country* + *side*. Make sure you pronounce *country* correctly. It is *country* not 'countery'.

47 *Marsupials* is a tricky word. It is an Australian word you must learn and remember how to spell.

48 *Parched* is the word *parch* with the suffix ***ed***. ***Arch*** is a fairly common letter combination. Get to know groups of words with ***arch*** spellings (e.g. *march*, *starch*).

49 Make sure you pronounce *regions* correctly. It is a word you must learn and remember how to spell.

50 Make sure you pronounce *carnivorous* correctly: ***car*** + ***niv*** + ***o*** + ***rous***. Remember that it comes from the word *carnivore*. This will help you keep the vowels in order.

Intermediate level

CONVENTIONS OF LANGUAGE

Sample Test 2

Pages 53–56

1 B (Intermediate level) **2 A** (Intermediate level) **3 A** (Standard level) **4 C** (Advanced level) **5 bright, yellow, small** (Intermediate level) **6 B** (Standard level) **7 D** (Intermediate level) **8 D** (Standard level) **9 A** (Intermediate level) **10 B** (Standard level) **11 C** (Advanced level) **12 C** (Intermediate level) **13 A** (Intermediate level) **14 B** (Standard level) **15 D** (Standard level) **16 A** (Intermediate level) **17 C** (Standard level) **18 B** (Intermediate level) **19 D** (Advanced level) **20 C** (Intermediate level) **21 B** (Advanced level) **22 A** (Standard level) **23 D** (Intermediate level) **24 C** (Intermediate level) **25 forward** (Intermediate level) **26 levelling** (Intermediate level) **27 leisure** (Intermediate level) **28 gravy** (Standard level) **29 busier** (Intermediate level) **30 territory** (Intermediate level) **31 javelin** (Advanced level) **32 parrot** (Standard level) **33 citizen** (Intermediate level) **34 forgetting** (Intermediate level) **35 audience** (Intermediate level) **36 weary** (Intermediate level) **37 straight** (Intermediate level) **38 wriggly** (Intermediate level) **39 carriage** (Advanced level) **40 perpendicular** (Advanced level) **41 notice** (Standard level) **42 contractors** (Advanced level) **43 plentiful** (Intermediate level) **44 where** (Intermediate level) **45 expect** (Intermediate level) **46 recent** (Intermediate level) **47 corner** (Standard level) **48 fibres** (Intermediate level) **49 flavour** (Intermediate level) **50 kidney** (Intermediate level)

1 *Ring* is an irregular verb. Most verbs in English form their past tenses by adding ***ed*** (e.g. *he walked*). There are a number of irregular verbs when this doesn't happen, so the past of *ring* is *rang* instead of 'ringed'.

2 The sentences are in past tense. The event happened yesterday. *Were* is the past tense of the verb. *You* may refer to a single person but it is a pronoun. The pronoun *you* takes a plural verb regardless of the number of people it refers to.

3 The word *hers* is a possessive pronoun and does not require an apostrophe ***s***. Using *hers* saves repeating the full phrase, which could sound awkward.

4 This is a sentence using indirect (or reported) speech. The actual words spoken are not recorded. A question is not asked but the reader is told a question was asked.

5 There are three adjectives in the sentence. Adjectives describe nouns, giving such information as size, shape and appearance.

6 Singular subjects (nouns) need singular verbs; plural subjects (nouns) need plural verbs. *Hot Water Beach* is the three-word name of a place and is singular. The correct verb is *has*. If there were several beaches, the verb would be *have*.

7 The word *your* is a pronoun. It is not a contraction for *you are*. 'Yer' is not a word.

8 Singular subjects (nouns) need singular verbs; plural subjects (nouns) need plural verbs. *Hot water* is singular. The correct verb is *comes*. *Water* is not often used in the plural form. When it is, the correct verb would be *come*.

9 The word *their* is a possessive pronoun. Using *their* saves repeating the full phrase, which could sound awkward. *Them* is usually the object of the verb.

10 Adjectives are words that describe people, places or things. *Top* in option B describes a place in the street.

11 *Each* is an indefinite pronoun which takes a singular form but often has the plural meaning of 'each one': in this case, every baker (i.e. all the bakers) gave a cake for the banquet.

12 *Low* is correct because it refers to a temperature below average. It is the opposite of *high*. *Small*, *short* and *little* have more to do with physical size.

13 The unnecessary word is *annual*. A wedding anniversary is a yearly (or annual) occurrence. *Annual* is redundant. No meaning is lost by omitting *annual*.

Year 5 Literacy Sample Online-style Test Answers

14 The full stop follows *house*. The next word is *It* with a capital letter, indicating the start of a new sentence.

15 The word *the* is called a definite article. It is used to refer to a particular person or thing. In this case it refers to the latest edition. *A* and *an* are incorrect because they are used for things in general.

16 *Think* is an irregular verb. Most verbs in English form their past tenses by adding ***ed*** (e.g. *he walked*). There are a number of irregular verbs when this doesn't happen, so the past of *think* is *thought* instead of 'thinked'.

17 *To* is a preposition (*to the library*). Prepositions tell about position. The preposition *to* refers to motion in general, in a certain direction. Certain prepositions tend to go with particular situations (e.g. *to a particular place* but *into the hut*). They have to be learnt and remembered.

18 *Had been* is past tense. It is called a past participle. It is made up of a verb and a helper (*had*). *Five dollars* is treated as a singular subject.

19 *Ponies* is a plural noun. The clue is in the word *tails* which shows there was more than one pony. To show ownership by more than one pony, the apostrophe goes after the ***s*** (***s'***).

20 Commas are used in lists where there are more than two items (*boxes, bags, cartons*). *And* is used between the last two items (*bags and cartons*) in the series or list. Don't be distracted by the adjectival phrases describing what is in each container (e.g. *boxes of toys*).

21 The word *clock* is the last word in a question asked by Bruce. Notice that the question mark comes before the closing speech mark.

22 The word *father* is a common noun and does not require a capital letter.

23 The word *they're* is an abbreviation for *they are*. The apostrophe shows that a letter (***a***) has been left out. *It* is incorrect because it refers to just one thing.

24 *Gently* is an adverb which refers to how Bruce should *push*. Many adverbs end in ***ly***. *Gentle* is an adjective. 'Gentlely' is not a word or the correct spelling for *gentle* + ***ly***.

25 The word *forward* is unnecessary. *Looking to the future* means 'looking forward'. Using both terms is simply a matter of repeating unnecessary information.

26 The double ***l*** ending in two-syllable words is uncommon. However, when adding a suffix, it is common practice to double the final ***l*** (e.g. *rebelling, cancelling, patrolling*).

27 *Leisure* is a tricky word to spell. In this question the ***i*** and the ***e*** have swapped positions. The Standard general rule is ***i*** before ***e*** except after ***c***. It means that, in words where ***i*** and ***e*** fall together, the order is ***ie***, except directly following ***c***, when it is ***ei***. Examples are *friend*, *thief* and *ceiling*, *receive*. Beware: There are a number of exceptions to this rule and this is one of them.

28 The word *gravy* does not come from the word *grave*. There is no ***e*** in *gravy* (the brown sauce poured on meat).

29 *Busier* is *busy* + ***er***. When a word ends with the consonant ***y***, you must change the ***y*** to ***i*** before adding the suffix ***er***.

30 Make sure you spell *territory* correctly. The word is *territory*, not 'territery'.

31 *Javelin* is a word commonly used at school which you need to learn and remember how to spell.

32 Make sure you spell *parrot* correctly: *parrot*, not 'paret'. Take care to include the double ***r*** (***rr***).

33 The word *citizen* comes from *city*. The ***y*** was changed to ***i*** before the unusual suffix ***zen*** was added.

34 *Forget* is a combination of *for* and *get*. *Fore*, *for* and *four* (4) are homonyms, words that sound the same but which are spelt differently. *Fore* has the meaning of being in front. When adding ***ing*** to short words ending with a single vowel and a consonant you double the final consonant. Examples are *get—getting* and *rub—rubbing*.

35 *Audience* is a tricky word. The basic general rule is ***i*** before ***e*** except after ***c***. It means that, in words where ***i*** and ***e*** fall together, the order is ***ie***, except directly following ***c***, when it is ***ei*** (e.g. *friend*, *thief* and *ceiling*, *receive*). Beware: There are a number of exceptions to this rule.

36 Many short words beginning with ***w*** are not spelt as they sound (e.g. *was*). *Weary* is a word you must learn and remember how to spell.

37 *Strait* and *straight* are homonyms, words that sound the same but which are spelt differently. A *strait* is a narrow strip of water that joins two larger bodies of water. *Straight* is an adjective meaning 'without bends'.

38 Before adding the suffix ***y*** to *wriggle* you must drop the ***e***.

39 The word *carriage* is: *carry* + *age*. When a word ends with the consonant ***y***, you should change the ***y*** to an ***i*** before adding the suffix ***age***.

40 Make sure you pronounce *perpendicular* correctly: ***per*** + ***pen*** + ***dic*** + ***u*** + ***lar***. It is a word commonly used at school which you must learn and remember how to spell.

41 ***Ice*** and ***ise*** are common suffixes. As a general rule, words that end with ***ice*** are nouns of some type and words that end with ***ise*** are verbs (e.g. *advice—advise*, *practice—practise*).

42 It is easy to confuse the word endings ***er*** and ***or***. The ***or*** ending often follows a ***t*** in many words (e.g. *actor*, *projector*, *visitor*).

43 *Plenty* + *full* is spelt *plentiful*. When adding the suffix ***ful*** to a word it is spelt with a single ***l***. If the word (*plenty*) ends with a consonant and ***y***, you must change the ***y*** to ***i*** before adding the suffix ***ful***.

44 *Wear* and *where* are homonyms, words that sound the same but which are spelt differently. *Wear* means 'having something on, such as clothes'. *Where* refers to a location. Learn to use each word correctly as they are both common words.

45 Make sure you pronounce *expect* correctly: *expect*, not 'expeck'. *Expect* has two syllables: ***ex*** + ***pect***. ***Pect*** is a common word ending (e.g. *suspect*, *respect*, *aspect*).

46 *Recent* has two syllables: ***re*** + ***cent***. *Recent* and *resent* are close to being homonyms. *Recent* refers to events happening not long ago. *Resent* can mean 'sent again' or 'having a feeling of being unjustly treated'. *Recent* and *resent* are words you need to learn and remember how to spell and use correctly.

47 *Corner* is a common word. Take time to learn to spell it correctly.

48 It is common in North America to spell many English words that end with ***re*** (e.g. *fibre*, *litre*, *theatre*) with ***er***. This is not acceptable in Australia.

49 It is common in North America to spell many English words that end with ***our*** (e.g. *honour*, *favour*, *labour*) with ***or***. This is not acceptable in Australia.

50 Make sure you pronounce *kidney* correctly: *kidney*, not 'kideny'.

Advanced level

CONVENTIONS OF LANGUAGE

Sample Test 3

Pages 57–60

1 later, peacefully (Advanced level) **2 D** (Intermediate level) **3 B** (Advanced level) **4 C** (Advanced level) **5 D** (Intermediate level) **6 D** (Advanced level) **7 A** (Intermediate level) **8 C** (Intermediate level) **9 C** (Advanced level) **10 B** (Intermediate level) **11 C** (Advanced level) **12 A** (Advanced level) **13 D** (Intermediate level) **14 B** (Advanced level) **15 D** (Advanced level) **16 D** (Advanced level) **17 A** (Intermediate level) **18 B** (Intermediate level) **19 C** (Advanced level) **20 A** (Advanced level) **21 D** (Advanced level) **22 C** (Intermediate level) **23 A** (Advanced level) **24 B** (Intermediate level) **25 D** (Advanced level) **26 actually** (Intermediate level) **27 cartridges** (Advanced level) **28 fluttered** (Intermediate level) **29 grieved** (Standard level) **30 aquarium** (Advanced level) **31 wishbone** (Standard level) **32 crater** (Standard level) **33 cyclones** (Standard level) **34 campaign** (Advanced level) **35 archery** (Intermediate level) **36 terrible** (Standard level) **37 parallel** (Advanced level) **38 oblique** (Advanced level) **39 hyphen** (Advanced level) **40 microscope** (Intermediate level) **41 automobile** (Intermediate level) **42 required** (Standard level) **43 refrigerator** (Advanced level) **44 palms** (Intermediate level) **45 unnecessary** (Advanced level) **46 compasses** (Intermediate level) **47 billabongs** (Advanced level) **48 submerged** (Advanced level) **49 varies** (Advanced level) **50 numerous** (Advanced level)

1 There are two adverbs in the sentence. Adverbs tell when and how things are done. Many *how*-type adverbs end in ***ly***.

2 Singular subjects (nouns) need singular verbs; plural subjects (nouns) need plural verbs. In this case *are* must be used because the subject is *prices*. There are many prices. The event is reported in the present tense.

3 The unnecessary words are *from view*. When an object disappears it is no longer in view. *From view* is superfluous. No meaning is lost by omitting *from view*.

4 *To* is a preposition. It is commonly accepted practice to use *to* with *similar* (*similar to*). Certain prepositions tend to go with particular situations (e.g. *different from*). They have to be learnt and remembered.

5 The comma separates items in a list or series (*small, medium*) if there are more than two items.

And is used between the last two items in a list (*medium and large*), and also if there are only two items in the list. A comma is not necessary. A series can be made up of adjectives as well as nouns.

6 It is usual for the first word in a line of poetry (limerick) to have a capital letter. *Who* is correct as it refers to a person (a young man). *Which* is used to refer to animals and things. *That* is more often used to refer to something special.

7 The word *he'd* is a shortened word for *he would*. An apostrophe is used to indicate letters (***woul***) have been left out.

8 *Eat* is an irregular verb. Most verbs in English form their past tenses by adding ***ed*** (e.g. *he walked*). There are a number of irregular verbs when this doesn't happen, so the past of *eat* is *ate* instead of 'eated'. 'Et' is not a word.

9 *Water* is an uncountable noun. We don't say *many water*. *Wasn't some* would be incorrect. *Wasn't no* would also be incorrect. In English we do not put two negative words together, such as *not* and *no*.

10 *Shine* is an irregular verb. Most verbs in English form their past tenses by adding ***ed*** (e.g. *he walked*). There are a number of irregular verbs when this doesn't happen, so the past of *shine* is *shone* instead of 'shined'. 'Shineded' is not a word.

11 *Anne* with an apostrophe ***s*** shows that the face belongs to Anne, and to Anne alone.

12 There is a full stop after *blinked*. *Suddenly* is the beginning of a new sentence. *Sudden* is incorrect as it is an adjective.

13 The comma indicates a pause and not the end of the sentence.

14 *Which* is a common pronoun used to refer to animals or things, such as *house*. *Which* often follows a comma. *Who* is used to refer to people. *What* is most often used to ask a question. *That* is used to refer to, or point out, a particular thing.

15 Adjectives are words that describe people, places or things. *Spring* in Option D describes the type of blossoms making the display.

16 *Me* is correct. Think of the example as having two sentences: *He will give them to Bobby* and *He will give them to me*. *Me* is the object of an action. (*I* is the subject.)

17 *Strange* is the last word in a question starting with *Why*. The following word (*She*) is the beginning of a new sentence and paragraph.

18 *By* indicates that the mother is *beside* or *close* to the stove. *To* is used to indicate a direction. Certain prepositions tend to go with particular situations (e.g. *by the roadside*). They have to be learnt and remembered.

19 The sentence starts with a quoted question (in speech marks) and ends with a full stop.

20 The statement *Anne said she hadn't* is an example of indirect, or reported, speech. The actual words Anne said are not used. If the actual words were used, Anne would have referred to herself as *I*. The next sentence is also in indirect speech.

21 *Them* is a pronoun. *Them* is used because it is the object of the verb. Using *them* saves repeating the full phrase, which could sound awkward. *They* is used as a subject, usually closer to the beginning of a sentence.

22 *Bravely* is an adverb describing how the players played their game. *Many* and *high* are adjectives describing specific actions.

23 Abbreviations that consist of more than one capital letter or of capital letters only do not require a full stop (e.g. *HMAS*, *WA*). *DVD* stands for *Digital Video (or Versatile) Disc*. The ***s*** indicates there is more than one. The ***'s*** is unnecessary.

24 Apostrophes can show ownership or belonging. As there is only one tray (*Mum's favourite*) the apostrophe comes before the ***s*** (***'s***). The plural form of *tray* is *trays*.

25 *Themselves* is a reflexive pronoun that refers to *the children*.

26 *Actually* has a double ***l*** (***ll***). It is *actual* with the suffix ***ly***.

27 Make sure you pronounce *cartridges* correctly. The word is *cartridges*, not 'caridges'.

28 Many longer words that end with ***er*** do not double the ***r*** before adding the suffix ***ed*** (e.g. *bothered*, *staggered*). Beware: There are a number of exceptions to this rule.

29 *Grieved* is *grieve* + ***d***. A Standard general rule is ***i*** before ***e*** except after ***c***. This means in words where ***i*** and ***e*** fall together, the order is ***ie***, except directly following ***c***, when it is ***ei***. Examples are ***ie*** in words like *friend* and *thief*, and ***ei*** in words like *ceiling* and *receive*. Beware: There are a number of exceptions to this rule.

30 *Aqua* means water and ***(r)ium*** is a common suffix referring to a particular place (e.g. *emporium*, *solarium*).

31 *Wishbone* is a compound word: *wish* + *bone*.

32 Make sure you read and pronounce *crater* carefully. A *creator* is someone who creates something, such as an artist. Remember: *crater* has an ***er*** ending.

33 *Cyclone* has a final ***e***. Get to know the group of words with the ***one*** spelling (e.g. *telephone*, *baritone*).

34 *Campaign* has a silent ***g***. There are a few common words that have a silent ***g*** before an ***n*** (e.g. *align*, *gnome*, *reign* and *foreign*).

35 Make sure you pronounce *archery* carefully: *archery*, not 'archary'. *Archery* is *archer* + ***y***. The ***y*** suffix is often used as a suffix of nouns which denote occupation, business or interest (e.g. *bakery*, *robbery*).

36 Make sure you pronounce *terrible* carefully: *terrible*, not 'terrable'.

37 *Parallel* is a tricky word. The only doubled letter is the ***l*** inside the word. *Parallel* is a word commonly used at school which you must learn and remember how to spell.

38 *Oblique* is a word commonly used at school which you must learn and remember how to spell.

39 The ***ph*** in *hyphen* has an ***f*** sound but is spelt with a ***ph***. ***Ph*** for ***f*** is common in English (e.g. *phone*, *photograph*). *Hyphen* is a word commonly used at school which you must learn and remember how to spell.

40 *Microscope* is *micro* + *scope*. ***Micro*** is a prefix relating to smallness. ***Scope*** suggests a type of instrument.

41 *Automobile* is *auto* + *mobile*. ***Auto*** is a prefix meaning 'self'. It is a common prefix (e.g. *automatic*, *autograph*). *Mobile* means 'moving'.

42 *Required* is not an ***ie*** word. *Required* is a common word which you should learn and remember how to spell.

43 Although the short word for *refrigerator* is *fridge*, which is spelt with a ***d***, it is incorrect in the full word.

44 *Palms* has a silent ***l***. A silent ***l*** is common before an ***m*** (e.g. *calm*, *almond*, *salmon*).

45 *Unnecessary* is the word *necessary* with the prefix ***un***. It has a double ***n*** (***nn***).

46 Make sure you pronounce *compasses* carefully: ***com*** + ***pass*** + ***es***. *Compasses* is a word commonly used at school which you must learn and remember how to spell.

47 *Billabongs* is an Aboriginal word that has become part of English vocabulary and which you must learn and remember how to spell.

48 *Submerged* is the word *merged* with the prefix ***sub***. There are no English words with the letter combination of ***rdge***.

49 Make sure you pronounce *varies* carefully. 'Veries' is not a word. *Very* and *vary* are similar-sounding words which are spelt differently. *Very* is an adjective (e.g. *very hot*) and *vary* is a verb meaning 'change something'.

50 The ***o*** and the ***u*** have swapped places in the incorrect spelling. The ***uos*** ending is rare in the English language.

READING Sample Test 1

Pages 61–67

Go to **inside back cover** for a guide to question types.

1 escape a bushfire (Standard level) **2 A** (Standard level) **3 C** (Standard level) **4 D** (Intermediate level) **5 A** (Intermediate level) **6 B** (Intermediate level) **7 D** (Standard level) **8 C** (Standard level) **9 A, C** (Intermediate level) **10 B** (Intermediate level) **11 D** (Intermediate level) **12 It is an explanation of how the valley evolved over centuries.** (Advanced level) **13 A** (Intermediate level) **14 C, E** (Standard level) **15 D** (Intermediate level) **16 B** (Standard level) **17 C** (Advanced level) **18 Greg Holfeld** (Standard level) **19 A** (Standard level) **20 B** (Standard level) **21 D** (Intermediate level) **22 A** (Intermediate level) **23 B** (Advanced level) **24 C** (Standard level) **25 A** (Standard level) **26 B** (Standard level) **27 D** (Advanced level) **28 A** (Standard level) **29 The narrator was too scared to move.** (Standard level) **30 C** (Standard level) **31 A** (Standard level) **32 D** (Advanced level) **33 (4, 3, 1, 2)** (Advanced level) **34 D** (Advanced level) **35 A** (Intermediate level) **36 B** (Standard level) **37 carried on a stretcher** (Standard level) **38 A** (Advanced level) **39** ***Scarecrow*** **A, D;** ***Normanby Woman*** **B, C** (Intermediate level)

A Dreamtime legend

1 This is a **fact-finding type of question**. The answer is a fact in the text. You read *In a short time the whole mountainside was on fire and the two young brothers were trapped* (see lines 12–13) and *The brothers were frantic, they could barely breathe because of the smoke, and with a great effort they began to climb higher up the cliff until they reached the uppermost tip* (see lines 16–17).

2 This is a **fact-finding type of question**. The answer is a fact in the text. You read that *they eventually decided to light a fire, hoping that the flames and smoke would drive the flies away. It did* (see lines 10–11).

3 This is a **fact-finding type of question**. The answer is a fact in the text. You read that *they eventually decided to light a fire, hoping that the flames and smoke would drive the flies away* (see lines 10–11).

4 This is an **inferring type of question**. To find the answer you have to 'read between the lines'. You read *The ancestors, who had been watching, had taken pity on them and given them the power of flight to escape the flames. With relief the two men realised they were at last safe and they made their camp in the sky world (see lines 22–24)*. Combine this information with your own knowledge and understanding of legends to work out the final answer. The ancestors must have been watching from a faraway place. The brothers' new camp was in the sky. The ancestors are people of generations who are no longer alive. They are spirits, not living people.

5 This is a **judgement type of question**. You read *the two men realised they were at last safe and they made their camp in the sky world where they remain till this day. At night their camp fires can still be seen as The Pointers, the two bright stars that point to the Southern Cross (see lines 23–25)*. Combine this information with your own knowledge to work out the final answer which is that the story is used to explain a natural event: why the two stars are in the sky.

6 This is a **fact-finding type of question**. The answer is a fact in the text. You read *the two men realised they were at last safe and they made their camp in the sky world where they remain till this day. At night their camp fires can still be seen as The Pointers, the two bright stars that point to the Southern Cross (see lines 23–25)*.

Wairere Boulders

7 This is a **fact-finding type of question**. The answer is a fact in the text. You read *Early settlers in the region had no explanation for how the hundreds of rocks were formed (see lines 13–14)*.

8 This is a **fact-finding type of question**. The answer is a fact in the text. You read *The rain fell through the Kauri leaves and branches, picking up a weak acid from the trees, which dripped onto the rocks below. Over many centuries the flutes developed (see lines 17–20)*.

9 This is a **language type of question**. To find the answer you have to read the text carefully: *The boulders in the valley have eroded in an unusual way. They have deep channels in them, called flutes or cuts. Some of the flutes are up to a metre deep and 35 centimetres wide (see lines 10–12)*. Combine this information with your own knowledge of word meanings: the word *channels* means 'grooves'. So the word *flutes* is a synonym for *grooves*.

10 This is a **fact-finding type of question**. The answer is a fact in the text. You read *The boulders in the valley are the eroded remains of a lava flow (see line 6)*. You also read *Lava on a clay base is unusual. As the clay washed away, large pieces of the basalt sheet broke off (see lines 7–8)*. The rocks became unstable because the clay ground became eroded.

11 This is an **inferring type of question**. To find the answer you have to 'read between the lines'. You need to look at the detail in the illustrations. You can see a person sitting next to the boulders. This gives an indication of the size of the boulders and the size of the grooves.

12 This is a **judgement type of question**. You read *The Wairere Boulders are an unusually large, chaotic mass of basalt boulders (see lines 1–2)*. You also read *The boulders in the valley are the eroded remains of a lava flow about three million years ago (see lines 6–7)*. The whole passage talks about how the boulders were created: the text is an explanation of how the valley was formed or how it changed/evolved over the centuries.

School Days

13 This is an **inferring type of question**. To find the answer you have to 'read between the lines' and look at the detail in the illustrations. You can see Kate saying *'I don't believe it! $50 million on pets' (see frame 2)*. From the way Kate says this and the look on her face you can see she feels the amount is unfair. She also complains that her allowance is *'just $5 a week!' (see frame 4)*. Ray feels it is all unfair: *'Pets get better, faster health care than people!' (see frame 5)*. The exclamation marks help show their feelings. The children feel the money spent on pets is unfair.

14 This is an **inferring type of question**. To find the answer you have to 'read between the lines' and look at the detail in the illustrations. You can see Kate querying the truth of the report *(see frame 1)*, then saying *'I don't believe it! $50 million on pets' (see frame 2)*. She is shocked. *Dubious* suggests a lack of willingness to believe something.

15 This is an **inferring type of question**. To find the answer you have to 'read between the lines' and look at the detail in the illustrations. You can see Kate saying *'I don't believe it! $50 million on pets' (see frame 2)*. From the way Kate has said this and the look on her face you can see she feels the amount is unfair. She also complains that her allowance is *'just $5 a week!' (see frame 4)*. This is nothing like the money spent on pets.

16 This is an **inferring type of question**. To find the answer you have to 'read between the lines' and look at the detail in the illustrations. The dog and the cat look very excited about their conditions and prospects.

17 This is a **judgement type of question**. Throughout the cartoon strip there is an ongoing comparison between pet welfare and human welfare. Combine this with your own knowledge to work out the final answer. Some people would assert that this is out of proportion.

Graphic novel review

18 This is a **fact-finding type of question**. The answer is a fact in the text. You read *Illustrated by Greg Holfeld (see line 2)*.

19 This is an **inferring type of question**. To find the answer you have to 'read between the lines'. You read *this new call takes the pair to India. They have been asked to investigate the sudden death of the Maharaja (see lines 10–11)*. The paragraph mentions *Asterix* and *Tintin* and the book's characters but it mainly discusses all the elements of the plot or storyline.

20 This is a **fact-finding type of question**. The answer is a fact in the text. You read *this new call takes the pair to India. They have been asked to investigate the sudden death of the Maharaja (see lines 10–11)*.

21 This is a **language type of question**. To find the answer you have to read the text carefully, especially the section that is quoted: *Rumours abound (see line 13)*. Use your own knowledge of word meanings to work out the answer. *Rumours* are stories that have little to do with facts. They are gossip.

22 This is a **judgement type of question**. You read *not-quite-so-courageous offsider Pug (see line 9)*. You also read *Pug (now cunningly—if reluctantly—disguised as a woman (see lines 13–14)* and *Pug is the reluctant sidekick, expected to shine in roles he would not choose (see lines 23–24)*. A *sidekick* is a companion and usually a subordinate or assistant. *Reluctant* means 'half-hearted'. So Pug was a half-hearted assistant.

23 This is a **judgement type of question**. You read *It is an adventure in grand style (see line 18)*. You also read *There is plenty of humour here, along with the cracking-pace adventure (see line 21)* and *Recommended for mid-primary and beyond (see line 25)*. The reviewer had much praise for the graphic novel. It is *in the style of Asterix and Tintin (see lines 16–17)* which are highly acclaimed graphic novels. All the reviewer's comments are positive; the reviewer has a highly favourable opinion of the novel.

Ducks' Ditty

24 This is a **fact-finding type of question**. The answer is a fact in the text. You read *Ducks are a-dabbling, / Up tails all! (see lines 3–4)* and *Heads down, tails up, / Dabbling free! (see lines 15–16)*. You also read *We are down a-dabbling, / Up tails all! (see lines 19–20)*. The ducks have their heads under water looking for food in their 'larder'. *Dabbling* has one meaning of ducks searching for food on the bottom of shallow water by using their bills.

25 This is an **inferring type of question**. To find the answer you have to 'read between the lines'. You read *We like to be, / Heads down, tails up, / Dabbling free! (see lines 14–16)*. It doesn't matter to the ducks what other birds do; the ducks enjoy *dabbling free*. There is a sense of being carefree. Combine this with your own knowledge and understanding and with the rhythm of the poem, and you have a very definite impression that the ducks are carefree.

26 This is an **inferring type of question**. To find the answer you have to 'read between the lines'. You read *Ducks are a-dabbling, / Up tails all! (see lines 3–4)* and *Heads down, tails up, / Dabbling free! (see lines 15–16)*. You also read *Yellow bills all out of sight / Busy in the river! (see lines 7–8)* and *We are down a-dabbling, / Up tails all! (see lines 19–20)*. The ducks spend much of their time with their heads under water.

27 This is a **language type of question**. To find the answer you have to read the text carefully, especially the section that is quoted: *We like to be, / Heads down, tails up, / Dabbling free! (see lines 14–16)* and *We are down a-dabbling, / Up tails all! (see lines 19–20)*. *We* is a pronoun referring to all the ducks. Combine this with your own knowledge of how language is used in the text to come to a final answer. *We* is in italics because the poet wants to emphasise that the ducks don't care what other birds like to do; they (*we*) really like to do their own thing.

28 This is a **language type of question**. To find the answer you have to read the text carefully, especially the section that is quoted: *High in the blue above, Swifts whirl and call (see lines 17–18)*. Swifts are birds that whirl (fly around in circles). The *blue above* is a poetic expression for the daytime sky.

The Night of the Scarecrow

29 This is an **inferring type of question**. To find the answer you have to 'read between the lines'. You read that the narrator awoke suddenly after hearing a sudden *Tap. Tap-tap. Tap.* (line 13). The narrator was already tense in the opening paragraph: *But I was still tense. I jumped at every little noise* (see lines 2–3). Combining this information with your own knowledge of how people react to unexpected noises, you can work out that the narrator was too scared to move or draw attention to himself.

30 This is a **language type of question**. To find the answer you have to read the text carefully, especially the section that is quoted: *Then I saw it* (see line 44). *It* is a pronoun referring to a frightening sight: *Suddenly lit up and in the frame of the window was the face of a scarecrow* (see lines 44–45). *It* refers to the scarecrow—the pronoun is used to build tension by not immediately revealing to the reader what the narrator had seen.

31 This is a **fact-finding type of question**. The answer is a fact in the text. You read *Then it happened. Tap. Tap-tap. Tap. I awoke abruptly* (see lines 13–14).

32 This is a **language type of question**. To find the answer you have to read the text carefully, especially the section that is quoted: *I toyed with the idea* (see lines 24–25). Toys are playthings, so *toying with the idea* suggests that the narrator was not really serious and unlikely to act on his idea. The term is a saying and a metaphor and not intended to be taken literally.

33 This is a **fact-finding type of question**. The answer is a fact in the text. By reading the text carefully and noticing the correct order of things you can find the answer: The narrator goes to sleep (1). The parents switch off the lights (2). There is a tapping sound on Jenny's window (3). The narrator falls out of bed (4).

34 This is a **synthesis type of question**. To find the answer you have to read the whole text. The text is mainly about the events leading up to the frightening discovery that there is someone outside the window. The best title for the passage would be 'Face at the window'. Do not be distracted by minor details.

Normanby Woman

35 This is a **fact-finding type of question**. The answer is a fact in the text. You read that first the Normanby Woman *was eventually captured* (see line 5), then she was *put on a horse, to take her to a new home in Cooktown. Angry Aboriginals attacked the party, demanding her release* (see lines 8–9) but *in the commotion the woman's horse bolted and she was thrown* (see lines 10–11).

36 This is a **fact-finding type of question**. The answer is a fact in the text. You read *She died of her severe head injuries at the hospital on 30 August 1887, the day after she arrived* (see lines 13–14). The Normanby Woman was in Cooktown about a day because she died the day after she arrived.

37 This is a **fact-finding type of question**. The answer is a fact in the text. You read *Two Chinese men were hired to carry her by stretcher on the two-day walk to Cooktown* (see lines 11–12).

38 This is a **judgement type of question**. You read *Interest in the woman was high in Cooktown and locals were charged one shilling (about ten cents) to view the 'Normanby Woman'* (see lines 14–15). She was treated as an oddity and even though she was dying, people came to have a look. Combine this with your own knowledge of human behaviour and good manners: the local people could be described as inconsiderate.

39 The *Night of the Scarecrow* text is a fictional narrative. It is written for reading enjoyment in the first person (the narrator is *I*). *Normanby Woman* is a factual report describing an incident that developed on the goldfields.

READING Sample Test 2

Pages 68–74

1 A (Intermediate level) **2 D** (Standard level) **3 B** (Advanced level) **4 Feed pets indoors, feed chickens and ducks in a secure pen, don't leave food scraps in the open or stop adding seed to bird feeders for native birds if mynas are around** (Intermediate level) **5 B** (Standard level) **6 A** (Intermediate level) **7 B, F** (Intermediate level) **8 D, E** (Intermediate level) **9 3** (Intermediate level) **10 D** (Intermediate level) **11 A** (Intermediate level) **12 *Coconut palm* A, B: *Dark rendezvous* C, D** (Intermediate level) **13 B** (Standard level) **14 C** (Intermediate level) **15 D** (Intermediate level) **16 B** (Intermediate level) **17 A** (Advanced level) **18 a lady** (Intermediate level) **19 B** (Advanced level) **20 D** (Advanced level) **21 (4, 2, 1, 3)** (Intermediate level) **22 A** (Advanced level) **23 D** (Intermediate level) **24 56 000** (Standard level) **25 B** (Intermediate level) **26 D** (Intermediate level) **27 A** (Standard level) **28 B** (Intermediate level) **29 D** (Standard level) **30 C** (Intermediate level) **31 D** (Intermediate level) **32 B** (Advanced level) **33 A** (Advanced level) **34 Suggested answers: Lisa feels school sport is unnecessary, a waste of time, or sport is best as a community activity** (Intermediate level)

Year 5 Literacy Sample Online-style Test Answers

35 A (Intermediate level) **36 doors must be removed** (Intermediate level) **37 C** (Intermediate level) **38 3** (Intermediate level) **39 A** (Standard level)

The Indian Mynas

1 This is a **synthesis type of question**. To find the answer you have to read the whole text. You read that mynas *eat almost anything (see line 5)* and *Mynas have adapted to Australian conditions and breed quickly (see line 11)*. The text is mainly about the features and behaviour of mynas. Mynas are very adaptable.

2 This is a **fact-finding type of question**. The answer is a fact in the text. You read *They prefer urban environments where food and nesting sites are plentiful (see line 4)*; *The mynas also scavenge unattended pet food from urban backyards (see line 6)*; *Hundreds of mynas can roost in a single tree or building near a regular food source (see lines 16–17)* and *Mynas thrive where food is easy to get (see line 20)*.

3 This is a **language type of question**. To find the answer you have to read the text carefully. You read *mynas join larger groups and move to communal roosts (see line 14)*. The word *communal* in this sentence refers to many mynas. A *roost* is a place where birds rest or sleep. So a *communal roost* is one where many birds perch.

4 This is a **fact-finding type of question**. The answer is a fact in the text. You read in the section *Stop the invasion* that it is important to *stop putting out birdseed immediately (see line 23)*; *Feed pets inside or, if that is not possible, put pet food inside during the day (see line 24)*; *Feed chickens and ducks in a secure pen (see line 25)*.

5 This is a **fact-finding type of question**. The answer is a fact in the text. You read *They evict animals and birds from their nests and leave tree hollows that are mite-ridden and unusable by other wildlife (see lines 10–11)*.

6 This is an **inferring type of question**. To find the answer you have to 'read between the lines'. You read *Mynas thrive where food is easy to get (see line 20)* and then you are advised what to do with birdseed, pet food and domestic animal food. These tactics may help stop the invasion. It will help control the myna population.

Summer fun

7 This is a **synthesis type of question**. To find the answer you have to read the whole poem. The poem relates activities that the sailors do. You read that they *sail to distant sunny isles (see line 3)*, *swim on palm-fringed beaches (see line 7)* and *we'll eat fish we catch (see line 9)*. The sailors have a life of relaxed enjoyment and satisfying leisure.

8 This is a **language type of question**. To find the answer you have to read the text carefully. You read that the beaches were *palm-fringed (see line 7)*. Palms are trees. The word *palm-fringed* refers to something that is bordered or edged with palms. Combine this with your own knowledge of how language is used in the poem to come to a final answer. *Palm-fringed beaches* are ones where palms grow along the land side of the beach. It is a way to describe the beach poetically.

9 This is a **fact-finding type of question**. The answer is a fact in the text. You read in stanza 3: *For dinner we'll eat fish we catch / And pawpaws freshly cut (see lines 9–10)*. Stanza 3 is about the partaking of local produce. *Partake* can mean 'eat'. *Local produce* is food available locally. There is plenty available.

10 This is a **synthesis type of question**. To find the answer you have to read the whole poem. The poem is about what life on a sailing boat might be like: *To sail to distant sunny isles (see line 3)*; *We'll drop our anchor by the reef (see line 5)*; *And when we're tired of swimming … We'll gently sail away (see lines 13 and 16)*. Combine this with your knowledge of text types and their purpose. It is a poem intended to entertain. It doesn't have a serious purpose of informing or educating.

11 This is a **synthesis type of question**. To find the answer you have to read the whole poem. The poem is about what life on a sailing boat might be like: *To sail to distant sunny isles (see line 3)*; *We'll drop our anchor by the reef (see line 5)*; *And when we're tired of swimming … We'll gently sail away (see lines 13 and 16)*. A suitable title would be: 'Life at sea'. The other options in the question focus on less important detail.

The coconut palm

12 *The coconut palm* is a factual text. It informs the reader as well as explains the importance of the palm. The *Dark rendezvous* text is a fictional recount of an incident. The text is to engage the reader in recreational reading for enjoyment.

13 This is a **fact-finding type of question**. The answer is a fact in the text. You read *If the head of the coconut palm snaps off in strong winds then the tree dies (see lines 15–16)*.

Year 5 Literacy Sample Online-style Test Answers

14 This is a **language type of question**. To find the answer you have to read the text carefully, especially the section that is quoted: *A good-sized coconut can be larger than an adult's head and weigh several kilograms. And they float! (see lines 21–22)*. Exclamation marks are used to express surprise. It is surprising that something that big can float.

15 This is an **inferring type of question**. To find the answer you have to 'read between the lines'. You read *Every part of the tree has a use: leaves, fruit, trunk, bark and roots (see lines 8–9)*. You also read *the coconut palm is called the Tree of Life (see line 8)* and that *They are a source of food and drink, a provider of building materials and materials for fishing and farming (see lines 9–10)*. The writer is mainly impressed by the coconut palm because of its many practical uses. The other options are minor aspects of the palm.

16 This is a **fact-finding type of question**. The answer is a fact in the text. You read *there are different types of coconut palms (see line 11)*.

17 This is a **language type of question**. To find the answer you have to read the text carefully. Words in certain contexts carry special meaning. You read *It has a long slender trunk that bends and sways, without snapping off during most tropical cyclones (see line 13)*. The word *slender* is what suggests that coconut palms can withstand high winds.

Dark rendezvous

18 This is a **fact-finding type of question**. The answer is a fact in the text. You read *He looks around expecting to see the lady (see line 22)*.

19 This is a **language type of question**. To find the answer you have to read the text carefully. Words in certain contexts carry special meaning. You read *It looms above his head (see line 15)* and *Across the ground is a tangle of struggling vines (see line 17)*. The words *struggling* and *looms* carry the suggestion of danger.

20 This is a **language type of question**. To find the answer you have to read the text carefully, especially the section that is quoted: *There is a low tide smell stealing up from the bay (see line 6)*. The words *low tide smell* suggest something nasty and foul. *Stealing* is a metaphor that suggests dishonesty. The overall suggestion is that the smell is sinister.

21 This is a **fact-finding type of question**. The answer is a fact in the text. Read the text carefully and notice the correct order of things: 1. Brett crosses a road near a major intersection. 2 Brett makes his way up an access ramp. 3. Brett waits for the lights to turn green. 4. Brett hears a goods train shunting.

22 This is a **synthesis type of question**. To find the answer you have to read the whole text to determine what mood (the atmosphere or feeling) the text has created. You read Brett went to a *mystery site (see line 2)*; *he looks around almost guiltily. He feels like an intruder (see lines 10–11)*; *Their little paw-like flowers, with torn fingernails, seem to be reaching out desperately for help (see line 18)*; *Their crashing makes him shudder (see lines 20–21)* and *He wonders if she might be watching him intruding into her special place (see lines 22–23)*. *Foreboding* means 'a feeling of something bad about to happen'. The passage has a foreboding mood.

23 This is an **inferring type of question**. To find the answer you have to 'read between the lines'. You read *He looks around expecting to see the lady and relaxes a little (see line 22)*. Brett is somewhat disappointed, as this was the purpose of his visit, but he is also relieved.

Volcano erupts

24 This is a **fact-finding type of question**. The answer is a fact in the text. You read *As many as 56 000 people were warned to leave their homes (see lines 27–28)*.

25 This is a **fact-finding type of question**. The answer is a fact in the text. You read *The volcano, located just 60 kilometres from Mexico City, had been rumbling and spewing smoke for almost 12 hours. According to a volcano expert this is an indication that the volcano was about to blow (see lines 6–12)*.

26 This is a **fact-finding type of question**. The answer is a fact in the text. You read *Two thousand soldiers were called in to control the evacuation of twenty villages in the danger zones (see lines 35–38)*.

27 This is a **fact-finding type of question**. The answer is a fact in the text. You read *These people are so poor they are afraid that their homes will be looted and that their basic possessions will take years to replace (see lines 55–59)*.

28 This is a **synthesis type of question**. To find the answer you have to read the whole text. The report is objective. It relates facts as they have happened. You read *huge traffic jams blocked roads (see lines 42–43)*. It also relates plans that have been put into place. You read *soldiers were called in to control the evacuation (see lines 35–37)*. Combining this with your own knowledge and understanding of newspaper reports you can work out that the report is concerned with facts as they happen.

29 This is a **fact-finding type of question**. The answer is a fact in the text. You read that the Red Cross *feared that without proper control there could be a major outbreak of disease (see lines 69–71)*.

Lisa's essay

30 This is a **synthesis type of question**. To find the answer you have to read the whole text. The essay gives details and reasons for Lisa's opinion. Points are firmly made and backed up with evidence. For example, you read *pupils are only getting lessons for around 920 hours per year (see line 17)* and *About one-eighth of each child's year is spent on real education (see line 19)*. Lisa's essay is well thought out.

31 This is a **fact-finding type of question**. The answer is a fact in the text. You read *longer lessons, are the only ways to stop students wasting time (see lines 22–23)*.

32 This is a **language type of question**. To find the answer you have to read the text carefully. You read *Children have plenty of opportunity to play (or do nothing) outside school hours (see lines 9–10)*. The bracketed words are an additional example and a facetious comment on another way time is wasted.

33 This is a **judgement type of question**. You read *You may need a calculator (see line 12)*. Lisa is not afraid to have her facts checked. She is confident she is correct.

34 This is an **inferring type of question**. To find the answer you have to 'read between the lines'. You read *The times not spent in class at primary school are wasted (see line 3)*. You also read *Take out at least an hour for organised sport, which is also an out-of-school hour activity for many families (see lines 15–16)*. By her comments Lisa shows that she believes organised school sport is unnecessary, a waste of time, and is better if organised as a family/community activity.

35 This is a **fact-finding type of question**. The answer is a fact in the text. You read *In the schoolyard there are times when pupils are bullied, called names or simply ignored. There is a lot of time being bored or waiting for the bell to ring. There are studies that have said that the benefits of playtime are small (see lines 4–6)*.

Council Clean-up Dates 2011

36 This is a **fact-finding type of question**. The answer is a fact in the text. You read *It is a legal requirement that the doors be removed from stoves and fridges (see line 27)*.

37 This is a **fact-finding type of question**. The answer is a fact in the text. You read *Uncollected items must be removed within two days after collection has been completed (see line 31)*.

38 This is a **fact-finding type of question**. The answer is a fact in the text. You read that Rowlands Creek in Council Zone 1 has three Council Clean-up days: the first weeks in February, June and October.

39 This is a **fact-finding type of question.** The answer is a fact in the text. You read *medicines (return to your chemist) (see line 9)*.

READING Sample Test 3

Pages 75–81

1 A (Intermediate level) **2 the cat's rarity and beauty** (Advanced level) **3 B** (Intermediate level) **4 C** (Intermediate level) **5 A** (Intermediate level) **6 B** (Advanced level) **7 C** (Intermediate level) **8 (1, 4, 3, 2)** (Intermediate level) **9 bark** (Standard level) **10 the production of herbal medicines** (Intermediate level) **11 flower** (Standard level) **12 B** (Advanced level) **13 mischievous, naughty, impish, rascally** (Advanced level) **14 C** (Standard level) **15 D** (Standard level) **16 D, F** (Advanced level) **17 A** (Advanced level) **18 D** (Standard level) **19 B** (Advanced level) **20 C** (Advanced level) **21 A** (Intermediate level) **22 B** (Advanced level) **23 A** (Advanced level) **24 A** (Intermediate level) **25 D** (Advanced level) **26 its colour** (Standard level) **27 C** (Standard level) **28 pink** (Standard level) **29 B** (Advanced level) **30 B** (Intermediate level) **31 C** (Advanced level) **32 B** (Advanced level) **33 D** (Advanced level) **34 A** (Intermediate level) **35 A** (Intermediate level) **36 D** (Advanced level) **37 C** (Advanced level) **38 B** (Intermediate level) **39 Raymond's speech A, C; *Black Mountain* B, D** (Advanced level)

The Brazilian cat

1 This is an **inferring type of question**. To find the answer you have to 'read between the lines'. You read *The whole afternoon was occupied by an inspection of Everard's menagerie (see lines 8–9)*. You also read *I am about to show you the jewel of my collection (see line 16)*. The fact that the two men spend so long looking at the collection and that Everard calls the Brazilian cat the jewel of his collection implies that he is generally proud of his collection. Everard has a feeling of pride.

2 This is an **inferring type of question**. To find the answer you have to 'read between the lines'.

Year 5 Literacy Sample Online-style Test Answers

You read *There is only one other specimen in Europe, now that the Rotterdam cub is dead. It is a Brazilian cat* (see lines 17–19). You also read *I am about to show you the jewel of my collection* (see line 16). The Brazilian cat was a very rare type of cat. It was not only found in a remote area of Brazil but there was only one other specimen in Europe since another captive cat had died. The fact that Everard calls the Brazilian cat the jewel of his collection implies that he felt especially proud of his rare and beautiful acquisition.

3 This is an **inferring type of question**. To find the answer you have to 'read between the lines'. You read *It was an enormous and very well-kept black cat, and it cuddled up and basked in that yellow pool of light exactly as a cat would do* (see lines 28–31). You also read that it *yawned and rubbed its round, black head affectionately against his side, while he patted and fondled it* (see lines 50–52). Combine this with your own knowledge and understanding of cats to work out that Marshall likens the Brazilian cat to a domestic pet cat.

4 This is a **language type of question**. To find the answer you have to read the text carefully. You read that *We came to a heavy door with a sliding shutter* (see lines 11–12) and *stout bars extended across the passage* (see lines 14–15). The heavy door and bars indicate the room needed to be secure. You also read that in the room in which the cat lived there were *small, barred windows on the farther wall* (see lines 24–25). This indicates that they were put there for protection. The animal inside could be dangerous.

5 This is an **inferring type of question**. To find the answer you have to 'read between the lines'. You read the Brazilian cats are the *most absolutely treacherous and bloodthirsty creatures upon earth. They prefer humans to game* (see lines 41–42). Marshall was astonished when Everard entered the room because he had just finished telling Marshall how dangerous the cat was and how they like human blood.

6 This is a **language type of question**. To find the answer you have to read the text carefully, especially the section that is quoted. You read *I am about to show you the jewel of my collection* (see line 16). Combine this with your own knowledge that jewels are precious. Jewels set in a crown would have very special significance. The term is a metaphor and is not intended to be taken literally.

Hibiscus facts

7 This is a **fact-finding type of question**. The answer is a fact in the text. You read *One of the most important pollinators of the hibiscus is the hummingbird* (see line 25).

8 This is a **fact-finding type of question**. The answer is a fact in the text. You read *The hibiscus is the fifth most popular garden plant in the world today. It comes after roses, azaleas, carnations and orchids in that order* (see lines 10–11). The correct order for the listed plants is azaleas (1), hibiscus (4), orchids (3) and carnations (2).

9 This is a **fact-finding type of question**. The answer is a fact in the text. You read *Hibiscus bark has been used to make fibre for weaving and for making cords and ropes* (see line 24).

10 This is a **fact-finding type of question**. The answer is a fact in the text. You read *Recently, the flower has become more important in Asia as an ingredient in herbal medicine* (see line 16).

11 This is a **fact-finding type of question**. The answer is a fact in the text. You read the *hibiscus is called the 'shoeshine' plant because the flower can be rubbed over leather* (see lines 12–13).

12 This is an **inferring type of question**. To find the answer you have to 'read between the lines'. You read of its many functional applications, some of them being that it *is the fifth most popular garden plant in the world* (see line 10); *the flower can be rubbed over leather to shine or blacken it* (see lines 12–13); *has been used as a dye, as an ink, and as colouring for alcoholic drinks* (see lines 14–15); *an ingredient in herbal medicine* (see line 16); *The fruit of one hibiscus is often eaten as a 'vegetable'—okra* (see line 18).

The dust elf

13 This is an **inferring type of question**. To find the answer you have to 'read between the lines'. You read *For he leaves a trail of dust around the place* (see line 3). The poet doesn't get angry. The tone of the poem suggests that the poet tolerates the dust elf without too much worry. Combine this with your own knowledge and understanding to work out the final answer. The poet finds the dust elf to be playfully wicked without causing any real harm.

14 This is a **fact-finding type of question**. The answer is a fact in the text. You read *There's a dust elf lives at our house … For he leaves a trail of dust around the place* (see lines 1 and 3). An elf is an imaginary creature.

15 This is a **fact-finding type of question.** The answer is a fact in the text. You read *And lays in wait until I've lost a shoe. / Then when I crawl beneath the bed / The dust gets up my nose, / And I have to scramble out with a 'Kerchoo!'* (see lines 15–18).

16 This is a **judgement type of question**. You read *He likes to climb on bookshelves, / And he loves the picture frames* (see lines 7–8). You also read *But I think the thing he likes best / Is to come into my room / And sprinkle my belongings with his grime* (see lines 10–12). The words used (*like, love, likes best*) suggest the dust elf isn't malicious but is just having fun. The poet wishes the dust elf would go away but she feels he is here to stay. The tone of the poem suggests that the poet tolerates the dust elf and she will go on dusting her home. The poet finds the dust elf's behaviour a cheeky prank and a frivolous ploy.

17 This is an **inferring type of question**. To find the answer you have to 'read between the lines'. You read *And I wish that he would leave and go away* (see line 21). You also read *But I fear that this dust elf is here to stay* (see line 24). The poet reluctantly accepts the dust elf's presence in her home. She has no plans to force him out.

Raymond's speech

18 This is a **fact-finding type of question.** The answer is a fact in the text. You read *I disagree with any form of Saturday school* (see lines 8–9). He is hostile to any change.

19 This is an **inferring type of question**. To find the answer you have to 'read between the lines'. You read S*ome students enjoy paid work on Saturday. This may be their only source of pocket money* (see lines 23–24). You also read *A lot can be done—and earned—in forty days* (see lines 41–42). Raymond has worked out that the extra forty days (all the Saturdays in a school year) could instead be spent earning pocket money.

20 This is a **language type of question**. To find the answer you have to read the text carefully, especially the section that is quoted: *For others, Saturday is the one time they can see family* (see lines 14–15). You also read *This would be true for students whose parents are separated or who both work unusual hours* (see lines 16–18). *Others* is a pronoun that refers to additional people. The other people are the students that have difficulty seeing a lot of their parents.

21 This is a **language type of question**. To find the answer you have to read the text carefully, especially the section that is quoted: *Sunday would not be a day of rest and a time to recharge batteries* (see lines 33–34). The term suggests Sunday is a time to regain fitness, build up energy and get over any tiredness. The term is a saying and a metaphor, and not intended to be taken literally.

22 This is a **synthesis type of question**. To find the answer you have to read the whole text. The text is about Raymond trying to convince his audience that his opinion is right. He is against Saturday classes. He lists all the arguments against Saturday classes: *What are the benefits for a family?* (see line 10); *Saturday classes would definitely reduce family time* (see lines 10–11); *The extra day of classes would cut down on competitive sports days* (see lines 20–21); *Saturday classes would also mean one less day of rest* (see lines 26–27). Raymond is trying to persuade his audience.

23 This is a **language type of question**. To find the answer you have to read the text carefully, especially the section that is quoted: *A lot can be done—and earned—in forty days* (see lines 41–42). You also read earlier in the text *Some students enjoy paid work on Saturday. This may be their only source of pocket money* (see lines 23–24). The term is a reference back to the students who work part-time for pocket money.

Black Mountain

24 This is an **inferring type of question**. To find the answer you have to 'read between the lines'. You read Black Mountain is *Known as 'Kalkajaka' (place of spear or place of death)* (see line 1). You also read of *Black Mountain's dramatic, sinister black appearance* (see line 13) and that *There have been many reported sightings of the 'Tiger'* (see line 9). All these details indicate that it is a place of mystery.

25 This is a **language type of question**. To find the answer you have to read the text carefully, especially the section that is quoted: *There have been many reported sightings of the 'Tiger' which, it is said, has mauled and killed cattle* (see lines 9–10). The phrase *which it is said* suggests that the writer is not entirely convinced of the truth of the statement. You are told what the writer has heard, but he hasn't seen evidence of the existence of the 'Tiger'.

26 This is an **inferring type of question**. To find the answer you have to 'read between the lines'. You read Black Mountain *is an imposing short range of massive, black granite boulders* (see lines 4–5). You also read of *Black Mountain's dramatic, sinister black appearance* (see line 13). Its name,

Black Mountain, reflects the fact that its colour is the noteworthy feature.

27 This is a **fact-finding type of question**. The answer is a fact in the text. You read *The solid core of the ancient volcanic site now lies beneath the jumbled cover of boulders* (see line 27).

28 This is a **fact-finding type of question**. The answer is a fact in the text. You read *The granite rock is actually a drab pinkish colour* (see line 13).

29 This is a **fact-finding type of question**. The answer is a fact in the text. You read there is an *entire absence of soil on the surface* (see line 19). Soil is organic material.

Cartoon

30 This is an **inferring type of question**. To find the answer you have to 'read between the lines'. Look at the expressions on the faces of the two people. Look at the headlines on the newspaper. Combine this with your own knowledge and understanding to work out the final answer. The lady is most likely shocked by the rats taking over their house.

31 This is a **synthesis type of question**. To find the answer you have to look at the whole cartoon. Look at the headlines in the paper. Combine this with your own knowledge and understanding to work out the final answer. The news report seems to be true in a most unexpected way.

32 This is an **inferring type of question**. To find the answer you have to 'read between the lines'. Look at the expression on the face of the rat with the briefcase. The stereotypical real estate agent does not have a good reputation. Combine this with your own knowledge and understanding to work out the final answer. The rat is probably involved in something shady, or not quite honest.

33 This is a **judgement type of question**. To find the answer you have to take in the whole cartoon. You can see that the real estate agent rat is trying to convince the pair of rats to move into a 'new home'. He'll say anything to convince them. This comment would be out of character or improbable for other characters to make. Combine this with your own knowledge and understanding to work out the final answer. The fat, real estate agent rat is most likely to say the suggested comment.

34 This is a **synthesis type of question**. To find the answer you have to take in the whole cartoon to determine what is actually happening. A caption is a bit like a title or label. For the human occupants the rats would be unexpected and unwanted residents.

How to change a light bulb

35 This is a **judgement type of question**. You read *Changing a light bulb can be dangerous … Before changing a light bulb, follow these tips* (see lines 6–7). These are safety instructions.

36 This is a **language type of question**. To find the answer you have to read the text carefully. You read *There is an ever-circulating light bulb joke* (see line 1). You also read *Before changing a light bulb, follow these tips* (see line 7). The information is clear, precise and in easy-to-follow short sentences and points. It is not too serious which is indicated by the introductory joke. The text is light but practical.

37 This is an **inferring type of question**. To find the answer you have to 'read between the lines'. You read *have an assistant hold the ladder steady. The assistant can take the removed bulb and pass up the replacement bulb, which saves unnecessary fiddling while on the ladder* (see lines 19–21). The person on the ladder doesn't have to climb down and then back up, which makes the task more efficient. The assistant also holds the ladder steady to prevent the person on the ladder falling. The second person makes the task safer and more efficient.

38 This is a **fact-finding type of question**. The answer is a fact in the text. You read *For bayonet-fitting bulbs: using your hand, put a little upward pressure on the glass bulb, and rotate it anticlockwise (as you look up at it). It will unlock the bulb shank from the metal frame* (see lines 22–23).

39 *Raymond's speech* is a persuasive text. It informs the reader of what he sees is a problem and tries to persuade listeners why there must be the change he advocates. The *Black Mountain* text is a factual description of a place. The text explains to the reader how the site evolved.

WRITING Sample Tests 1 , 2 and 3 Pages 82–84

Go to **pages 133–141** for Standard, Intermediate and Advanced Writing samples for Sample Tests 1, 2 and 3.

Go to **pages 105–107** for Marking Checklists for Sample Tests 1, 2 and 3:

- Persuasive text (pages 105–106)
- Narrative text (page 106)
- Recount text (page 107).

Writing Mini Test 1

Mother's Day—a day of celebration

Mother's Day is a special day for mothers. It is enjoyed in many countries. It is the day when flowers or chocolates or presents are given to mothers to make them feel special. This seems a good idea but I don't like what it has become.

Firstly, not all women are mothers. Simply saying mothers are good people ignores the fact that many women do caring work for children. There are carers of the elderly, as well as foster parents and nurses in hospitals. These women do as much as some mothers do.

Secondly, what was meant to be a family day has become a big day for shops. Some shops make a fortune. They have spoilt it for everybody. The sale of flowers, cards and chocolates skyrockets! It is a money-making event, just like Easter and Christmas. It's lost its true meaning.

I have to ask: why do we have to remember our mother on just one day? We should be considerate towards our mother all the time. Every day should be mother's day!

Finally, the old idea to remember individual mothers and the important role they played 'behind the scenes' has been forgotten. Once girls grew up to be housewives with few opportunities. Now women have more opportunities. Many good women do not become mothers at all. Times have changed.

We have moved on from mothering being the important job for women. We don't need the selling that goes with Mother's Day. If we must have a special day it should be International Women's Day. It's a worldwide celebration. Will the shops change? I doubt it, but maybe we can start people thinking about the real meaning behind Mother's Day.

Structure

Audience

The audience is readily identified (mothers, children).

Background information is provided to give context to the points raised.

There is a brief statement outlining the issue to be discussed.

Persuasive techniques

Arguments for the writer's reaction are in separate paragraphs. The points raised are obviously important to the writer in a personal way.

Evidence and examples are provided to support the argument. Objectivity is maintained throughout the writing.

Text structure

The text contains a well-organised introduction, body and conclusion. The writer refers regularly to words used in the topic.

Paragraphing

New paragraphs are used for each new argument and a summary.

Cohesion

The final paragraph establishes where the writer stands on the issue, with a concluding sentence that provokes the reader to think about the issue.

Language and ideas

Vocabulary

A good variety of precise verb types are used to establish strong, informed arguments.

Nouns are used to make generalised statements.

Adverbs and adjectives are well selected to qualify words. The pronoun *I* is not overused.

Sentence structure

Logical sentence beginnings are used (e.g. *firstly, finally*).

There is variety in sentence types and lengths.

A topic sentence introduces each paragraph's main idea.

Questions and exclamations are used to good effect.

Ideas

Ideas are well balanced to create a sense of rational, logical argument.

A strong viewpoint is expressed with careful choice of words.

Ideas are presented with confidence.

Punctuation

Punctuation, including apostrophes and full stops, is correctly applied.

Spelling

There are no spelling mistakes of common or unusual words.

These writing samples have been analysed based on the marking criteria used by markers to assess the NAPLAN Writing Test.

Writing Mini Test 1

Mother's Day—a day of celebration

Mother's Day is a special day for mothers It is celebrated in many countries. It is the day to show appreciation of a mother's importance in the lives of children. This seems a good idea but I don't like what it has become.

Firstly, mothers are a small percentage of the population. Simply recognising mothers as good people ignores the fact that many women do caring work. There are carers of the elderly, as well as foster parents. Surely these women do as much as many mothers.

Secondly, what was meant to be a family day has become a selling spree. Companies make fortunes out of what was intended to be a private family thing. The sale of flowers, cards and chocolates skyrockets! The day has become a money-making exercise just like Easter and Christmas. It's lost its true meaning.

I have to ask: why do we have to remember our mother on one particular day? We should value our mother all the time. Every day should be mother's day!

Finally, the original idea to recognise individual mothers and the important role they played 'behind the scenes' has been lost. Women were stuck in the home with few opportunities. Now women have more opportunities. Many women may not become mothers. Times have changed.

We have moved on from mothering being the important role for women. We don't need excessive selling that goes with Mother's Day. If we must have a special day, let's focus on International Women's Day. It's a worldwide celebration. Will the shops accept a change? I doubt it, but maybe we can put a better perspective on the day.

Please note that this sample has not been written under test conditions. However, it gives you a standard to aim for.

Structure

Audience

The audience is readily identified (mothers, children).

Background information is provided to give context to the points raised.

There is a brief statement outlining the issue to be discussed.

Persuasive techniques

Arguments for the writer's reaction are in separate paragraphs.

The points raised are obviously important to the writer in a personal way.

Evidence and examples are provided to support the argument.

Text structure

The text contains a well-organised introduction, body and conclusion.

The writer refers regularly to words used in the topic.

Paragraphing

New paragraphs are used for each new argument and a summary.

Cohesion

The final paragraph establishes where the writer stands on the issue, with a forceful concluding sentence.

Language and ideas

Vocabulary

A good variety of precise verb types are used to establish strong, informed arguments.

Nouns are used to make generalised statements.

Adverbs and adjectives are well chosen to qualify statements.

The pronoun *I* is not overused.

Sentence structure

Sentence beginnings are logical (e.g. *firstly*, *finally*).

There is variety in sentence types and lengths.

A topic sentence introduces each paragraph's main idea.

Questions and exclamations are used to good effect.

Ideas

Ideas are well balanced to create a sense of rational, logical argument.

A strong viewpoint is expressed with careful choice of words.

Ideas are presented confidently.

Punctuation

Punctuation, including apostrophes and full stops, is correctly applied.

Spelling

There are no spelling mistakes of common or unusual words.

Writing Mini Test 1

Mother's Day—a day of celebration

Mother's Day is a day honouring mothers, celebrated on various days in different countries. It is the day to show appreciation of a mother's importance in the lives of children. This seems a good idea but I don't agree with the present situation.

Firstly, mothers are a small percentage of the population. Simply recognising mothers as good people ignores the fact that many women do caring work. There are carers of the elderly, those who provide respite care, as well as foster parents. Surely these women do as much as many mothers.

Secondly, what was meant to be a family day has become a selling spree. Commercial interests make fortunes out of what was intended to be a private family thing. The sale of flowers, cards and chocolates skyrockets! The day has become a money-making exercise just like Easter and Christmas. It has lost its true meaning.

Thirdly, I have to ask: why do we have to remember our mother on *one* particular day? We should value our mother (and father) all the time. Every day should be mother's day!

Finally, the original idea to recognise individual mothers and the important role they played 'behind the scenes' has been lost. Women were stuck in the home with few opportunities. Now women, whether mothers or not, have more opportunities. Many women may not become mothers. Times have changed.

We have moved on from mothering being the only important role for women. We don't need excessive selling that goes with Mother's Day. If we must have a special day, let's focus on International Women's Day. It's an international day of celebration. Will the shops accept a change? I doubt it, but maybe we can put a better perspective on an important day.

Structure

Audience
The audience is readily identified (mothers, children).
Background information is provided to give context to the points raised.
There is a brief statement outlining the issue to be discussed.

Persuasive techniques
Arguments for the writer's reaction are in separate numbered paragraphs.
The points raised are obviously important to the writer in a personal way.
Evidence and examples are provided to support the argument.
Objectivity is maintained throughout the writing.

Text structure
The text contains a well-organised introduction, body and conclusion.
The writer refers regularly to words used in the topic.

Paragraphing
New paragraphs are used for each new argument and a summary.

Cohesion
The final paragraph establishes where the writer stands on the issue, with a forceful concluding sentence.

Language and ideas

Vocabulary
A good variety of precise verb types are used to establish strong, informed arguments.
Nouns are used to make generalised statements.
Adverbs and adjectives are well chosen to qualify statements.
The pronoun *I* is not overused.

Sentence structure
Sentence beginnings are logical (e.g. *firstly, finally*).
There is variety in sentence types and lengths.
A topic sentence introduces each paragraph's main idea.
Questions and exclamations are used to good effect.
Italics is used for emphasis.

Ideas
Ideas are well balanced to create a sense of rational, logical argument.
A strong viewpoint is expressed with careful choice of words.
Ideas are presented confidently.

Punctuation
Punctuation, including apostrophes, brackets and full stops, is correctly applied.

Spelling
There are no spelling mistakes in common or unusual words.

Please note that this sample has not been written under test conditions. During a test you might not have the time to produce such a polished piece of writing. However, this sample gives you a standard to aim for.

Writing Mini Test 2

Left-handed Lenny

Lenny was a left-hander. His father tried to get him to change hands—to use the right hand—but sometimes that could be embarrassing. He'd have silly little accidents. Lenny always found it easier to do things with his left hand.

"I don't know what we can do with you," his father would often say.

At home Lenny would sit at the table with his brother on the right. That way he didn't keep clipping Jake's elbow when he was eating or drinking. His parents always had to think about where he sat, even at parties.

When he started school, teachers made sure his writing arm didn't accidentally bump the writing hand of his desk partner.

For everything he did, there had to be 'arrangements for Lenny'. Scissors are made for right-handed people. Scissors are used all the time at school!

In Year 3 the teacher announced they were going to have a visit from a popular soccer coach.

"Our visitor wants the whole class to be on the school oval when he arrives. He will show us a few tricks and watch you kick the ball around," Ms Pol explained.

Lenny felt nervous. He knew that being left-handed also meant he was also left-footed. He didn't want to do something embarrassing.

The next day the class went out onto the oval. Lenny kept to one side at the back of the class.

Suddenly the coach kicked the ball to Lenny. Lenny trapped the ball and hesitated. He carefully tapped it back to the visitor.

"Well done," clapped the visitor, "and you're a left-footer just like me!"

Lenny hadn't noticed. He had been too worried about his problem.

"You know, there are lots of left-handed people that play sport. Take the great golfer Greg Norman," called the coach, tapping the ball back to Lenny.

This time Lenny didn't hesitate. He gave the ball a solid kick with his left foot.

"It looks like you and me, and Bart Simpson, are something special," said the coach.

Structure

Audience

The main character (Lenny) is introduced quickly in the first paragraph and the reader becomes aware of a personal concern.

Character and setting

In the beginning, the reader is quickly told what, who, when and where.

The problem (orientation) is introduced early in the writing: Lenny has to cope with being a left-hander.

Text structure

The middle is a series of events that are related in the order in which they happen. Lenny has to face an embarrassing situation.

The reader has to read on to find out how Lenny copes.

Paragraphing

Paragraphs are used to show different time periods and to show when actual words are spoken (direct speech).

Cohesion

The story has an obvious beginning, middle and end.

The 'problem' is resolved.

The final two sentences neatly round off the story in an amusing way.

Language and ideas

Vocabulary

Adjectives and adverbs are used to enhance the story.

Verbs are used imaginatively.

A variety of 'said' words are used (e.g. *called*), helping with characterisation.

Sentence structure

A variety of sentence beginnings add interest.

A variety of sentence lengths keeps the story flowing.

The story is written in the past tense using the third person.

The use of correct grammar makes the story flow smoothly.

Ideas

Interesting detail is included (e.g. scissors for right-handers).

An exclamation sentence highlights the problem.

Punctuation

There are no errors in punctuation. All direct speech is correctly punctuated.

Apostrophes are correctly used for contractions.

Capital letters are used correctly (e.g. *Bart Simpson*).

Spelling

There are no spelling errors in commonly used words or in more unusual words (e.g. *nervous*).

These writing samples have been analysed based on the marking criteria used by markers to assess the NAPLAN Writing Test.

Writing Mini Test 2

Left-handed Lenny

Lenny was a left-hander. He couldn't remember when he first became aware that he was different. He did remember that his father sometimes tried to get him to hold his mug in the other hand—the right hand. He could remember his embarrassment when he spilled his drink or couldn't cut meat using a knife in his right hand.

"I don't know what we can do with you," his father would often complain, with a smile.

At home Lenny would sit at the table with his brother on the right. That way he didn't keep clipping Jake's elbow when he was eating or drinking. It meant that his parents always had to think about where he sat, even at parties.

When he started school, teachers had to make sure his writing arm didn't accidentally bump the writing hand of his desk partner.

For everything he did, there had to be 'arrangements for Lenny'. Scissors are made for right-handed people. They just don't cut as well with the left hand. Scissors are used all the time at school!

In Year 3 the teacher announced they were going to have a visit from a popular soccer coach.

"Our visitor wants the whole class to be on the school oval when he arrives. He will show us a few tricks and watch you kick the ball around," Ms Pol explained.

Lenny felt as if hornets had invaded his stomach. Only a few months earlier he had realised that being left-handed also meant he was also left-footed. He didn't want to do something embarrassing.

The next day the class assembled excitedly on the oval. Lenny kept to one side at the back of the group.

Suddenly the coach kicked the ball to Lenny. Lenny trapped the ball and hesitated. He carefully tapped it back to the visitor.

"Hey! That's great," clapped the visitor, "and you're a left-footer just like me!"

Lenny hadn't noticed. He had been too worried about his problem.

"You know there are many left-handed people that play sport. Take the great golfer Greg Norman," called the joyful coach, tapping the ball back to Lenny.

This time Lenny didn't hesitate. He gave the ball a solid kick with his left foot.

"It looks like you and me, and Bart Simpson, are something special," grinned the coach.

Lenny grinned back. If it's okay for Bart Simpson, it's okay for me, reckoned Lenny.

Structure

Audience
The main character (Lenny) is introduced quickly in the first paragraph, and the reader becomes aware of a personal concern.

Character and setting
In the beginning, the reader is quickly told what, who, when and where.

The problem (orientation) is introduced early in the writing: Lenny has to cope with being a left-hander.

Text structure
The middle is a series of events that are related in the order in which they happen. Lenny has to face an embarrassing situation.

The reader has to read on to find out how Lenny copes.

Paragraphing
Paragraphs are used to show different time periods and to show when actual words are spoken (direct speech).

Cohesion
The story has an obvious *beginning, middle* and *end.*

The 'problem' is resolved.

The final two sentences neatly round off the story in an amusing way.

Language and ideas

Vocabulary
Adjectives and adverbs are used to enhance the story.

Verbs are used imaginatively.

A variety of 'said' words are used (e.g. *grinned*) helping with characterisation.

Sentence structure
A variety of sentence beginnings add interest.

A variety of sentence lengths and types keep the story flowing.

The story is written in past tense using third person.

The use of correct grammar makes the story flow smoothly.

Ideas
An exclamation sentence highlights the problem.

A simile adds clarity to the description.

Interesting detail is included (e.g. *even at parties*).

Punctuation
There are no errors in punctuation. All direct speech is correctly punctuated.

Apostrophes are correctly used for contractions.

Spelling
There are no spelling mistakes in common or unusual words.

Please note that this sample has not been written under test conditions. However, it gives you a standard to aim for.

Writing Mini Test 2

Left-handed Lenny

Lenny was a left-hander. He couldn't remember when he first became aware that he was different. He did remember that his father sometimes tried to get him to hold his mug in the other hand—the right hand. He could remember his embarrassment when he spilled his drink or couldn't cut meat using a knife in his right hand. The right hand was the wrong hand!

"I don't know what we can do with you," his father would often complain, with a smile.

At home Lenny would sit at the table with his brother on the right. That way he didn't keep clipping Jake's elbow when he was eating or drinking. It meant that his parents always had to think about where he sat, even at parties.

When he started school, teachers had to make sure his writing arm didn't accidentally bump the writing hand of his desk partner.

For everything he did, there had to be 'arrangements for Lenny'. Scissors are made for right-handed people. They just don't cut as well with the left hand. Scissors are used all the time at school!

In Year 3 the teacher announced they were going to have a visit from a popular soccer coach.

"Our visitor wants the whole class to be on the school oval when he arrives. He will show us a few tricks and watch you kick the ball around," Ms Pol explained.

Lenny felt as if hornets had invaded his stomach. Only a few months earlier he realised that being left-handed also meant he was also left-footed. He didn't want to do something embarrassing.

The next day the class assembled excitedly on the oval. Lenny kept to one side at the back of the group.

Suddenly the coach kicked the ball to Lenny. Lenny trapped the ball and hesitated. He carefully tapped it back to the visitor, hardly daring to watch the ball.

"Hey! That's great," clapped the visitor, "and you're a left-footer just like me!"

Lenny hadn't noticed. He had been too worried about his problem.

"You know there are many left-handed people that play sport. Take the great golfer Greg Norman," called the joyful coach, tapping the ball back to Lenny.

This time Lenny didn't hesitate. He gave the ball a solid kick with his left foot.

"It looks like you and me, and Bart Simpson, are something special," grinned the coach.

Lenny grinned back. If it's okay for Bart Simpson, it's okay for me, reckoned Lenny.

Please note that this sample has not been written under test conditions. During a test you might not have the time to produce such a polished piece of writing. However, this sample gives you a standard to aim for.

Structure

Audience

The main character (Lenny) is introduced quickly in the first paragraph. The reader understands Lenny's personal concerns, and is familiar with the problem.

Character and setting

In the beginning, the reader is quickly told what, who, when and where.

The problem (orientation) is introduced very early in the writing: Lenny has to cope with being a left-hander.

Characterisation is revealed through actions and speech.

Text structure

The middle is a series of events that are related in the order in which they happen. Lenny has to face an embarrassing situation.

The reader has to read on to find out how Lenny copes.

Paragraphing

Paragraphs are used to show different time periods and to show when actual words are spoken (direct speech).

Cohesion

The story has an obvious beginning, middle and end.

The 'problem' is resolved.

The final two sentences neatly round off the story in an amusing way.

Language and ideas

Vocabulary

Adjectives and adverbs are used to enhance the story.

Verbs are used imaginatively.

A variety of 'said' words are used (e.g. *grinned*), helping with characterisation.

Sentence structure

A variety of sentence beginnings add interest.

A variety of sentence lengths and types keep the story interesting.

The story is written in the past tense using the third person.

The story flows smoothly because grammar is used correctly.

Ideas

A pun is used to show Lenny's frustration.

Exclamation sentences highlight the problem.

A simile adds clarity to the description of a feeling.

Interesting detail is included (e.g. *even at parties*).

Punctuation

There are no errors in punctuation.

All direct speech is correctly punctuated.

Apostrophes are correctly used for contractions.

Spelling

There are no spelling mistakes in common or unusual words.

Writing Mini Test 3

A new sporting event

Sport! Our family is good at sport. I belong to the swimming club. Mum plays tennis. Dad has his golf. We watch our sports on TV.

One day Dad decided I should try something new. He didn't say what. That was a worry!

We got into the car and headed for the lake. As we pulled into the car park Dad announced we were all going kayaking.

Dad hired three kayaks from the boatshed. The kayaks were at the water's edge. I looked at the boats and frowned.

"Don't worry Kerry," said Mum, as she got into her kayak. "Dad will help you."

First, Dad pushed the nose of the kayak into the water. He told me to get in and sit down as he held it steady. It still wobbled a lot.

Dad gave me a paddle. It had a blade on each end. I had to dip one end in the water, then the other end.

"Just watch your mother and do what she does," Dad advised as he gave the kayak a push into deeper water.

I started off by trying to row too quickly. My paddle made large splashes in the water. I wasn't a good paddler.

It was not a swimming race. I had to take my time. I had to dip the paddle deep into the water and pull steadily. The kayak still wanted to curve one way, then the other.

Later I got the hang of going straight. Then Mum showed me how to make sharp turns by keeping one paddle blade in the water while the kayak drifted along.

Finally it was time to return the kayaks. I had enjoyed my first try at kayaking. Learning a new sport can be fun and I'll become good at that too.

Structure

Audience
The title informs the reader of the event to be recounted.

The first word (an exclamation) 'grabs' the reader's interest.

The situation is quickly established in the first paragraph.

The past tense is used.

The use of the pronoun *I* indicates that this is a personal recount.

Character and setting
Time, place and characters are established quickly.

The narrator is aware of the help provided by parents.

Text structure
Events happen in order using adverbs of time.

Precise words are used for detail.

The reader is made aware of the family relationships.

Paragraphing
New paragraphs begin with changes in time or subject.

New paragraphs are used for a personal opinion and speech.

Cohesion
A personal comment is used to round off the recount, with a reference to being *good*.

Language and ideas

Vocabulary
Adverbs are well chosen.

There is a suitable selection of adjectives.

A variety of verbs are used, including an interesting 'said' word (e.g. *advised*).

Sentence structure
The narrator uses a variety of sentence beginnings including 'time' adverbs.

The narrator has used a variety of sentence types and lengths and has not overused *I* as a sentence beginning.

Ideas
The narrator is writing fluently about a familiar subject.

Precise details make the recount feel authentic.

Two exclamation sentences are used effectively.

Punctuation
Punctuation is well handled.

Capital letters for the start of sentences are correctly applied.

Direct and indirect speech are used without errors.

Apostrophes are used correctly.

Spelling
There are no spelling mistakes in common or unusual words.

These writing samples have been analysed based on the marking criteria used by markers to assess the NAPLAN Writing Test.

Writing Mini Test 3

Structure

Audience
The title informs the reader of the event to be recounted

The first word (an exclamation) 'grabs' the reader's interest.

The situation is quickly established in the first paragraph.

Past tense is used.

The use of the pronoun *I* indicates that this is a personal recount.

Character and setting
Time, place and characters are established quickly.

The narrator is aware of the help provided by parents.

Text structure
Events happen in order using adverbs of time.

Precise words (e.g. *dip*) are used for details.

The reader is made aware of the family relationships.

Paragraphing
New paragraphs begin with each change in time or subject.

New paragraphs are used for a personal opinion and speech.

Cohesion
A personal comment is used to round off the recount, with another reference to being *good*.

A new sporting event

Sport! Our family just loves sport and we are good at our sports. I belong to the swimming club. Mum plays tennis. Dad has his golf. We watch our sports on TV. We like our sports so much we don't play anything else. Playing is better than being a spectator.

One day Dad decided I should try something new. He didn't say what. That was a worry!

We all climbed into the car and headed for the lake. As we pulled into the car park Dad announced we were all going kayaking. Mum smiled quietly.

Dad hired three kayaks from the boatshed. The kayaks were at the water's edge. I looked at the boats and frowned. Maybe I wouldn't be a good kayaker. I hoped no one was going to watch.

"Don't worry Kerry," said Mum as she stepped into her kayak. "Dad will show you what to do."

First, Dad pushed the nose of the kayak into the shallow water. He told me to get in and sit down as he held it steady. It still wobbled a lot.

Dad gave me a paddle. It had a blade on each end. I had to dip one end in the water, then the other end.

"Just watch your mother and do what she does," Dad advised as he gave the kayak a push into deeper water.

I started off by trying to row too quickly. My paddle made wild splashes in the water as if I was a pelican trying to take off from the water. I wasn't very good at it.

It was not a swimming race. I had to take my time. I had to dip the paddle deep into the water and pull steadily and calmly. The kayak still wanted to curve one way, then the other.

Later I got the hang of making it go straight ahead. Then Mum showed me how to make sharp turns by keeping one paddle blade in the water while the kayak drifted along.

Finally it was time to return the kayaks. I had enjoyed my first attempt at kayaking. Learning a new sport can be fun. I decided I was going to be good at kayaking too.

Language and ideas

Vocabulary
Adverbs are well chosen.

There is a suitable selection of adjectives.

A variety of verbs are used, including an interesting 'said' word (e.g. *advised*).

Sentence structure
The writer uses a variety of sentence beginnings including 'time' adverbs.

The narrator has used a variety of sentence types and lengths.

The narrator has not over-used *I* as a sentence beginning.

Ideas
The narrator is writing fluently about a familiar subject.

Precise details make the recount feel authentic.

Two exclamation sentences are used effectively.

A simile helps describe the narrator's attempt to paddle.

Punctuation
Punctuation is well handled.

Capital letters for the start of sentences are correctly applied.

Direct and indirect speech are used without errors.

Apostrophes are used correctly.

Spelling
There are no spelling mistakes in common or unusual words.

Please note that this sample has not been written under test conditions. However, it gives you a standard to aim for.

Writing Mini Test 3

A new sporting event

Sport! Our family just loves sport and we are competent at our sports. I belong to the swimming club. Mum plays tennis. Dad has his golf. We watch our sports on TV. We like our sports so much we don't play anything else. It is better to be an active player than an inactive spectator.

One day Dad decided I should try something new. He didn't say what. That was a worry!

We all climbed into the car and headed for the lake. As we pulled into the car park Dad announced boldly we were all going kayaking. Mum smiled quietly. Suddenly I felt nervous.

Dad hired three kayaks from the boatshed. The kayaks were at the water's edge. I looked at the boats and frowned. Maybe I wouldn't be a competent kayaker. I hoped there were no spectators.

"Don't worry Kerry," said Mum as she stepped into her kayak. "Dad will show you what to do."

First, Dad pushed the nose of the kayak into the shallow water. He told me to get in and sit down as he held it steady. It wobbled like a jelly on a plate.

Dad handed me a paddle. It had a blade on each end. I had to dip one end in the water, then the other end.

"Just watch your mother and do what she does," Dad advised as he gave the kayak a push into deeper water.

I started off by trying to row too quickly. My paddle made wild splashes in the water as if I was a pelican trying to take off from the water. I wasn't very competent at it—and getting wet.

It was not a swimming race. I had to take my time. I had to dip the paddle deep into the water and pull steadily and calmly. The kayak still wanted to curve one way, then the other.

Later I got the hang of making it go straight ahead. Then Mum showed me how to make sharp turns by keeping one paddle blade in the water while the kayak drifted along.

Finally it was time to return the kayaks. I had enjoyed my first try at kayaking. Learning a new sport can be fun. My arms might have ached but I had decided I was going to be competent at kayaking too.

Structure

Audience

The title informs the reader of the event to be recounted.

The first word (an exclamation) 'grabs' the reader's interest.

The situation is quickly established in the first paragraph. The past tense is used. The use of the pronoun *I* indicates that this is a personal recount.

Character and setting

Time, place and characters are established quickly.

The narrator is aware of the help provided by parents.

Text structure

Events happen in order using adverbs of time.

Precise words (e.g. *dip*) are used for detail.

The reader is made aware of the family relationships.

The narrator makes reference to senses other than sight.

Paragraphing

New paragraphs begin with each change in time or subject. New paragraphs are used for a personal opinion and speech.

Cohesion

A personal comment is used to round off the recount, with another reference to being *competent*.

Language and ideas

Vocabulary

Adverbs are well chosen.

There is a suitable selection of adjectives.

A variety of verbs are used, including an interesting 'said' word (e.g. *advised*).

Sentence structure

The narrator uses a variety of sentence beginnings including 'time' adverbs.

The narrator has used a variety of sentence types and lengths.

The narrator has not overused *I* as a sentence beginning.

Ideas

The narrator writes fluently about a familiar subject and those who are involved.

Precise details make the recount feel authentic.

Two exclamation sentences are used effectively.

Similes help describe the narrator's experiences.

Punctuation

Punctuation is well handled.

Capital letters for the start of sentences are correctly applied.

Direct and indirect speech are used without errors.

Apostrophes are used correctly.

Spelling

There are no spelling mistakes in common or unusual words.

Please note that this sample has not been written under test conditions. During a test you might not have the time to produce such a polished piece of writing. However, this sample gives you a standard to aim for.

Writing Sample Test 1

Testing in schools

Testing is very common in schools. There are two main types of tests—those written by the teacher and tests written by people outside the school (e.g. NAPLAN). There is now much too much testing in schools.

How many tests do pupils have? There are weekly tests, monthly tests, term tests and half-yearly tests. Time used for testing would be better spent teaching. Classroom teachers should know how well their students are doing without all the testing. I reckon some tests are given to keep students busy!

External tests include government tests that every pupil must do. Then there are tests for special classes or special schools, as well as tests run by universities and businesses, such as banks. Teachers gently push students to sit for the tests but they are still stressful. They are given under strict test conditions. If a student doesn't do well on the day then an opportunity may be lost forever.

An advantage of tests written by the teacher is that they are held regularly. Nerves play no part. If a mistake is made, then it is a small part in a whole string of tests. An assessment is not made on one result—but there are still too many tests.

Finally, multiple-choice tests—tests where the student has to pick the correct answer out of four choices—can give incorrect results. Even hopeless students have a one-in-four chance of guessing the right answer!

Testing no longer reflects a student's ability. Students are numbers for education departments. It's time to get rid of most tests and get back to teaching. Has the value of testing been lost? Yes!

Structure

Audience

The audience is readily identified (schools, pupils).

Background information is provided to give context to the arguments raised.

Brief statements outline the issue to be discussed.

Persuasive techniques

Arguments for the writer's opinion are in separate paragraphs.

Points raised are obviously important to the writer in a personal way.

Evidence and examples support the argument.

Objectivity is maintained throughout the writing.

Text structure

The text contains a well-organised introduction, body and conclusion.

The writer refers regularly to words used in the topic.

Paragraphing

New paragraphs, with topic sentences, begin with each new argument and the summary.

Cohesion

The final paragraph refers to the topic and re-establishes how the writer feels. The writing ends with a strong, personal, concluding sentence.

Language and ideas

Vocabulary

A good variety of precise verb types are used to establish strong, informed arguments. Nouns are used to make generalised statements. Adverbs and adjectives are well selected to qualify statements.

The pronoun *I* is used sparingly.

Sentence structure

There is a good variety of sentence beginnings (e.g. *Time*, *Finally*), types and lengths.

A topic sentence is used to introduce each paragraph's main idea.

Questions and exclamations are used effectively. A rhetorical question is used to full effect.

Ideas

Ideas are well balanced to create a sense of rational, logical argument.

A strong viewpoint is expressed with careful choice of words and use of repetition.

Arguments are presented with confidence.

Punctuation

Punctuation, including apostrophes, commas and full stops, is correctly applied.

Spelling

There are no spelling mistakes in common or unusual words.

These writing samples have been analysed based on the marking criteria used by markers to assess the NAPLAN Writing Test.

Writing Sample Test 1

Testing in schools

Testing is now a big part of school life. There are two main types of tests—those written by the teacher and external tests written by people outside the school (e.g. NAPLAN). There is now too much testing in schools.

Look at the number of tests schools have. There are weekly tests, monthly tests, term tests and half-yearly tests. Time used in testing would be better spent teaching. Classroom teachers should have a solid knowledge of a student's ability without all this testing. I suspect some tests are given to keep students occupied!

External tests include compulsory government tests. Then there are tests for special classes and special schools, as well as tests run by educational organisations, subject teachers' groups (e.g. Mathematics), and businesses, such as banks. These tests are stressful. They are given under strict test conditions. If a student doesn't do well on the day then an opportunity may be lost forever.

An advantage of school-based tests is that they are held regularly. Nerves play no part. If a mistake is made, then it is a minor part in a whole string of tests. A judgement is not made on a single result—but there are still too many tests.

Finally, multiple-choice tests—tests where the student has to pick the correct answer out of four choices—can give inaccurate results. Even hopeless students have a one-in-four chance of getting the right answer!

Testing no longer reflects a student's potential. Students are statistics for educational authorities. It's time to get rid of most tests and focus on teaching. Has the value of testing been lost? Yes!

Structure

Audience

The audience is readily identified (schools, pupils).

Background information is provided to give context to the points raised.

Brief statements outline the issue to be discussed.

Persuasive techniques

Arguments for the writer's opinion are in separate paragraphs.

Points raised are obviously important to the writer in a personal way.

Evidence and examples are used to support the argument.

Objectivity is maintained throughout the writing.

Text structure

The text contains a well-organised introduction, body and conclusion.

The writer refers regularly to words used in the topic.

Paragraphing

New paragraphs, with topic sentences, are used for each new argument and the summary.

Cohesion

The final paragraph refers to the topic and re-establishes how the writer feels. The writing ends with a strong, personal, concluding sentence.

Language and ideas

Vocabulary

A good variety of precise verb types are used to establish strong, informed arguments.

Nouns are used to make generalised statements.

Adverbs and adjectives are well selected to qualify statements.

The pronoun *I* is used sparingly.

Sentence structure

There is a good variety of sentence beginnings (e.g. *Nerves*, *Finally*), types and lengths.

A topic sentence is used to introduce each paragraph's main idea.

Questions and exclamations are used to good effect. A rhetorical question is used to full effect.

Ideas

Ideas are well balanced to create a sense of rational, logical argument.

A strong viewpoint is expressed with careful choice of words.

Ideas are presented forcefully.

Punctuation

Punctuation, including apostrophes, commas and full stops, is correctly applied.

Spelling

There are no spelling mistakes in common or unusual words.

Please note that this sample has not been written under test conditions. However, it gives you a standard to aim for.

Testing in schools

Testing is now an important part of school life. There are two main types of tests—those written by the teacher and external tests written by people outside the school (e.g. NAPLAN). There is now too much testing in schools.

Look at the number of tests schools have. There are weekly tests, monthly tests, term tests and half-yearly tests. Time used in testing would be better spent teaching. Classroom teachers should have a solid knowledge of a student's ability without all this testing. I suspect some tests are given to keep students occupied!

External tests include compulsory government tests. Then there are tests for special classes and special schools, as well as tests run by educational organisations, subject teachers' groups (e.g. Mathematics), and businesses, such as banks and newspapers. These tests are stressful. They are conducted under strict test conditions. If a student doesn't perform well on the day then an opportunity may be lost forever.

An advantage of school-based tests is that they are held regularly. Nerves play no part. If a mistake is made, then it is a minor part in a whole string of tests. A judgement is not made on a single result—but tests seem to be as regular as TV commercials.

Multiple-choice tests—tests where the student has to pick the correct answer out of four choices—can give inaccurate results. Even hopeless students have a one-in-four chance of getting the right answer!

Finally, another worry about school testing is whether teachers are teaching to get good test results for their class or school, and not for a good education.

Testing no longer reflects a student's potential. Students are statistics for educational authorities. It's time to get rid of most tests and focus on teaching. Has the value of testing been lost? Yes!

Please note that this sample has not been written under test conditions. During a test you might not have the time to produce such a polished piece of writing. However, this sample gives you a standard to aim for.

Structure

Audience

The audience is readily identified (schools, pupils).

Background information is provided to give context to the points raised.

Brief statements outline the issue to be discussed.

Persuasive techniques

Arguments for the writer's opinion are in separate paragraphs.

Points raised are obviously important to the writer in a personal way.

Evidence and examples are used to support the argument.

Objectivity is maintained throughout the writing.

Text structure

The text contains a well-organised introduction, body and conclusion.

The writer refers regularly to words used in the topic.

Paragraphing

New paragraphs, with topic sentences, are used for each new argument and the summary.

Cohesion

The final paragraph refers to the topic and re-establishes how the writer feels. The writing ends with a strong, personal, concluding sentence.

Language and ideas

Vocabulary

A good variety of precise verb types are used to establish strong, informed arguments.

Nouns are used to make generalised statements.

Adverbs and adjectives are well selected to qualify statements.

The pronoun *I* is used sparingly.

Sentence structure

There is a good variety of sentence beginnings (e.g. *Nerves*, *Finally*), types and lengths.

A topic sentence is used to introduce each paragraph's main idea.

Questions and exclamations are used to good effect. A rhetorical question is used to full effect.

Ideas

Ideas are well balanced to create a sense of rational, logical argument.

A strong viewpoint is expressed with careful choice of words.

Ideas are presented forcefully. A simile is used for impact.

Punctuation

Punctuation, including apostrophes, commas and full stops, is correctly applied.

Spelling

There are no spelling mistakes in common or unusual words.

Writing Sample Test 2

Night camp-out

The five scouts were ready for their camp, but even as they got into Skip's van, Bobby was reading his book. The other scouts worried that Bobby might not be very helpful.

After a long dusty trip, they finally came to a clearing in the bush. Skip said, "This is going to be a good camp. Nothing will go wrong. The time for fun comes after you put up the tents."

The boys soon had their tents up. Skip made a safety check of the nearby bush. They all hoped nothing would spoil their fun.

"No snakes. I've checked the weather. No rain this weekend," Skip said. "Nothing to spoil our camp. No mobile phones. No other campers! No TV. We don't want any accidents, or being frightened by silly horror stories!"

Four of the boys frowned but Bobby was more interested in his insect book!

By nightfall Skip had everything organised. He had a gas cooker and a gas light. He had lamps to kill mosquitoes. While the boys sat on logs eating sausages, Skip sat in his camp chair. He was pleased with himself! Nothing could go wrong.

Suddenly Josh, the youngest scout, cried, "There's something in the bush. I saw two eyes."

The other scouts looked up. They could all see two eyes in the darkness. "There's someone over there!" exclaimed Glen, another camper.

Skip quickly stood up and stared into the darkness. "Can't be," he said. "There's no-one else here."

"We all saw them!" whispered Josh. Glen gasped when the eyes moved closer.

"Into your tents immediately," ordered Skip. "This is dangerous. Bobby, put your book down!"

"Don't worry, Skip," said Bobby, "They're not eyes. They're just two happy fireflies!"

Skip sighed, then said, "Thanks Bobby. Thought we had our own horror story!"

"Nothing horrible about fireflies," said Bobby, closing his book.

Structure

Audience

The main characters are introduced quickly in the first short paragraph. The title gives the subject of the story. Readers can relate to a camping situation.

Character and setting

The reader is quickly told what, who, when and where.

The problem (orientation) is introduced early in the writing—how successful will the camp be?

Text structure

The middle is a series of events that are related in the order in which they happen.

Characters make an effort to foresee possible problems.

The reader has to read on to find out if they succeed.

Paragraphing

Paragraphs are used to show different time periods and to show when actual words are spoken (direct speech).

Cohesion

The story has an obvious flow, and a beginning, middle and end.

The 'problem' is resolved.

The ending ties in with the beginning (Bobby is helpful).

Language and ideas

Vocabulary

Adjectives and adverbs are used to enhance the story.

Verbs are well chosen.

The 'said' words help develop characterisation.

Some interesting words are used (e.g. *nearby*, *gasped*).

Sentence structure

A variety of sentence beginnings adds interest.

A variety of sentence lengths keeps the story flowing. Direct speech creates a sense of urgency.

The story is written in the past tense using the third person.

Personal pronouns are used correctly, creating a smooth flow of action.

Ideas

Some information about the trip is withheld to encourage the reader to read on.

Interesting detail is included (e.g. *gas light*).

Punctuation

There are no punctuation errors. All direct speech is correctly punctuated.

Apostrophes and exclamation marks are used correctly.

Spelling

There are no spelling mistakes in common or unusual words.

These writing samples have been analysed based on the marking criteria used by markers to assess the NAPLAN Writing Test.

Writing Sample Test 2

Structure

Audience
The main characters are introduced quickly in the first short paragraph. The title gives the subject of the story. Readers can relate to a camping situation.

Character and setting
The reader is quickly told what, who, when and where.

The problem (orientation) is introduced early in the writing—how successful will the camp be?

Text structure
The middle is a series of events that are related in the order in which they happen.

Characters make an effort to foresee possible problems.

The reader has to read on to find out if they succeed.

Paragraphing
Paragraphs are used to show different time periods and to show when actual words are spoken (direct speech).

Cohesion
The story has an obvious flow, and a beginning, middle and end.

The 'problem' is resolved.

The ending ties in with the beginning (Bobby is helpful).

Night camp-out

The five scouts were ready for their weekend camp, but even as they climbed into Skip's van, Bobby was still reading. The other scouts worried that Bobby might not be very helpful.

After a long dusty trip, the van finally bumped over the last few ruts into a grassy clearing. Skip ordered the scouts out to set up camp. "This will be a trouble-free camp. Nothing will go wrong. The time for fun comes after the hard work is done," he said.

The boys pretended to groan, but soon had their tents up. Skip did a safety check of the nearby bushland. The boys hoped nothing would spoil their fun.

"No snakes. I've checked the weather. No rain coming," Skip later told the boys. "There will be nothing to spoil our camp. No mobile phones. No other campers! No TV. We don't want any accidents," he said, "or being frightened by silly horror stories."

Four of the boys frowned but Bobby was more interested in his insect book.

By nightfall, Skip had done everything to make the camp a success. He had a gas cooker and a gas light. While the boys sat on the logs to eat their sausages, Skip had his camp chair. He felt very pleased with himself! Nothing could go wrong.

Suddenly Josh, the youngest scout, cried, "There's something in the bush. I saw two eyes."

The other scouts looked to where Josh was pointing. They could all see two bright eyes in the dark bushes. "There's someone over there!" exclaimed Glen, another camper.

Skip quickly stood up and stared into the darkness. "Can't be," he said. "There's no-one else here."

"We all saw them!" whispered Josh. Glen gasped when the eyes moved towards the camp.

"Into your tents immediately," ordered Skip. "This could be dangerous. Bobby, put your book down!"

"Don't worry, Skip," said Bobby calmly, "They're not eyes. They're just a pair of happy fireflies! My book says they are often seen at night."

Skip gave a soft whistle, then said, "Thanks Bobby. Thought we had our own horror story!"

"Nothing horrible about fireflies," smiled Bobby, closing his insect book.

Language and ideas

Vocabulary
Adjectives and adverbs are used to enhance the story.

Verbs are well chosen.

The 'said' words help develop characterisation.

Some interesting words are used (e.g. *bumped, darkness*).

Sentence structure
A variety of sentence beginnings adds interest.

A variety of sentence lengths keeps the story flowing. Direct speech creates a sense of urgency.

The story is written in the past tense using the third person.

Personal pronouns are used correctly, creating a smooth flow of action.

Ideas
Some information about the trip is withheld to encourage the reader to read on.

Interesting detail is included (e.g. *gas light, dark bushes*).

Punctuation
There are no punctuation errors. All direct speech is correctly punctuated.

Apostrophes and exclamation marks are used correctly.

Spelling
There are no spelling mistakes in common or unusual words.

Please note that this sample has not been written under test conditions. However, it gives you a standard to aim for.

Writing Sample Test 2

Night camp-out

The five scouts were ready for their weekend camp, but even as they clambered into Skip's van, Bobby still had his head in a book. The other scouts worried that Bobby might not be very helpful.

After a long trip, the van finally rattled over the last few dusty ruts of the bush track into a flat, grassy clearing. Skip ordered the scouts out to set up camp. "This is going to be a trouble-free camp. Nothing will go wrong. The time for fun comes after the hard work is done," he said.

The boys pretended to groan, but soon had their tents up. Skip did a safety check of the nearby bushland. The boys hoped nothing would spoil their fun.

"No snakes. I've checked the weather. No rain and no wind on the forecast," Skip later told the boys. "There will be nothing to spoil our camp. No mobile phones. No other campers! No TV. But we must be sensible. We don't want any accidents," he said, "or being frightened by silly horror stories."

Four of the boys looked at each other and frowned. Bobby was more interested in his insect book!

By nightfall, Skip had done everything to make the camp successful. He had a gas cooker and a gas light. He had lamps to kill mosquitoes. While the boys sat on a log to eat their sausages, Skip had his camp chair. He felt very pleased with himself! Nothing could go wrong.

Suddenly Josh, the youngest scout, cried, "There's something in the bush. I saw two eyes."

The other scouts looked to where Josh was pointing. They could see two pinpoints of flickering light like evil eyes in the darkness. "There's someone over there!" exclaimed Glen, another camper.

Skip stood up abruptly and stared into the darkness. "Can't be," he said. "There's no-one else here."

"We all saw them!" whispered Josh. Glen gasped when the eyes moved towards the camp.

"Into your tents immediately," ordered Skip. "This could be dangerous. Bobby, put your book down!"

"Don't worry, Skip," said Bobby calmly, "They're not eyes. They're just a pair of happy fireflies! My book says they are often seen at night."

Skip gave a soft whistle, then said, "Thanks Bobby. Thought we were part of a real horror story!"

"Nothing horrible about fireflies," smiled Bobby, closing his insect book.

Structure

Audience
The main characters are introduced quickly in the first short paragraph. The title gives the subject of the story. Readers can relate to a camping situation.

Character and setting
The reader is quickly told what, who, when and where.

The problem (orientation) is introduced early in the writing—how successful will the camp be?

Text structure
The middle is a series of events that are related in the order in which they happen.

Characters make an effort to foresee possible problems.

The reader has to read on to find out if they succeed.

Paragraphing
Paragraphs are used to show different time periods and to show when actual words are spoken (direct speech).

Cohesion
The story has an obvious flow, and a beginning, middle and end.

The 'problem' is resolved.

The ending ties in with the beginning (Bobby is helpful).

Language and ideas

Vocabulary
Adjectives and adverbs are used to enhance the story.

Verbs are well chosen.

The 'said' words help develop characterisation.

Some interesting words are used (e.g. *pinpoints*, *clambered*).

Sentence structure
A variety of sentence beginnings adds interest.

A variety of sentence lengths keeps the story flowing. Direct speech creates a sense of urgency.

The story is written in the past tense using the third person.

Personal pronouns are used correctly, creating a smooth flow of action.

Ideas
Some information about the trip is withheld to encourage the reader to read on.

Interesting detail is included (e.g. *gas light*, *dusty ruts*).

The simile is effective.

Punctuation
There are no punctuation errors. All direct speech is correctly punctuated.

Apostrophes and exclamation marks are used correctly.

Spelling
There are no spelling errors in commonly used words or more unusual words.

Please note that this sample has not been written under test conditions. During a test you might not have the time to produce such a polished piece of writing. However, this sample gives you a standard to aim for.

Standard level — Sample of Recount Writing

Writing Sample Test 3

My holiday

Just before the last school holiday my parents were invited to my Uncle Herb's fiftieth birthday party. They decided to drive all the way to Gilgang. Dad said it was a good chance to see the country.

We left early on Monday morning. We headed off over the hills just out of town. The scenery wasn't too bad, but anything interesting was blocked out by houses or trees. At least I had my Playstation to pass some of the time.

On the first night we stayed at a motel. It was very small and the television didn't work. Food from the café next door was uninteresting.

On the second day we were onto the flat country. I soon got very tired of just sitting. Even my Playstation had lost its interest. We just cruised along hour after hour.

That night it was another motel, in another small town way out in the bush. I wondered what my friends were doing.

On Wednesday it was more of the same flat country, but the trees were smaller. I had a mountain of boredom to live with. Mum gave me a dirty look when I sighed loudly.

We had an early start on Thursday morning to beat the summer heat. Later in the morning we saw Gilgang in the distance. Suddenly I felt a bit better. The trip was almost over!

When we arrived my uncle suggested we all go for a swim in his new pool.

"How was the trip to Gilgang?" Uncle Herb said to me.

"Really great!" I grinned, but I was thinking more of the pool than the trip.

Structure

Audience

The title informs readers of the subject to be recounted.

The situation is quickly established in the title and the first paragraph (who, where and when).

The past tense is used.

Personal pronouns (*I, my, we*) indicate that this is a personal recount.

Character and setting

Time and place are quickly established.

The narrator begins to lose interest in the trip.

Text structure

Events happen in order using adverbs of time.

Precise words are used for detail.

The reader is made aware of the conditions at the time.

Indirect speech is used correctly.

Paragraphing

New paragraphs begin with changes in time.

Cohesion

Well-selected pronouns and adverbs keep the recount flowing.

A personal comment is used to conclude the recount.

Language and ideas

Vocabulary

Adverbs and adjectives are well chosen.

Interesting verbs are used, including 'said'-type words.

Sentence structure

The narrator uses a variety of sentence beginnings, including 'time' adverbs.

The narrator has used a variety of sentence types and lengths.

There is a controlled use of *I* as a sentence beginning.

Ideas

Repetition is used to indicate boredom.

A metaphor is also used to highlight the narrator's boredom.

The writer is recounting a familiar subject.

Punctuation

Punctuation is well handled.

Direct speech has the correct punctuation.

Capital letters for proper nouns and sentence beginnings are correctly applied.

Spelling

There are no spelling mistakes in common or unusual words.

These writing samples have been analysed based on the marking criteria used by markers to assess the NAPLAN Writing Test.

Writing Sample Test 3

My holiday

Just before the last school holiday my parents were invited to my Uncle Herb's fiftieth birthday party. They decided to drive from our home town all the way to Gilgang, in the outback. Dad said it was a good chance to see the country.

We left early on Monday morning. We headed off over the hills just out of town. The scenery wasn't too bad, but anything interesting was blocked out by houses or trees. At least I had my Playstation to pass some of the time.

On the first night we stayed at a motel. It was very small and the television didn't work. The picture was snowy. Food from the café next door was uninteresting. Dad warned not to expect too much.

On the second day we were onto the flat country. I soon got very tired of just sitting. Even my Playstation had lost its interest. We just cruised along hour after hour. I was a prisoner in the back seat of our car!

That night it was another motel, in another small town way out in the bush. I wondered what my friends were doing.

On Wednesday it was more of the same flat country, but the trees were smaller. I had a mountain of boredom to live with. Mum gave me a dirty look when I sighed loudly.

We had an early start on Thursday morning to beat the summer heat. Later in the morning we saw Gilgang in the distance. Suddenly I felt a bit better. The trip was almost over. We had seen enough country!

When we arrived my uncle suggested we all go for a swim in his new pool.

"How was the trip to Gilgang?" Uncle Herb asked me.

"Really great!" I grinned, but I was thinking more of the pool than the trip.

Please note that this sample has not been written under test conditions. However, it gives you a standard to aim for.

Structure

Audience
The title informs readers of the subject to be recounted.

The situation is quickly established in the title and the first paragraph (who, where and when).

The past tense is used.

Personal pronouns (I, my, we) indicate that this is a personal recount.

Character and setting
Time and place are quickly established.

The narrator begins to lose interest in the trip.

Text structure
Events happen in order using adverbs of time.

Precise words are used for detail (e.g. *The picture was snowy*).

The reader is made aware of the conditions at the time.

Indirect speech is used correctly.

Paragraphing
New paragraphs begin with changes in time.

Cohesion
Well-selected pronouns and adverbs keep the recount flowing.

A personal comment is used to conclude the recount.

The narrator suddenly changes his attitude.

Language and ideas

Vocabulary
Adverbs and adjectives are well chosen.

Interesting verbs are used, including 'said'-type words

Sentence structure
The narrator uses a variety of sentence beginnings, including 'time' adverbs.

The narrator has used a variety of sentence types and lengths.

There is a controlled use of *I* as a sentence beginning.

Ideas
Repetition is used to indicate boredom.

Metaphors are also used to highlight the narrator's boredom.

Exclamation sentences are used effectively.

The writer is recounting a familiar subject.

Punctuation
Punctuation is well handled.

Direct speech has the correct punctuation.

Capital letters for proper nouns and sentence beginnings are correctly applied.

Spelling
There are no spelling mistakes in common or unusual words.

My holiday

Don't tell me about country holidays. I've had one!

It all started just before the last school holidays when my parents were invited to my Uncle Herb's fiftieth birthday party. They decided to drive from our home town all the way to Gilgang, in the outback. Dad said it was a good chance to see the country.

We left early on Monday morning. We headed off over the hills just out of town. The scenery wasn't too bad, but anything interesting was blocked out by houses or trees. At least I had my Playstation to pass some of the time.

On the first night we stayed at a motel. It was very small and the television didn't work. It looked as if the cameraman had spent his life in a snowstorm. Food from the café next door was uninteresting. Dad warned not to expect too much.

On the second day we were onto the flat country. I soon got very tired of just sitting. Even my Playstation had lost its interest. We just cruised along hour after hour. I was a prisoner in the back seat of our car!

That night it was another motel, in another small town way out in the bush. I wondered what my friends were doing.

On Wednesday it was more of the same flat country, but the trees were smaller. I had a mountain of boredom to live with. Mum gave me a dirty look when I sighed loudly.

We had an early start on Thursday morning to beat the summer heat. Later that morning we saw Gilgang in the distance. Suddenly I felt a bit better. The trip was almost over. I had seen enough country!

When we arrived my uncle suggested we all go for a swim in his new pool.

"How was the trip to Gilgang?" Uncle Herb asked me.

"Really great!" I grinned, but I was thinking more of the cool pool than the hot trip.

Please note that this sample has not been written under test conditions. During a test you might not have the time to produce such a polished piece of writing. However, this sample gives you a standard to aim for.

Structure

Audience

The title informs readers of the subject to be recounted.

The situation is quickly established in the title and the first paragraph (who, where and when).

The past tense is used.

Personal pronouns (*I, my, we*) indicate that this is a personal recount.

Character and setting

Time and place are quickly established.

The narrator begins to lose interest in the trip.

Text structure

Events happen in order using adverbs of time.

Precise words are used for detail (e.g. *snowstorm*).

The reader is made aware of the conditions at the time.

Indirect speech is used correctly.

Paragraphing

New paragraphs begin with changes in time.

Cohesion

Well-selected pronouns and adverbs keep the recount flowing.

A personal comment is used to conclude the recount.

The narrator suddenly changes his attitude.

Language and ideas

Vocabulary

Adverbs and adjectives are well chosen.

Interesting verbs are used, including 'said'-type words.

Sentence structure

The narrator uses a variety of sentence beginnings, including 'time' adverbs.

The narrator has used a variety of sentence types and lengths.

There is a controlled use of *I* as a sentence beginning.

Ideas

A suitable simile is used.

Repetition is used to indicate boredom.

Metaphors are also used to highlight the narrator's boredom.

Exclamation sentences are used effectively.

The writer is recounting a familiar subject.

The comparison works well.

Punctuation

Punctuation is well handled.

Direct speech has the correct punctuation.

Capital letters for proper nouns and sentence beginnings are correctly applied.

Spelling

There are no spelling mistakes in common or unusual words.

SPELLING WORDS FOR REAL TESTS

To the teacher or parent

First read and say the word slowly and clearly. Then read the sentence with the word in it. Then repeat the word again.

Give the student time to write their answer. If the student is not sure, then ask them to guess. It is okay to skip a word if it is not known.

Spelling words for Mini Test 1

Word	Example
1 hungry	The hungry dog ate all the dog food.
2 city	The car broke down in a city street.
3 forget	"Don't forget to take your homework," called Mel's mother.
4 answer	I got every answer right except the first one.
5 cruise	My grandparents went on a cruise to the South Pacific.
6 flashes	There were flashes of lightning in the western sky.
7 diaries	The new school diaries were given out on the first day of Term 1.
8 tadpoles	The tadpoles were trapped in a small pool in the creek.

Spelling words for Mini Test 2

Word	Example
1 trail	A snail left a slimy, silver trail right down the window.
2 different	My sister and I are in different schools in the same street.
3 dreadful	Take a bucket and brush and clean up the dreadful mess.
4 birthday	Mark's birthday is on the first day of the second month.
5 animals	The hollow tree is a safe home for many bush animals.
6 string	The string was knotted through the wire and I couldn't undo it.
7 cheese	We put cheese and pickles on the sandwich.
8 happiness	"You don't need money to find happiness," stated Mum.
9 flooring	The flooring on the back deck was rotting.
10 worst	That is the worst result for a science test I have ever seen.

Spelling words for Mini Test 3

Word	Example
1 health	Good health is more important than working late into the night.
2 reach	Mum cannot reach the magazine, but I can get it for her.
3 canary	A yellow canary whistled sadly in its cage.
4 decide	David can't decide which shirt to wear to the party.

5 evening	Every evening fruit bats head to the orchards for food.
6 hollow	Lizards were hiding in a hollow log to escape the winter frosts.
7 knives	Don't play with knives. You could cut yourself.
8 learning	The school has a new computer and I am learning keyboard skills.

Spelling words for Mini Test 4

Word	Example
1 flavour	The flavour of the meat was too strong for me.
2 agents	All the players had agents when they turned professional.
3 amateur	Our netball team was an amateur team when we won last year's final.
4 flooded	The water flooded the oval and the assembly area.
5 kangaroo	Have you ever seen a red kangaroo?
6 reindeer	There were cut-out reindeer along the fence over Christmas.
7 varnish	I used almost a whole tin of varnish when I painted the floor.
8 volume	Turn the volume down! I can't think with that noise.

Spelling words for Mini Test 5

Word	Example
1 elastic	The elastic in my trousers has lost its spring. I need a leather belt.
2 handwritten	Meg is smart at science but her handwritten reports are messy.
3 delayed	I was delayed for work yesterday but I'm early today.
4 orchids	Our neighbour grows roses but my parents prefer orchids.
5 galah	The galah is a grey and pink parrot.
6 janitor	Every warehouse in this district has a janitor.
7 sandals	Mum wonders if sandals will be better than joggers for our walk.
8 cherries	What do you want with your breakfast? Cherries or a banana?
9 porridge	We had a choice of porridge or muesli each morning.
10 potatoes	Mr Jones grows potatoes and cabbages in his back garden.

Spelling words for Mini Test 6

Word	Example
1 driveway	The driveway cracked when a driver parked a council truck on it.
2 orbits	The moon orbits the Earth every twenty-four hours.
3 graphs	In our last test we had to answer questions on graphs and tables.

SPELLING WORDS FOR REAL TESTS

4 parcels	The parcels were left in the middle of the alley!
5 innocent	"Is the woman innocent or guilty?" asked the judge.
6 attic	The chest was found in a far corner of the dusty attic.
7 necessary	It is not necessary to complete the project before Friday.
8 eventually	"To my way of thinking," said the captain, "we will eventually win."
9 weary	The soldiers were weary after their jungle march.
10 truth	Tell the youth to tell the truth!

Spelling words for Mini Test 7

Word	Example
1 easily	Graham was easily distracted during the last half of the game.
2 performed	Grace performed well in her half-yearly test.
3 torpedoes	The enemy submarine fired its torpedoes from ten kilometres away.
4 unnoticed	David went unnoticed at the school concert.
5 vanishes	Dad complains that Mum vanishes every time they go shopping.
6 eclipse	An eclipse of the moon is when the earth's shadow is on the moon.
7 ascended	As the climbers ascended the mountain they became sick.
8 information	The school is having an information night for the parents.
9 lottery	Tessa's mother won a lottery prize.
10 nocturnal	The possum is a nocturnal animal.

Spelling words for Mini Test 8

Word	Example
1 blossom	The wattle blossom made some people sneeze.
2 shoulder	A dislocated shoulder can be very painful.
3 surfacing	After surfacing the diver gasped for air.
4 ostrich	An ostrich is a bird that cannot fly.
5 naughty	Have you ever been naughty in class?
6 foul	There was a foul smell coming from the dry creek bed.
7 odours	Animals can detect odours people cannot smell.
8 products	Many products at the sales were at half price.
9 favouritism	Teachers should not show favouritism when they give out awards.
10 astronaut	An astronaut is a spaceman or spacewoman.

SPELLING WORDS FOR REAL TESTS

Spelling words for Mini Test 9

Word	Example
1 burglar	The reported burglar was caught in a police operation.
2 disappear	Did the circus magician make the rabbit disappear?
3 delighted	I was delighted to be chosen as class captain in the election.
4 neighbourhood	Our neighbourhood is a very safe place even during the holidays.
5 film	The film star was relaxing under a palm tree during a short break.
6 famous	Colin Brown was a famous gymnast but now he is an announcer.
7 midday	There are twelve hours between midday and midnight.
8 author	Who was the author of the adventure story set in the forest?
9 parsley	Some popular herbs are parsley, mint and chives.
10 discussing	"We are not discussing this any longer," declared the park ranger.

Spelling words for Mini Test 10

Word	Example
1 probably	You probably know how to complete this survey form.
2 propeller	Propeller driven aircraft are not normal but can be seen at country air shows.
3 barrel	The sights on the barrel of the rifle were aligned.
4 athletics	An athletics carnival has a variety of different events.
5 queried	"Why is there a pile of gravel on the lawn?" queried Dad.
6 lagoon	The lagoon at the western end of the swamp is polluted.
7 relief	No relief was available for the miners trapped underground.
8 eaves	The painters had to repaint under the eaves of the garage roof.
9 gardener	A landscape gardener can make the outside of a cottage very attractive.
10 intersection	The residents demanded lights at the busy intersection.

Spelling words for Conventions of Language Test 1

Word	Example
26 born	Lester was born in a country hospital in 1987.
27 because	"I hosed the garden because it was covered in ants!" said Julie.
28 coming	If you are coming with us to the shop then you must hurry!
29 enemies	The shadows on the hill were our enemies.
30 blossom	The rose blooms were great but I prefer the blossom of wattles.

SPELLING WORDS FOR REAL TESTS

31 vacant	The vacant block of land near our house is covered in trees!
32 beautiful	The high clouds were the reason for a beautiful sunset.
33 rattling	The old car was rattling over the rough ground.
34 speeding	A speeding train rushed through the station.
35 quitting	Are you quitting for good, or will you start again tomorrow?
36 broken	Alan's bike had broken down on the crest of the hill.
37 clubs	We have two netball clubs in town.
38 diamonds	Mum has two diamonds in her ring.
39 hearts	Most of the cards in my hand were hearts.
40 spades	Hoes and spades were in the garden shed.

Spelling words for Conventions of Language Test 2

Word	Example
26 levelling	Craig said, "We were levelling the grass when the storm struck."
27 leisure	Our team had leisure after a week of intense training.
28 gravy	Do you want gravy on your meat or will you have sauce?
29 busier	Smith Street is far busier than any other street in the area.
30 territory	Rugged territory in the north caused the death of three hikers.
31 javelin	Justin is in the javelin event but I am in the archery.
32 parrot	A small parrot was feeding near the wheat silo before flying off.
33 citizen	Did every citizen receive a council letter?
34 forgetting	After forgetting his pen, James then lost his pencil.
35 audience	The audience clapped loudly at the end of the first act.
36 weary	"Judy has been tired and weary since the exams," said Mum
37 straight	It is eight o'clock. You must go straight to bed!
38 wriggly	Jess drew wriggly lines on the book cover.
39 carriage	We found a few seats in the last carriage of the express.
40 perpendicular	A wall must be perpendicular to the floor.

SPELLING WORDS FOR REAL TESTS

Spelling words for Conventions of Language Test 3

Word	Example
26 actually	Gail was actually kept in after class today!
27 cartridges	The police found empty cartridges at the scene of the robbery.
28 fluttered	Birds fluttered through the canopy of thick leaves.
29 grieved	The mourners grieved for weeks after the funeral.
30 aquarium	An aquarium is for fish as a sty is for pigs.
31 wishbone	The wishbone is part of a chicken's skeleton.
32 crater	The crater was formed by a meteor impact, millions of years ago.
33 cyclones	Many countries, including Australia, experience cyclones.
34 campaign	Class 5H had a campaign to raise money for the surf club.
35 archery	You can take up archery when you get older!
36 terrible	The last match of the day was a terrible display of fairness.
37 parallel	The highway runs parallel to the rail track.
38 oblique	Is an oblique line a slanting line?
39 hyphen	A hyphen is a dash that can join two words.
40 microscope	We used a microscope to study insects.